Rock 'n' Roll Wisdom

Recent Titles in
Sex, Love, and Psychology
Judy Kuriansky, Series Editor

Relationship Sabotage: Unconscious Factors that Destroy Couples, Marriages, and Family
William J. Matta

The Praeger Handbook of Transsexuality: Changing Gender to Match Mindset
Rachel Ann Heath

America's War on Sex
Marty Klein

Teenagers, HIV, and AIDS: Insights from Youths Living with the Virus
Maureen E. Lyon and Lawrence J. D'Angelo, editors

ROCK 'N' ROLL WISDOM

What Psychologically Astute Lyrics Teach about Life and Love

Barry A. Farber

Sex, Love, and Psychology
Judy Kuriansky, Series Editor

Westport, Connecticut
London

Library of Congress Cataloging-in-Publication Data

Farber, Barry A. (Barry Alan), 1947–
Rock 'n' roll wisdom : what psychologically astute lyrics teach about
life and love / Barry A. Farber.
    p. cm. — (Sex, love, and psychology, ISSN 1554–222X)
  Includes bibliographical references and index.
  ISBN-13: 978-0-275-99164-7 (alk. paper)
  ISBN-10: 0-275-99164-4 (alk. paper)
  1. Conduct of life. 2. Rock music—History and criticism. I. Title.
  BJ1595.F27 2007
  782.42166'0268—dc22   2007008322

Library of Congress Catalog Card Number: 2007008322
ISBN-13: 978-0-275-99164-7
ISBN-10: 0-275-99164-4
ISSN: 1554-222X

First published in 2007

Praeger Publishers, 88 Post Road West, Westport, CT 06881
An imprint of Greenwood Publishing Group, Inc.
www.praeger.com

Printed in the United States of America

The paper used in this book complies with the
Permanent Paper Standard issued by the National
Information Standards Organization (Z39.48–1984).

10 9 8 7 6 5 4 3 2 1

To April: "you're my soul and my heart's inspiration"

CONTENTS

PART IV ON COPING WITH LIFE

PART V ON AGING AND GROWTH

PREFACE

Wisdom comes from many sources. Most often, we think of wisdom as emanating from philosophers, social critics, writers, poets, or religious leaders. We might also throw in a few humorists (Mark Twain and Will Rogers come to mind) and political statesmen (Lincoln, Churchill, and Gandhi are good examples). Some psychological thinkers (Freud, Jung, and Rogers) and scientists (Darwin and Einstein) have also been considered wise. Bartlett's book of famous quotations is full of pithy and astute observations about the human condition from the ranks of these groups. We also commonly find wisdom in the words of family, friends, or respected community members. These days, many individuals, especially those in the younger generations, seem to seek wisdom in the daily postings of Internet blogs.

There are those who study the Bible or Shakespeare their whole lives. Others pore over the works of James Joyce, Virginia Woolf, Toni Morrison, Martin Luther King, or so many other notable writers and speakers. There are those who belong to book and film groups that scrutinize the themes, plots, and words of the great or popular works of these traditions. But one doesn't hear much about those who seek wisdom in the words of rock music. I suspect that the usual, or at least the most natural, response to this is something on the order of, "Well, of course not, there's not much wisdom there to find." And, in fact, there may not be, if we were simply calculating the proportion of wise words to trite (or inane) words over the history of rock music. But there are wise words here, more than even most rock music lovers would suspect. No, not as many as in the works of the great writers or poets or spiritual leaders, but I don't have a contest in mind. My goal is far simpler: to show that there have been hundreds of rock lyrics that are not just clever (though many are) but also wise. These are the lyrics from which we can learn a great deal about a good many subjects, including such all-important ones as love, identity, money, sex, religion, social justice, and the search for meaning. At their best, lyrics in the rock tradition embody the same kinds of enduring truths found in other, more respectable media such as books or plays. For example, the Beatles' line, "She's leaving home after living alone for so many years," is beautifully crafted, perfectly ironic, and as good a reflection of our psychological knowledge about adolescence as can be found in any source.

A number of Internet sites are devoted to the study of rock lyrics. Some concentrate on individual songs and act as a forum for fans to debate whether a particular tune or lyric is really about drugs or the songwriter's own life, or just random words that fit a melodic structure. Some sites offer the stories behind individual songs, purporting to reveal (often via previously documented interviews with the songwriters) what the song is meant to convey. Other sites have collected seemingly thousands of lyrics categorized among dozens of topics; most of these sites even allow one to enter a keyword or phrase that results in a display of various lyrics that contain these words. Most of these sites are enjoyable, but none are particularly discriminating. Lyrics pop up regardless of whether they're clever, mediocre, or downright awful. My task in this book has been to find those relatively few lyrics that are worth lingering over and learning from.

I grew up in a household where the music we listened to—mostly show tunes, some easy listening of the likes of Andy Williams, and a smattering of classical—was played on a record player. (Records, of course, had two sides, a fact that mystified my son years later when he tried unsuccessfully to find a particular cut of a Beatles' song that was on their *Abbey Road* album). I never really learned to play a musical instrument—a major regret in my life—but once I found rock 'n' roll, I became a consistent listener.

I also became good at a young age at remembering the words to songs. In college and later, friends would call and ask me for the title, artist, or lyrics of songs, and, more often than not, I'd come through. I half-kiddingly think of this as my own so-called idiot savant ability (now more sensitively termed *savant syndrome*). As an elementary school teacher in New York City and Westchester County, I used lyrics from Motown songs and the Who's rock opera *Tommy* to teach reading. Later, as a college professor, I also started using lyrics in graduate psychology courses, for classes on such topics as depression (Otis Redding: "I have nothing to live for, look like nothing gonna come my way"), child abuse (Pearl Jam: "She holds the hand that holds her down"), and the psychological effects of poverty (Marvin Gaye: "Mother, mother there's too many of you cryin'; brother, brother, there's too many of you dying"). I liked doing this, my graduate students seemed to enjoy starting classes with this kind of material, and many of them started sharing their own favorite lyrics with me. And so my collection grew, especially of lyrics with some psychological relevance, and thus the idea was born of a book on psychologically astute rock lyrics.

One of the powerful lessons I've learned about life came from my good friend (and former graduate school professor), Jesse Geller: you can find knowledge and wisdom in all sorts of places—in a phrase from some obscure poet, a riff about life from a street musician, or a line from a rock song. So, I thank Jesse for this lesson and also for his careful readings of early versions of this book. I have many others to thank, including some terrific graduate assistants. Jesse Metzger, to whom I turned for help on a previous book on therapist self-disclosure, was a great source for ideas, contemporary lyrics, and editorial advice. It is a wonderful thing to have a research assistant who can write well, think well, and who loves music. Amy Blume was instrumental in crafting excellent first versions of the chapters on aging and mortality, money, and growing up; Arielle Farber combined her fine writing skills and interest in policy issues to write an impressive draft of the chapter on the search for social justice; and Tanya Peters used her clinical skills and great love of music to write a personally meaningful draft of the chapter on religion and spirituality. Larissa Stodghill did an extraordinary job on the difficult task of tracking down the credit and copyright information on more than 500 songs.

Many music-loving colleagues contributed lyrics and friendship over the years, including Dr. Susan Alexander (lots of Rolling Stones), Dr. Clarissa Bullitt (Joni Mitchell), Dr. Sam Menahem (Bob Dylan), and Dr. David Roe (Simon and Garfunkel). Other colleagues and friends contributed a great deal of enthusiasm and useful advice, including Dr. Betsy Glaser, Dr. Robin Lippert, Phyllis Meissel, Dr. Billie Pivnick, Dr. Dinelia Rosa, and Dr. Roni Beth Tower. Many music-loving students sent occasional lyrics and consistent support my way, including Ben Adams, Kathryn Berano, Jason Karageorge, Dan Laukitis, Inessa Manevich, Emily Rosenthal, Erica Saypol, Arielle Shanok, Alice Sohn, and Traci Stein. In the early stages of this project, Andrew Witkin and Arthur Baraf did a great job of going through reams of sheet music and musical collections in search of psychologically astute lyrics. Neal, Varda, Dani, Wayne, Jean, and Jamie have been there during the proverbial "good times and bad." To all, my sincere thanks. I'd also like to express my appreciation to Judy Kuriansky, aka, Dr. Judy of radio, television and newspaper fame—who once played in a rock band—for her belief in this project and her enormous help in connecting me to the very patient and supportive senior editor of Praeger Publishers, Ms. Debora Carvalko.

My deepest appreciation and love go to my very supportive, very musical family: my daughter, Alissa (formerly on the piano and guitar, now focused on dance); my very new son-in-law, Dan (clarinet); my son, David (guitar and musical composition); his girlfriend, Genna (music lover and great dancer); my father-in-law, Bernie (harmonica); my mother (music lover); and my wife, April (piano). They have read, critiqued, edited, and affirmed my efforts; they have (usually) tolerated well my increasingly annoying habit of finding a lyric to accompany every conversation.

Stevie Wonder (in *Sir Duke*) said it very well: "Music is a world within itself with a language we all understand." There's always music, and sometimes, even great lyrics.

FOREWORD

We are a nation of music lovers, with listening made even more accessible in contemporary times with technological advances like iPods and cable radio. But a deeper look at our favorite playlist can bring valuable lessons about who we are—as Dr. Barry A. Farber so poignantly shows us in this new book, *Rock 'n' Roll Wisdom: What Psychologically Astute Lyrics Can Teach about Life and Love.*

This is a read that is surely fun, as all these rock couplets trigger us to sing the complete songs and recall cherished memories. But it is also illuminating, as the learned psychologist/author guides us to understand the deeper meanings behind the tunes.

What do musical giants like Bob Dylan, Bob Marley, Paul Simon, Joni Mitchell, Bruce Springsteen, Billy Joel, the Eagles, and U2 have to do with psychological geniuses like Freud, Jung, Maslow, and Erikson? Plenty, as Farber elucidates the connection between lyrics and psychological concepts like the search for identity, conflicts over commitment, and the hierarchy of needs—all of which underlie our everyday experience and behavior, self-image, relationships, and place in the world.

Brilliantly weaving rock lyrics with stages of life, Farber explains songs using well-established concepts from the field of psychology. For example, "Self Psychology" explains our need for others to affirm us and help us define who we are. Bruce Springsteen likely did not know just how effectively he was tapping into these principles, invoking the yearning for friendship to affirm ourselves, when he penned, "Wendy, let me in, I wanna be your friend. I wanna guard your dreams and visions," or when Bill Withers crooned, "Just call on me brother, when you need a hand."

Musicians are often heroes of generations, with legions of faithful fans, and Farber gives us insight into their magic. Consistent with various psychological aspects of love, we long wistfully as 3 Doors Down implores a lover to "love me when I'm wrong, hold me when I'm scared," and despair with fear of losing love as The Shirelles ask, "Will you still love me tomorrow?" Carole King triggers our own existential angst as she notes that the tapestry of life is "impossible to hold," and John Lennon's longing to "give peace a chance" resonates in our own heart and soul. The experience can be an individualized journey or a more collective and socially conscious one, as when we sing along with the group of artists brought together for *We Are the World* or for *We Are Family*—the latter produced by my friend Nile Rodgers, whose musical imprint is on the likes of Madonna and Eric Clapton, and whose foundation now builds schools in Africa.

Farber knows of what he speaks on both professional and personal levels. A clinical psychologist and head of one of the most prestigious graduate psychology programs in the country, at Teachers College (Columbia University), he has also been a music lover for nearly half a century and can impressively name artists and quote lyrics from thousands of songs.

Similarly, for both professional and personal reasons, I am proud to be series editor of this book and part of bringing it to light. Professionally, I admire and applaud Farber's product: it is a well-thought out, academically sound, and a meaningful contribution to the literature about one of the most important cultural arts of our time. It is also the first book of its kind to bring a psychological depth to the study and understanding of our captivation with rock lyrics. Further, associating rock lyrics to psychological models, like those of Robert Sternberg on the different components of love and of Erik Erikson on stages of development, makes perfect psychological sense, particularly as a developer of psychological models myself. Known as a relationship counselor in the media for years, giving call-in advice to thousands of men and women of all ages around the world, I have heard many people discuss the issues that Farber raises in his book. I have developed and highlighted concepts about life and love documented in *The Complete Idiots Guide to a Healthy Relationship* and *The Complete Idiots Guide to Dating*, including the "mirror law of attraction" and the "Madonna-prostitute syndrome"—concepts that I was delighted to see analyzed in rock lyrics in Farber's book.

I have also often been called on in workshops and lectures to explain the miscommunication in relationships, which Farber chronicles so well in rock lyrics. While the perils of miscommunication had been pointed out in bestsellers by friends like Warren Farrell in *Women Don't Hear What Men Don't Say,* and Deborah Tannen in *You Just Don't Understand: Women and Men in*

Conversation, such problems persist and have even become more complicated in contemporary times, with changes in male-female roles and definitions.

On a personal level, as a psychologist, friend, and colleague of Farber's—from our days at Bayside High School together to contemporary times in clinical psychology—I know of his passion for this topic and am delighted to see it come to fruition in a public forum and for posterity. As a fellow psychologist with an analytic and humanistic/existential bent, I have always been fascinated and drawn to deeper understanding of commonplace events. Further, as a musician and music lover, I am delighted to read his unique perspective. This book takes me back through the decades of my own pleasure in music, bringing new depth to early experiences of relishing my 45s, with songs like *16 Candles* evoking growing pains of adolescence and The Everly Brothers' *Bye Bye Love* presaging the pains of infatuations.

Farber's book further evokes my experience over so many years when hosting call-in radio advice shows, like the popular *Love Phones,* which was syndicated on music radio stations around the country. So many men and women of all ages, and especially young people, called me with problems about their life, love, sex, and relationship problems, which related to the issues in the music that aired during the other programmed segments. Music stars who were guests on the show served as "honorary love doctors," adding their personal advice to the callers' questions that I was addressing and chronicled in *Generation Sex.* As a psychologist, I had great admiration and appreciation for artists when they shared their personal experiences to help the audience not only deal with their own issues but also understand the musicians' messages. Powerful examples included Tori Amos acknowledging that her experiences of having been abused served as the motivation for setting up a foundation to help others similarly suffering, and Alanis Morissette explaining how her chart-topping song reflected personal experience of being blinded by love at first sight and learning to be more discriminating in evaluating potential lovers.

In so many interviews with rock stars, I have pointed out kernels of wisdom in their words, many of which they had not even realize themselves. Surprised, they would remark, "I didn't know that" or "That's deep." Farber's book elaborates on such deep musical revelations so well. Fans can gain from seeing connections between words and phrases that linger in their minds, and deeper messages gleaned from those phrases, which can improve their daily lives. Popular songs are, after all, about the songwriter's experiences—struggling with independence, wanting to be loved, healing from disappointment—all of which resonate with our own experiences. Thus, we can understand and heal ourselves through listening and singing along. In this journey, Farber picks perfect issues to explore, including struggles for identity, depression, aging, and striving to find meaning in life.

The impact of music on our hearts, minds, and souls has been explored in much research. The Mozart Effect has become a popular term referring to the power of music to faciliate health and well-being by reducing stress, depression, and anxiety; inducing relaxation or sleep; activating the body; and improving memory and awareness. Other studies have explored uses of music and sound to treat such psychological disorders as learning disabilities, attention deficit disorder, and even autism. Many people know from personal experience how retreating into music helps heal personal pain. In my disaster relief work, I've even seen the healing power of music in helping people—and cultures—recover from disasters.

No analysis of rock 'n' roll is complete without reference to the classic triad of "sex, drugs, and rock 'n' roll." Farber explores this well. These connections appeal to me not only as a sex therapist in the media for many decades but also personally, having lived out the all-too-common adolescent dream of wanting to play in a rock band (by playing bass and singing in a band of six women called "Artemis: Band of Women," named for Artemis, the goddess of the hunt). At that time, I had to confront my parents' fears of sex, drugs and rock 'n' roll affecting their daughter. Despite their realistic concerns—since so many musicians get caught up in that vicious cycle with devastating results—Farber now arms me with a reassurance: that rock lyrics can serve as a warning against such dangers.

Of course, sex is a basic staple of rock 'n' roll—who can deny that given Elvis' erotic gyrations or Barry White's throaty admission, "can't get enough of your love, baby?" While I once found myself repulsed at a 2LiveCrew concert when band mates pushed women to their knees on stage in simulated sex scenes, I also now find new appreciation for the value of Marvin Gaye's "Sexual Healing," which turns out to be perfectly in tune with my own and others' revival of ancient teachings of tantric sex arts from India and China that facilitate sexual healing—and also enlightenment. As a peace activist now who travels the world giving workshops, including in troubled regions like Israel and Iran, I further hail Farber's chapter on rock lyrics that serve to heal the planet in the search for social justice in the world, throughout the decades from Peter, Paul, and Mary to Bono, Sting, and U2.

Reading the chapters of Farber's book can be mere enjoyment or a walk down memory lane triggered by familiar and beloved lyrics. For me, these include memories of night after night at Studio 54 disco, dancing until the wee hours, with the fervor reaching a pitch to songs like Gloria Gaynor's "I Will Survive"—a song that Farber reminds us triggers our own defiance against callous rejection. Earlier memories emerge of junior high school parties, trying out the first French kiss while slow dancing to Johnny Mathis's velvety seductive tones in "Misty," "Chances Are," and "The Twelfth of Never," or as the end of the party draws near, imploring a crush along with The Drifters to "Save the Last Dance for Me."

Why are these early memories so precious and poignant? Farber offers explanations and research, like a survey of 1,500 adults that showed that their favorite songs were ones they liked from ages 16 to 21. As I am often called on to comment in the media about cultural trends, I was asked to comment on this study by a reporter doing a story for the New York CBS-TV affiliate. Then, asked to sing my favorite, songs from many genres passed my mind—Peter, Paul, and Mary folk; The Rolling Stones rock; Poison heavy metal; Aerosmith hard rock; Sex Pistols punk; and even Nirvana grunge. Not surprisingly, though, the favorite I blurted out was consistent with the study results: "Under the Boardwalk" indeed came from my youth. Consistent with the analysis of favored music as so-called comfort food and a reminiscence bump, is the psychobiological explanation that words become associated with significant or pleasurable experiences and burned into long-term recall memory in our brain.

An important part of the experience of listening to rock lyrics, as Farber points out so wisely, is that they normalize our own feelings, letting us know we are not the only one. I know this from my work for years on the radio: everyone wants to know that they are not the only one going through a particular, or painful, experience. Knowing so reduces the anxiety and upset of any personal problem. Lyrics give us permission for our feelings and comfort in sharing. When Leslie Gore sang "it's my party," she reassured us all of our common humanity, that "you would cry too, if it happened to you."

For all these reasons, this book is not only for academics, psychologists, and cultural analysts, but for all music lovers. The illuminating and enjoyable analysis makes for the self-awareness that psychologists advise as well as what all people want and enjoy: personal reflection and interesting interpersonal conversation. Ask yourself, and others, about your favorite rock lyrics and explore what they mean. I have often asked myself why can I still now sing all the words to a very little-known 1959 song "Running Bear" about an Indian brave whose love for Little White Dove "couldn't die" and was "big as the sky" but could never be, so they both jumped into the raging waters and sealed their love with a kiss as they drowned to their death. The story evokes the tragic love between Romeo and Juliet, and it's now up to me to explore what that says about my own life.

After reading Farber's book, you may not be able to listen to songs mindlessly anymore, but this should be a good thing. As Farber guides us to learn lessons from rock lyrics, I invite you to apply the 3 Rs: Read this book thoroughly, Recall lyrics that come to your mind, and Reflect on lessons you can learn from them to improve and fulfill all aspects of your life.

Dr. Judy Kuriansky, Series Editor

INTRODUCTION: LISTENING TO LYRICS

Every one of them words rang true and glowed like burning coal.
—Bob Dylan, "Tangled up in Blue"

They're only words, unless they're true.

—Madonna, "Words"

There are some great lyrics in rock music. Whether or not they're poetry, whether or not they're the equal of great lines in novels, plays, or movies, whether or not they're best considered with their musical accompaniment—all this is secondary. These are issues of far more interest to scholars than to those who simply love rock music, including the words.

I'm one of those people who love rock 'n' roll, especially phrases that are psychologically smart. I've been a fairly serious rock 'n' roll fan for at least 45 years—the kind who, as a kid, would listen to the radio and compare top-10 lists of different New York radio stations. That was in the late 1950s/early 1960s, back in the era when there were only AM stations. No FM, no MTV, no Walkmans, no iPods. The first "45" single I bought was in 1961, the Marcels' "Blue Moon." It was probably at least 10 years later when I learned that this doo-wop recording was a remake of a song written by Rogers and Hart in 1934, and one that had been recorded previously by, among others, Billie Holiday, Frank Sinatra, and Elvis Presley. Since then, I've had collections of 45s, record albums, 8-tracks, cassettes, CDs, and mp3s. I've also gone to scores of concerts and hosted karaoke parties in my home. I also take perverse pride in being one of those adults whose kids, even as teenagers, asked me to turn the music down in the car.

Much of this, though, is standard stuff for a music lover growing up in the age when rock 'n' roll was developing. The more unusual, somewhat obsessive part is that for at least 10 years I've been collecting noteworthy rock lyrics: jotting them down after I've heard them, reading lyrics from albums and CD inserts, following up references or recommendations made by novelists or music reviewers, asking friends, colleagues, and students for their favorite lines—and then compiling and sorting them all, most recently on a series of computers. This hobby has been filtered over the years through a particular professional lens—that of a clinical psychologist. That is, the words that I've considered smart and worthy of saving are those that I've felt are psychologically wise. These are the words that ring true to me as a psychologist who has had a full-time academic career in a clinical psychology program (at Teachers College, Columbia University) since 1979 and who has also been in a part-time private practice of psychotherapy for all those years. Thus, this book on psychologically astute lyrics represents the merger of two great interests in my life.

There are lines in many rocks songs in every decade since the 1950s, across every genre from doo-wop to folk rock to hard rock, that are remarkably good. Some of these lines are beautiful, some really clever, and some so very wise. These great lyrics may well represent a very small proportion of the words that have been written, but considering the enormous output of music within the rock tradition, it should be no wonder that some words, metaphors, and phrases are exceptional. In the preface to this book, I offered the Beatles' words in "She's Leaving Home" as an example. Another of the great lines in rock history was written in 1962; the words are almost a cliché by now, but their power should still be evident: "How many roads must a man walk down before they call him a man?" This of course is from Bob Dylan's "Blowin' in the Wind." Despite the fact that Dylan consistently discounts the power or genius of the song, claiming it was written in five minutes and represents nothing special, it is poetic, moving, and politically and psychologically insightful. Yet another example of an extraordinary lyric is from a song ("Both Sides Now") by Joni Mitchell, another gifted songwriter and among the first to use her own struggles to illustrate feelings we've all experienced: "It's life's illusions I recall, I really don't know life at all." A favorite—and quite smart—lyric of Generation Xers (those born between the mid 1960s to late 1970s) comes from a song by the Indigo Girls, "Closer to Fine": "Darkness has a hunger that's insatiable, and lightness has a call that's hard to hear." In a few words, they've expressed the psychological essence of depression. There are hundreds, if not thousands, of other remarkably good lyrics. Still, many serious rock fans probably still don't realize the wisdom that's contained in some of their favorite songs.

Many baby boomers remember Dick Clark and his long-running TV show, *American Bandstand*. Those of us in this generation remember the part in the show when he'd ask audience members to rate a new song he had just played. "I give it a 7," someone would invariably say and explain why, with reasons like, "I like the beat." It seems unlikely that any song was ever rated a "10" (or even a "7") on the basis of its lyrics. This book, though, is about finding those lyrics that are worth appreciating and savoring—lyrics that are smart and psychologically astute. It is about a search for great lyrics in rock 'n' roll music, especially among those songs in the two decades between the 1960s and the 1980s that helped define a generation.

For the most part, we tend to judge the value of a rock song by its beat, rhythm, melody line, instrumentation, and performance—how well we can dance to it, how the music grabs us viscerally, or how much fun it is to sing along and belt out the chorus. In addition, a great voice (for example, Joan Baez, Aretha Franklin, and, more recently, Norah Jones) or even an unusual one (for example, Rod Stewart, Freddy Mercury of Queen, or Robbie Robertson of the Band) may enhance our appreciation of a piece of music. Contemporary listeners also tend to judge songs by the creative quality of their music videos.

Most songs judged among the so-called best of all time by critics or fans either have great opening notes—like those first few memorable bars of "Satisfaction" (recently judged the number one rock song of all time by a panel of consultants for the cable TV music network, VH1) or "Stairway to Heaven" or "Billy Jean"—or alluring hooks (repetitive catchy musical lines) like "Respect," "Born to Run," "Light My Fire" or, more recently, REM's "Losing My Religion" or U2's "I Still Haven't Found What I'm Looking For." It's easy to evoke the melodies of each of these songs. Other songs have been considered great because they've broken new ground musically, at least in the realm of rock 'n' roll. For example, the Beach Boys' "Good Vibrations" has extraordinary harmonies and a lushness of sound that was new to its time; Queen's "Bohemian Rhapsody" featured an intricate, ambitious musical structure; and Jimi Hendrix's "Foxy Lady" contains some extraordinary guitar playing and innovative chords.

In addition, some songs have also been considered great, or at least memorable, because their theme strikes just the right political or socially conscious note at the right time. This is especially true if sung by a supergroup like the Beatles, or, in their time, Buffalo Springfield, or, in contemporary times, U2. "Hey Jude" (an ode to love and togetherness), "Imagine" (a call for universal harmony), "For What It's Worth" (a testament to the profound social changes in the late 60s), and "One" (U2's plea to "carry each other") are all in this category. It's even tempting to add Gloria Gaynor's "I Will Survive" to this list because of its enduring message (backed by a highly danceable melody) that life does go on after a painful breakup. If we're in the right mood, all these songs are capable of making us feel more wistful, introspective, empowered, or politically or spiritually conscious. *Time* magazine reported that, in 2006, an Episcopal priest in Maine designed a service in which U2 songs are used as hymns.

And then there are those rock songs, rare though they are, that feature beautifully crafted, psychologically astute lyrics. Dylan's "Like a Rolling Stone" and the Eagles' "Hotel California" are two good examples of songs in this category. In each, there are a number of really smart, evocative phrases. Among the great lines from Dylan's song about the illusion of success and the shock of the fall: "When you got nothing, you got nothing to lose." (Of course, it might be argued that an even better, more psychologically astute line, would have been "when you've got nothing, you still have something to lose.") In "Hotel California"—a song primarily about the enduring emotional power of special times and places—there are some wonderfully clever puns and phrases: "Her mind is Tiffany twisted, she got the Mercedes Benz," and "You can check out any time you like, but you can never leave."

Lyrics, though, have rarely been the focal point of rock music, and it shows. Most lyrics of most songs are banal, employing simple rhymes and trite metaphors to express familiar themes of needing, finding, and losing love. The lack of emphasis on lyrics, by both songwriters and rock listeners, is even reflected in books about rock 'n' roll. They tend to describe rock's history and genres, present biographical sketches of its major artists, or feature lists of the best-selling or highest-charting songs or albums by decade or year; but, remarkably enough, most contain few or no specific lyrics. There are books of the collected lyrics of the most notable rock stars, but their inclusion of accompanying notes and chords suggests that they are designed so that those who know how to play a bit can try their hands at these songs. In short, lyrics are seemingly beside the point, of little interest in comparison to the power of the music itself or its staged presentation. In fact, from Chuck Berry and Elvis through the Rolling Stones, Alice Cooper, Kiss, David Bowie, James Brown, Prince, Madonna, and Britney Spears, rock has more often than not focused on the show rather than the words. In his book *Sex, Drugs, and Cocoa Puffs* (2003), Chuck Klosterman suggests that the most important part of rock has always been the "iconography and the posturing and the idea of what we're supposed to be experiencing" (p. 44).

Surprisingly, even those who love listening to rock music are often unaware of the lyrics, meaning that even when we are able to sing virtually every word of a particular song, we are oblivious to just what we are singing. Something akin to what Simon and Garfunkel referred to (in "Sounds of Silence") as "people hearing but not listening." The rhythm and orchestration of a song may generate a reflexive ability to sing along, but for the most part, the words are considered as sounds that go along with the music rather than meaningful in their own right. Sometimes, of course, we know the basic theme of the song or the essential meaning of the chorus—we can say what the song is about—but few of us tend to listen to the words of a rock song in a thoughtful way.

Thus, most of us have had the experience of listening to a very familiar song with another person who speaks of the meaning of the song in a way that absolutely stuns us: "Oh, of course, you're right—this song *is* about depression [or drugs, or sex, or the aftermath of a nuclear holocaust]. Never thought of that; I must have heard this song 500 times but never really listened to the words." Or, we have the experience of someone actually citing a line from a song we know well and we react with amazement; suddenly the line—heard out of context, without the familiar previous line, without the familiar rhythm—has an entirely new meaning. Or more likely, the line has meaning for the first time. An example exists in the long and musically intricate song, "Suite: Judy Blue Eyes" (Crosby, Stills, and Nash). The line, "fear is the lock and laughter the key to your heart," is one that many baby boomers have probably sung along to (or at least heard) multiple times. It's a beautiful, poetic, and psychologically astute phrase, but one, like many others, that probably hasn't been attended to across all those years of listening.

We all have our favorite songs. Usually, these feature both a melody line we love and words that we have actually taken in—words that "speak to us," that resonate with our experiences during a certain time of life. In fact, we can often remember when a song was popular because we remember hearing it or singing along to it during a certain grade or year in college. Sometimes the words are not especially poetic or well crafted, but they nevertheless touch a well of powerful feelings. What, after all, is more powerful than longing for or experiencing love for the first time? Moreover, the raw power of these words and feelings often gets further intensified as a result of their shared experience. That is, often these songs were heard or sung along to or danced to when we were part of a group. Strong feelings of communion and friendship make certain phrases especially meaningful. Songs we first heard during adolescence seem to continue to have an emotional hold on us even 30 or 40 years later. In fact, a recent study by a University of Amsterdam researcher found that most adults' favorite songs are those they loved between the ages of 16 and 21 (Deligiannakis & Greene, 2006). Our powers of memory are most astute at this point in life. Thus, lines from these songs have the strange and lovely ability to evoke feelings, images, and memories that perhaps no other stimuli can generate. Stated somewhat differently: these defining songs are those that evoke powerful feelings and then serve to store the whole experience so that hearing the song brings it all back—the feelings, the people, the hopes, the person we thought we were.

The therapist in the TV show *Ally McBeal* ("Dr. Tracy Clark," played by Tracey Ullman) liked asking her clients about their theme song—the song that reflects a key aspect of themselves. Similarly, one of my favorite questions in getting to know another person in a social situation is to ask about his or her favorite songs. Wonderfully enough, most people's first response is to smile. Then they think a bit, go "hmm," and their minds seem to go back in time in search of an answer. Answers are often remarkably self-revealing, placing a person back to a certain period of time, a certain mood, and often a certain important person. For me, that song is Simon and Garfunkel's "For Emily, Wherever I May Find Her"—a song reminiscent of college and first love. The lyrics are romantic and vivid, if a bit ornate ("What a dream I had, pressed in organdy, clothed in crinoline of smoky burgundy"), but far more expressive than typical songs about finding love. For a favorite cousin of mine, that song is the Indigo Girls' "Watershed," a lovely, moving, contemplative reflection on the choices we need to make throughout life: "every tree limb overhead just seems to sit and wait, until every step you take becomes a twist of fate."

In 1966, when "For Emily" was released as part of Simon and Garfunkel's *Parsley, Sage, Rosemary, and Thyme* album, the number-one song of the year was the Monkees' "I'm a Believer" (written by Neil Diamond)—one of those incredibly infectious songs with a great hook and mediocre lyrics ("And then I saw her face, now I'm a believer"). Why do so many hit songs have such unremarkable lyrics? Or phrased differently, why have lyrics been secondary in the rock tradition? The answer lies primarily in what I alluded to earlier—that, from the beginning, rock was more about the beat or the show than it was about words. What was important was the electricity, the rawness and sexuality of the rhythms. Elvis was compelling—and dangerous—because of the perceived sensuality of his music and movements; he was hardly radical or wise in regard to the lyrics he sang ("Are you lonesome tonight, do you miss me tonight?"; "Well since my baby left me, I've been so all alone"; "Love me tender, love me true, never let me go"; "I want you, I need you, I love you, with all of my might"). Interestingly enough, "Are You Lonesome Tonight?" was actually written in 1926 and first popularized by Al Jolson.

Thus, with a few exceptions—most notably, the songs of folk rockers, singer-songwriters, and rap musicians—rock has traditionally emphasized rhythmic and musical rather than lyrical innovations. In fact, judging from the lyrics of most of the early rock songs (extending well into the 60s), little attention was paid at all to creative imagery or phrases. Most songs were about finding or losing love, and lyrics were simple and earnest. From the top-10 songs of 1960: "I'm sorry, so sorry, please accept my apologies" (Brenda Lee, "I'm Sorry"); "Don't want your love anymore, don't want your kisses that's for sure" (the Everly Brothers, "Cathy's Clown"); and "Everybody's somebody's fool, everybody's somebody's plaything" (Connie Francis). The popular 1956 song by Frankie Lymon and the Teenagers, "Why Do Fools Fall in Love" has been called by one rock critic "everything you'd expect of the third-prize entry in a junior high poetry contest" (Hansen, 1992, p. 96).

At best, early rock lyrics might feature a moderately clever couplet, like "Is this a lasting treasure, or just a moment's pleasure?" (the Shirelles' "Will You Love Me Tomorrow?"), or a somewhat creative story line, like that in The Rays' "Silhouettes" (1957) where the singer, crazed with jealousy after having seeing his girlfriend and another man in silhouette embracing in the front of her house, ultimately realizes that he's on the wrong street ("Said to my shock, you're on the wrong block"). Somewhat similarly, in "Beep Beep" (1958) a cute song about a little Nash Rambler that somehow keeps gaining on an ultrafast, high-powered Cadillac, the last line offers us the surprise that the driver in the little, supposedly underpowered car wants to catch up in order to ask a simple question, "Buddy, how do I get this car out of second gear?" And in "Memphis" (1964), we find out in the last verse that this apparent love song is aimed at "Marie [who's] only six years old." And yes, to be fair, every once in a while, lyrics from this era might be soulful and even sneak in a bit of social consciousness: In 1961, Ben E. King and the Drifters sang of "a rose in Spanish Harlem…that's never seen the sun." Even earlier, in 1958, Eddie Cochran sang a song ("Summertime Blues"), later covered by Blue Cheer, that contained these politically savvy words: "Well I called my congressman, he said, quote, 'I'd like to help you son, but you're too young to vote'."

The point is that, exceptions aside, most rock songs, particularly those in the pre-1965 era, have been lyrically challenged. Harris (1993) wrote that pre-60s lyrics were "at best, superficial and shallow, and, at worst, silly and meaningless" (p. 4). While this judgment is a bit harsh—rock was just finding its way into the cultural mainstream in the late 1950s and hadn't yet found its lyrical voice—it is essentially true. Broadway tunes of the same era (e.g., those of *Carousel, My Fair Lady, Kismet,* or *Oklahoma*) featured far more sophisticated and clever lyrics—and those of Cole Porter were even cleverer and more sophisticated than these. Porter, in fact, was the first lyricist of any kind to have had a volume of his songs published in the Library of America's poetry series. So, yes, most rock lyrics pale in comparison to the great works of Cole Porter or, for that matter, Stephen Sondheim. Early rock songwriters especially tended to play it safe; the creativity and ingenuity of this form of expression were almost always located in the music. Criticism of rock lyrics is not, however, confined to songs written 50 years ago. Many journalists suggest that rock lyrics are still typically dreadful. Nick Hornby, in his very entertaining 2003 novel, *Songbook,* wrote: "I can understand people dismissing pop music. I know that a lot of it, nearly all of it, is trashy, unimaginative, poorly written, slickly produced, inane, repetitive and juvenile" (p. 15). He added: "all sorts of people knock up a neat tune and then can't furnish it with anything but a few tatty secondhand lines about eagles flying and love dying" (p. 49). Hornby, a great fan of rock 'n' roll and author of the wonderful rock-inspired novel, *High Fidelity*, contends that "lyrics are the literate pop fan's Achilles' heel" (p. 74). A similar, though more tempered view is offered by Robert Christgau (1992). In his essay on the Rolling Stones, he suggests that Mick Jagger's lyrics challenged "conventional perceptions more by their bite than by any notable eloquence or profundity" (p. 246)—a judgment that could well be extrapolated to most of rock music. The medium—the music itself—is the essential message; the lyrics, whether cynical and angry (hard rock, rap) or tender and loving (soft rock), usually play a secondary role in the production. The Who ("Gettin' in Tune") essentially made the same point: "I can't pretend there's any meaning here or in the words I'm saying, but I'm in tune."

Still, with literally millions of recordings over at least five decades of rock 'n' roll history, it is not surprising that some songs, or at least a few lyrics within some songs, have greatly transcended the norm. Smart lyrics sometimes exist throughout a song—like the earlier-mentioned "Hotel California" and "Like a Rolling Stone"; or, to name a few others from the classic rock era, Joni Mitchell's "Circle Game," Paul Simon's "Flowers Never Bend with the Rainfall," Billy Joel's "She's Always a Woman," and Jackson Browne's "I Thought I Was a Child." Some songwriters, like those noted above, consistently (though not invariably) turn out wonderful lines.

Occasionally, too, relatively unknown songwriters create a song with particularly powerful lyrics, for example, from "The Rose" (written by Amanda McBroom, popularized by Bette Midler): "It's the heart afraid of breaking that never learns to dance/It's the dream afraid of waking that never takes the chance." Note how these metaphors capture so well the risk and glory of lived experience. Sometimes, too, fine lyrics can be found scattered in otherwise unremarkable songs. Examples? How about in "Maniac" (from the movie *Flashdance*): "She has danced into the danger zone where the dancer becomes the dance." Or in Elton John and Bernie Taupin's "Daniel": "Do you still feel the pain of the scars that won't heal, your eyes have died but you see more than I." This latter lyric contains a truth about the consequences of abuse that would take most psychologists a few dense paragraphs or even pages to explain.

It was the blending of several other musical traditions with rock music that elevated at least some lyrics to a level considerably above the insipid and others to a level of genuine psychological or political astuteness. First, and most importantly, was the influence of folk music, more specifically, protest folk music in the tradition of Woody Guthrie. It was Dylan, a staunch admirer of Guthrie, who challenged and changed everything about typical rock song structure, rhyme schemes, and lyrics—his music wasn't necessarily two to three minutes long, and it sure wasn't about puppy love.

Dylan was and probably remains the single best lyricist within the general rock tradition. As Jon Pareles noted in a 1997 article in *The New York Times* chronicling Dylan's career, "Dylan taught folk singers how to transcend the topical, then taught rock songwriters how to think about something more than the next romance" (p. 1). Early in his career Dylan showed that he could write well and think broadly. His lyrics range from the deceptively simple to the seriously obtuse, and his domain of interest ranges from familiar issues of love lost (e.g., "Don't Think Twice, It's Alright") to politics ("Blowin' in the Wind") and the nature of authority ("My Back Pages"). Dylan was the first figure in rock to be deemed a poet. Indeed, the esteemed British literary critic and Oxford Professor of Poetry, Christopher Ricks, contends that Dylan is among the greatest poets in the English language. In stark contrast, the esteemed American novelist Norman Mailer has been quoted as saying, "If Dylan's a poet, I'm a basketball player" (cited in Leland, 2001, p. 36).

Among others following Dylan in the so-called folk-rock tradition were Paul Simon and Joni Mitchell—neither as politically incisive as Dylan but nonetheless brilliant in their lyrical depictions of adolescent angst and the problematic nature of commitment and connection. Others in this genre also contributed psychologically astute observations about the development of self and relationships, including Jackson Brown, Neil Young, Harry Chapin, Van Morrison, Don McLean, Carly Simon, and James Taylor. An equivalent group of a more recent vintage would include Tracy Chapman, Ani DiFranco, Melissa Etheridge, Mary Chapin Carpenter, Tori Amos, Gary Jules, John Mayer, Jack Johnson, Lucinda Williams, and, my own favorite, Sarah McLachlan. Bruce Springsteen, of course, also needs to be mentioned in this list because of both his enduring popularity and his ability, according to Springsteen observer Jimmy Gutterman (*Runaway American Dream,* 2005), to tell powerful and "unflinching stories" of ordinary, out-of-luck, working-class people. Springsteen is not in the same league as Dylan in terms of being able to turn out a poetic, complex line—who among songwriters is?—but he nonetheless has a compelling, gritty voice and a gift for metaphor, talents especially evident in his earliest ("Born to Run") and more recent ("The Rising," "Devils and Dust") work. Among his more oft-quoted lines (from "Thunder Road"): "Show a little faith, there's magic in the night/You ain't a beauty but, hey you're all right." These lines are neither elegant nor sophisticated, but their ability to evoke a knowing emotional response—a slight affirming shake of one's head or perhaps a bittersweet smile—is nonetheless impressive and rare.

A second influence on rock lyrics was the tin-pan alley, pop music tradition in which smart or at least clever lyrics were appreciated. Singer-songwriters like Carole King, Billy Joel, and, particularly in the beginning of their collaboration, the Elton John/Bernie Taupin duo contributed lyrics that made listening to the words of their songs worthwhile. Ironically, they (along with many of the folk-rock singers) were often vilified for this approach, with critics claiming that this wasn't genuine rock music because it wasn't true to rock's down-and-dirty rhythm and blues roots. That is, intelligent and/or clever lyrics, especially in the context of non-heavy-metal musical arrangements, have been regarded by some as antithetical to the essential rawness of what rock 'n' roll "should be" about. The late Lester Bangs, a former writer for *Rolling Stone* and among the most infamous rock critics of all time, felt that "grossness" was the truest criterion for great rock 'n' roll music. In one of his more infamous essays, "James Taylor Marked for Death" (1971), he caricatured these songs as "Jesus-walking-the boys-and girls-down-a Carolina-path-while-the dilemma-of-existence-crashes-like-a-slab-of-hod-on J.T.'s-shoulders." Thus, despite their enormous popularity and songwriting skills, groups like the Eagles and individual artists like Billy Joel have been dismissed by many prominent rock critics. The ethos underlying this unfortunate indictment is "if it ain't subversive, it ain't rock"—as if "subversive" guarantees authenticity or musical appeal and nonsubversive (i.e., "soft rock") necessarily reduces to intellectual or musical shallowness. Thus was born Billy Joel's playful but ultimately sarcastic message in "It's Still Rock 'n' Roll to Me" (1980): "Ev'rybody's talkin' 'bout the new sound, funny, but it's still rock and roll to me."

A third influence on songwriting, one that overlapped with the infusion of folk music into the rock tradition, was the rapidly changing nature of American culture in the late 1960s. Meaningful or at least socially topical lyrics began to be featured prominently in popular music as part of the 60s era of heightened political and individual consciousness. Indeed, the Beatles (in *Sgt. Pepper*); the Doors; the Who; Jefferson Airplane; Buffalo Springfield; and Crosby, Stills, Nash, and Young, among others, penned lyrics that continue to have the power to re-evoke the expansiveness, passions, hopes, fears, and excesses of that generation.

Two more recent influences on lyrics must also be noted. The punk movement—David Bowie, Patti Smith, Lou Reed and the Velvet Underground, and The Sex Pistols, for example—led to occasionally memorable song lyrics (and rhythms) that reflected the alienated, strung-out youth culture of the 1970s. And rap/hip-hop music of the 1980s onward, with its clever, often profane-filled rhymes about inner-city problems and struggles (e.g., violence; misogyny, poverty, racism), pushed listeners' attention to issues rarely dealt with in other rock formats. It's worth noting, too, that despite legions of followers (who would probably argue the point), neither heavy metal, disco, nor techno music have left memorable lyrical traces. In this regard, the pop music critic, Stephen Holden, suggested that the musical tradition that Dylan invented "nearly died with the arrival of punk rock and the macho rock climate that regarded singer-songwriters as self-pitying wimps" (1994, Section 2, p. 1).

Finally, what of MTV? How has its extraordinary influence on the music industry affected our experience of musical lyrics? Here I'd argue (with the help of younger colleagues and students of mine) that there's been strong, but almost contradictory effects. On the one hand, music videos, with their focus on creative imagery, production, technology, and dance, have likely lessened contemporary fans' interest in lyrics. After all, the power of these videos lies in the visual sphere. On the other hand, these videos are linked to the words of the songs, heightening at least passing awareness of what the song is about and what the words are intended to convey.

There are rock music critics who disparage any intellectual or even aesthetic focus on lyrics (without the accompanying music). Chief among this group are Dave Marsh and James Bernard who, in *The New Book of Rock Lists* (1994), suggest that the notion of rock lyrics as poetry is a "discredited" theory. "Rock lyrics," they wrote, "are verse and generally rhyme, but they aren't poetic, except in the rarest cases, and certainly, the best of them have little or no emotional impact when laid on the page, unadorned by music" (p. 128). Similarly, Scott Buchanan (1994) contends that "rock lyrics were meant to be heard and not seen" (p. 11). Even the lyrics of a master songwriter like Dylan tend to "feel awkward when read from a page," claims Alan Light. They do so, Light continues, because they were written as "genuine components of songs" and are best appreciated in the context of "Dylan's unparalleled phrasing, visionary arrangements and still-underappreciated melodic craft" (1992, p. 302).

These are strong words from knowledgeable and influential critics. But except for the observation that rock lyrics are rarely poetic, they have greatly overstated their thesis. Rock lyrics can be appreciated on the printed page, and they can be analyzed, enjoyed, and prized. They are, after all, words, and as such they can be evaluated (like any string of words) on the basis of their creativity, meaning, and wisdom. I agree entirely with what John Leland wrote in the *New York Times* magazine section a few years ago: "No populist definition [of poetry] could exclude the lyrics of rock songs, any more than it could exclude the songs of Sappho or the 'hey nonny nonny' nonsense of Shakespeare; any high-cultural guardians who exclude rock have the lost the authority to do so" (p. 36).

Do we lose something in the absence of the music? Yes, the music often intensifies or inflects meaning; or, stated somewhat differently, in good songs the total package is far greater than the sum of its parts. But, in the case of well-known songs, we supply the music—that is, the tunes are in our heads as we read the lyrics. We get the whole picture although we're shifting figure and ground. The words now become primary, the music secondary. And, in forcing this shift, we often get to hear, and sometimes even delight in, what we've never really heard before. Moreover, too many rock critics have underestimated the impact of smart or clever phrases on those who are willing to accept the possibility that such words exist in rock songs—especially those words that tell us something about ourselves, that are psychologically sharp. In fact, based on the reactions of many people who read these lyrics as I collected them, I would argue that the best of rock lyrics, unadorned by the accompanying music, often startle people with their brilliance (or at least near brilliance).

As noted earlier, most people simply have not paid attention to the lyrics even in familiar songs. In contrast to critics who get paid to attend to both music and words, ordinary listeners have often never really heard the words before and thus, not surprisingly, may have powerful reactions to words that have never really been taken in. Moreover, in the case of lyrics that are embedded in songs they've never heard, many individuals read these words as they would read anything of potential psychological or personal value—that is, with interest and perhaps with skepticism as well. But far more often than not, I have found that readers' reactions are in the "wow, that is good" or "that really is smart" category. And some have truly been moved by the way that rock lyrics—much like wonderful combinations of words in the form of prose or poetry—can bring us back to poignant moments or heighten current feelings in our lives.

The juncture of psychology and music has not been well explored by either field. Psychology, like most academic disciplines, generally fails to treat popular culture with any significant degree of seriousness. (There are, of course exceptions: David Michaelis's [2002] essay in *The American Scholar* about the Beatles' *Sgt. Pepper's* album is beautifully written and reflects a great awareness of both psychology and sociology). University scholars rarely bother learning what other academic disciplines have to say about their areas of interest, much less learn about what popular culture (music, dance, art) might contribute to their knowledge. This is unfortunate, of course, and a bit ironic given Freud's oft-repeated observation that "Everywhere I go I find a poet has been there before me."

Conversely, books and reviews generally fail to appreciate the psychological acumen of individual artists or songs. Although lyrics and album themes are often interpreted and critiqued, these attempts tend to treat the words as extensions of the artist's life or sensibility. These reviews rarely consider the accuracy or perceptivity of the words or message, that is, the extent to which the songwriter has tapped into a vein of wisdom that has been recognized as valid by psychological research or theory. Like fine poets and novelists, some songwriters have expressed vital psychological truths with a clarity and sharpness that have eluded all but the most accomplished writers among social scientists. Indeed, most academics learn to write in an overly intellectualized, jargon-filled style that, while rewarded by journal editors, feels deadly to virtually all readers outside the field. The point is that most rock critics have failed to appreciate just how good, how psychologically wise, some rock lyrics truly are.

I noted earlier that books about rock 'n' roll rarely attend to lyrics. The three significant exceptions to this rule are Richard Goldstein's *The Poetry of Rock* (1969),

James Harris' *Philosophy at 33 1/3* (1993), and Scott Buchanan's *Rock 'n' Roll: The Famous Lyrics* (1994). As enjoyable as this first book is with its commentary on the complete lyrics from many classic rock songs, it's now nearly 40 years old; moreover, its focus is on entire songs rather than specific, evocative lyrics from a wide array of sources. Harris' book contains a fair number of lyrics but is focused only on the 1960s; in addition, his interest was not on great lyrics per se but rather on themes in rock songs that reflected the nature of this era. Similarly, Buchanan's book, though containing a good many lyrics from 1955 to 1984, is not particularly discriminating—his goal was to sample broadly, and so mundane lyrics far outnumber the psychologically meaningful in his work.

This book focuses on lyrics that are smart, creative, and reflect significant psychological truths. Sometimes these are in the form of evocative metaphors, sometimes clever rhymes, and sometimes lovely, powerful, and/or startling phrases. Specifically, I have looked for lyrics that illustrate in particularly insightful ways common human longings and concerns. The phrases I have culled are necessarily pithy—copyright laws are usually interpreted to mean that one can have unrestricted use of only one to two lines—but their impact is often the stronger for this. Two lines of rock lyrics cannot compete with the depth of understanding of an essay, novel, or movie, but this is the lyricist's challenge—to create meaning, recognition, or pleasure using a very limited number of words. Leland (2001) made the interesting observation that rock lyrics actually generate "more good lines than coherent works."

Some readers will wonder why their favorite lyrics have been left out of this book. The answer is probably one of the following:

a) I or my research staff—which includes individuals ranging in age from 17 to more than 60—haven't looked at this particular song. It's obviously quite impossible to review every song published in the past 40–50 years. In 1996 alone, more than 500 albums per week were released, meaning that in recent years about 5,000 mostly new songs have been introduced each week, and that just for the five-year period between 1996 and 2000, more than one million recordings (although some instrumental) have entered the marketplace. Moreover, each of us has our favorite groups or genres; rap, for example, is not strongly represented in this volume, whereas classic rock hits from the 1965–1985 era are probably overrepresented. This bias is also one that *Rolling Stone* magazine was criticized for after compiling their 2004 list of the 500 greatest songs of all time.

b) For the most part, I've reviewed mainstream rock 'n' roll songs (not country, nor other related genres like folk, punk, or rap), perusing the lyrics in songs represented in such lists as VH1's top 100 greatest rock 'n' roll songs, the Amusement and Music Operations Association of top 40 jukebox singles of all time, the Rock and Roll Hall of Fame's list of the 500 most influential songs in rock history, *Rolling Stone's* list of the 500 greatest songs of all time, and Motown's Top 40. I've also reviewed the lyrics in almost all songs recorded by the most influential artists and groups in rock history. I've also checked out several Web sites that are devoted to lyrics and have gotten some good ideas, especially in regard to contemporary music, from these sources. And, finally, I've asked lots of friends, including students, to share their favorite lyrics with me. In general, though, I've stuck with the more popular tunes and more popular bands. Lyrics are more fun to read and easier to appreciate when one is familiar with the song.

c) I have reviewed a song or a particular set of lyrics and simply have come to the conclusion that these lyrics aren't as wise, compelling, or distinguished as some readers think. (Favorite lyrics—like favorite movies, books, or flavors of ice cream—are so subjective). There are many favorite songs that contain beautiful phrases or imagery but are not especially psychologically compelling. There are also favorite songs that are memorable in their tone, message, structure, or sentiment but have no one special phrase or verse—some of the Beatles' songs fit into this category.

d) I do think these lyrics are extraordinary, but to do them justice, I would need to quote more lines than copyright laws permit. Sometimes I have paraphrased a particularly evocative set of lyrics, but for the most part I have only included exact quotes in this book.

The beginning of the century seems to be a good time to look back at the top achievements in many fields; indeed, there have been numerous lists of the top-10 (or 100) movies, TV shows, books, or songs of the twentieth century. It's time for lyrics—or at least rock lyrics that are psychologically wise—to be recognized in this way. Moreover, this is a particularly good time to highlight psychological phenomena. In contrast to earlier (1950s/1960s) periods, contemporary clinical psychology is more accessible, that is, less often framed in obtuse psychoanalytic terminology. Individuals are no longer viewed from an almost exclusively pathological perspective but from a framework that recognizes people's healthy strivings toward mastery, creativity, spirituality, and acceptance and admiration from others. Psychological concepts (for example: defenses, attachment, autonomy, ambivalence, and stress) have increasingly become a part of our everyday vocabulary, informing our understanding of everything from the arts to business and finance to personal relationships. Rock lyrics, I believe, can be a lighthearted but engaging means to think about some profound issues of living.

These lyrics have been grouped into five broad categories, each representing a significant theme in contemporary life: friendship and love; pain and despair; sex, drugs, and money; psychological and spiritual ways of coping with life; and aging and growth. Each of these categories also reflects typical concerns that clients bring to their therapists. These categories are further subdivided into 18 smaller chapters (for example, one on "Finding Love" and another on "Losing Love"), each of which includes some discussion of the importance of this topic and the ways in which it's been thought about by psychologists and other social scientists. Most of each chapter, though, reflects my attempts to integrate into the discussion those rock lyrics that illuminate, often in more incisive ways than professionals have, the drama of love, the allure of drugs, the difficulty of change, the pain of aging, and the nature of many other psychological phenomena. The last chapter of the book is one in which I attempt to draw some conclusions about the power and influence of rock lyrics; I also speculate about how current developments in the field (for example, the growing market for "indie" music) may change the way songs and lyrics are heard, and shared with others. Lastly, I've included my list of the 50 best lyrics of all time (drawing heavily, as you'll see, on Bob Dylan, Billy Joel, Paul Simon, Joni Mitchell, Bruce Springsteen, the Beatles, and the Eagles). I hope you'll enjoy, learn, and ponder, even as you occasionally (or frequently) disagree with my choices of great lyrics throughout this book.

Part I

ON FRIENDSHIP AND LOVE

One of the more famous, and succinct, literary quotes is from E. M. Forster's (1910) *Howards End:* "Only connect." Perhaps the closest rock equivalent is the Beatles' classic line, "All you need is love." This section features lyrics that speak to our need to connect and love, both through friendship and more overtly romantic relationships. It also includes lyrics that address the dilemmas, complications, and heartaches that inevitably arise in our search for meaningful, lifelong relationships.

The first two chapters in this part are about "friendship" (Chapter 1) and "love" (Chapter 2). Virtually everyone has experienced the comfort of friendship and felt its capacity to nurture, heal, teach, and delight. Most everyone has also experienced the extraordinary power of love and felt its transformative capacity. There are many rock lyrics that speak to these parts of life, and some of the best ones (like those of Joni Mitchell) do so with a keen awareness of our psychological need for close human relationships. These lyrics, as you'll see, transcend greatly the "ooh, baby, I love you" music that defined all too well the early days of rock 'n' roll.

The final two chapters in this section include lyrics that focus on the painful, conflictual aspects of our need for others. The third chapter is on the near-universal experience of losing love, an ordeal that is generally far more traumatic than implied in the classic Neil Sedaka phrase that "breaking up is hard to do." The lyrics in this chapter reflect the range of reasons that relationships end—including fundamental differences between what men and women want or need in a relationship—and, at their best, also capture the sad and angry emotional tones that accompany this process.

Chapter 4 deals with one of the most basic conflicts in life: that between the need or wish to commit fully to another (as in a permanent loving relationship) and the need for personal freedom. The wisest lyrics in this chapter (especially those of the Eagles and Bruce Springsteen) are able to convey two often unrecognized truths: that freedom often comes with a great price, and that the needs for commitment and freedom are often far more complementary than truly opposite.

Chapter 1

FRIENDSHIP

When you're down and troubled and you need a helping hand…
—Carole King, "You've Got a Friend"

Although Carole King's "You've Got a Friend" ("When you're down and troubled and you need a helping hand") may be the most recognizable of all rock songs that have embraced the theme of friendship, it's hardly the only one to address this special part of life. While not quite as prevalent as songs about finding and losing love or about feeling depressed and alienated, a number of classic rock songs have addressed the nature of adult friendships. Some of these songs, such as "You've Got a Friend" (also recorded by James Taylor) and Bill Wither's infectious "Lean on Me" ("Lean on me when you're not strong, I'll be your friend, I'll help you carry on"), have essentially paid homage to the loving aspects of friendship, focusing on one person's willingness to always be there for the other. While the lyrics of neither of these songs are particularly creative, they are nonetheless moving. The image of good friends, there for us in Carole King's words to "brighten up even the darkest night," is powerful indeed. Others songs, though, have reflected the more complex, darker parts of this relationship, implying—quite accurately—that friendship can include significant doses of annoyance, jealousy, competition, fear of rejection, disappointment, ambivalence, and even cruelty. "I gotta friend," Bob Dylan sang, "who spends his life, stabbing my picture with a bowie knife" ("I Shall Be Free").

Let's focus on the positive aspects first. For most of us, good friends are critical to our mental and physical health. They serve a number of vital functions in our lives and act toward us in ways that even spouses or other family members cannot. They are often more patient, accepting of our flaws, and except for the honeymoon part of a romantic relationship, more eager to see us and more complimentary than those who see us on a daily basis. These are some of the advantages of what psychologists call "voluntary relationships." Friends, of course, have the advantage of (usually) not having to live with us, enabling them (usually) to ignore our more annoying qualities and be more attentive to who we are and the stories we like to tell. Time spent with friends is carved out and special, not part of the regular, taken-for-granted time spent at work or with family. Moreover, friends, along with family, make us feel like we have a place in the world, that we are cared for. "I get by with a little help from my friends" famously sang the Beatles. And although this line, from the 1967 *Sgt. Pepper's Lonely Hearts Club Band* album, is explicitly associated with drugs ("I get high with a little help from my friends"), it also implies a more basic truth: that we count on friends to help us through the inevitable rough spots in life.

Stated from the opposite perspective: a life without friends is difficult; it is hard to make it in this world alone. We are essentially social creatures and need supportive others in our lives from childhood on, a fact that psychologists have increasingly recognized in the past few decades. Social isolation hurts deeply and is often associated with depression. In the song that first brought fame to James Taylor, "Fire and Rain", he admits to "lonely times when I could not find a friend." We may wonder whether his assumed depression (or drug addiction, for that matter) led to his isolation and lack of friends, or whether a lack of friends resulted in depression and desperate measures to cope; but either way, his words remind us that being alone exacts a great emotional price. In one research study (Burt, 1986), those who were able to list five or more intimate friends to whom they could discuss important matters were 60 percent more likely to feel "very happy" in their lives.

In "Fire and Rain," James Taylor also lets us know about the suicide of a friend—reportedly, someone who was in the same group therapy he was in—who killed herself following an argument with her psychiatrist over medication. Here, his words reflect the expectation that intimate friends are to be forever: "But I always thought that I'd see you again." We may well take friends for granted, we may neglect to tell them how much they mean to us, but we nevertheless assume that those to whom we've bared our souls will somehow be in our lives forever. I suspect we all have friends in this category—those who we only rarely see or communicate with who we nonetheless assume will always be there for us if we need them. This eternal aspect of friendship is captured beautifully in Cyndi Lauper's "Time after Time": "If you fall I will catch you, I will be waiting/Time after time."

Let's consider the multiple roles that friends play in our lives. For starters, friends are there when we need them—in that Carole King and Bill Withers way. Sentimental though they may be, the words of Burt Bacharach in "That's What Friends Are For" (sung by, among others, Dionne Warwick) are also a good reflection of our wish for friends to care about us "in good times and bad times," to be on our side "forever more." Arguably, though, the most moving lyrics about friends being there for us are from two classic songs by Simon and Garfunkel. "Homeward Bound" features a graceful simile: "Like emptiness in harmony, I need someone to comfort me." "In Bridge over Troubled Water," the emotional sharpness of the imagery allows us to feel the power of a friend's reaching out: "When you're weary, feeling small/When tears are in your eyes, I will dry them all." Friends are on our side, especially when we're down. Friends can, and often do, buffer the negative parts of our relationships with significant others and other family members.

Similarly, friends believe in us when we cannot, helping us to achieve goals that we may have considered out of reach. This sentiment is expressed metaphorically in the words from "Wind beneath My Wings" (sung by many, but popularized by Bette Midler): "I could fly higher than an eagle, for you are the wind beneath my wings." Friends, these lines suggest, may have a better opinion of us than we ourselves do, a fact that we should appreciate and take advantage of when necessary.

This need for friends to care about us, believe in us, and make us feel good about ourselves is psychologically accurate. According to the tenets of Self Psychology—a currently popular, modified version of traditional Freudian thought—we all desperately need people to frequently affirm us, and we need this throughout our lives, from childhood on. In fact, this theory holds that this need is equal to the motivational power of sex and aggression, the two major drives posited by Freudian psychology. Heinz Kohut, the founder of Self Psychology and probably the most influential psychologist of the twentieth century whom no one outside the field has heard of, believed that such affirmation was initially the task of our parents, but that later the responsibility needed to fall to our significant others and friends. Kohut's (1971) theory suggests that we need people to affirm us in multiple ways: to tell us we're wonderful, to compliment us on something we've done or the way we look, to confirm that we've made the right decision, to agree with us regarding the people or politics we love or detest, and, perhaps most importantly, to unconditionally believe in us. We need such people in our lives—family, friends, and lovers who are also friends—to make us feel special and eminently lovable. Springsteen said all this in a far more poetic way in one of his signature songs, "Born to Run": "Wendy, let me in, I wanna be your friend. I wanna guard your dreams and visions." What a great line—a friend as someone who guards our dreams and visions, who holds them even when we struggle to believe them ourselves.

Another enormously important role of a friend is that of confidant. We need friends to disclose to. Sometimes this takes the form of just dumping all our anger and frustration and resentments on those who can bear it, a function of friendship well described by the Rolling Stones ("Let It Bleed"). Not only, noted the Stones, do we need someone to lean on, dream on, and feed on, but "we all need someone we can bleed on." And, Mick Jagger added, "you can bleed on me." But most of us also need friends to really listen to what we are saying. In fact, good friends often have the ability not just to respond well to what we say but also to how we're saying it. They seem attuned to our pauses, body language, and especially our moods. Moreover, good friends, like good therapists, have the uncanny ability to know when to leave things alone and when to pursue something further. That is, these friends know when to just listen and accept that we've said all we want to at the moment, and when to ask questions, gently pushing us to disclose more about what's really on our minds. Smart friends know that it's often most loving to be there to listen. Here I'm reminded of a wonderful couplet by the Canadian folksinger, Gordon Lightfoot ("Rainy Day People"): "Rainy day people always seem to know when it's time to call/Rainy day people don't talk, they just listen till they've heard it all."

So good friends are good listeners, a task far harder than most realize. Joni Mitchell ("Songs to Aging Children Come") was so very right: "So much said in listening." This is a wise phrase, one that speaks to the exquisite skill and caring involved in being a good listener. What is said in listening is that I care enough to devote all my attention to what you need and are trying to convey. Perhaps the most difficult yet most powerful aspect of listening is the need to put aside our own narcissism—to listen to another without needing to be listened to. Although it's sometimes loving and helpful for us to share our own story with another, especially if it's in the service of normalizing a friend's feelings or behavior ("I too have felt that way"), most of us tend to underestimate the value of well-attuned listening. In particular, men often come late to the task of being a good listener, not really learning how until late adolescence, when the demands of love and lust propel them to do so.

Still another role of friends is to offer new perspectives, to teach us. Good friends can tell us when we're making that big mistake about love or money or career because most of the time it's far easier being told by a friend that we're being foolish than it is by a significant other or other family member. Sometimes by reflecting our own words, sometimes by challenging us, sometimes by offering their own stories, sometimes by introducing us to new experiences, and sometimes through dialogue, friends teach us things about the world and ourselves that we hadn't known nor realized. Some psychologists (e.g., Wright, 1978) call this the "stimulation value" of friendship.

Back to "That's What Friends Are For" and some maudlin but essentially accurate lyrics about this aspect of friendship: "Well you came and opened me, and now there's so much more I see." These words could also be said about psychotherapists. A book written about therapy even referred to it as *The Purchase of Friendship* (Schofield, 1964). Good friends, like good therapists, enrich our vision. Both find ways of holding us that allow us the safety to see the world more fully. Especially when we're frightened or depressed, our vision tends to be constricted; we see the world in very narrow terms and can't imagine a future for ourselves that's different from the present. Friends (and therapists) help us see the world from new and often less self-defeating perspectives. The Dave Matthews Band ("Say Goodbye") offered a wise variation on this theme: "In your eyes, I see what's on my mind." In this song, the clear implication is that what's being seen is sexual desire. Still, these words reflect a more general truth: that we can learn about ourselves, especially those aspects of our presentation to others that we're mostly unaware of, through what our friends reflect back to us. This occurs frequently in terms of body language. Until friends react, we may have little or no idea of the signals we're giving off.

Friends also serve as problem-solvers, especially when we are too emotionally distraught to think clearly ourselves. This may often happen in the aftermath of relationship problems. These smart words are from the Indigo Girls' song, "Power of Two": I'm…smarter than the tricks played on your heart/we'll look at them together then we'll take them apart." What we can't do alone very well, like understanding why someone has hurt us, we can do in the presence of a loving, trusted friend. And perhaps this is a good place to use another Indigo Girls' lyric, to illustrate how friends keep us grounded emotionally by showing us the light parts of life when the world seems too heavy. These words are from what is probably their most famous song ("Closer to Fine"): "The best thing you've ever done for me is to help me take my life less seriously/It's only life after all." They've found a wise way to convey the obvious but often unnoted fact that we need friends with whom we can laugh and share the absurdities of life. This aspect of friendship is reminiscent of Billy Joel's line in "Piano Man" about going to a bar to "forget about life for a while." And it's also reminiscent of the lines of a great contemporary country song ("Friends I Can't Forget") by Toby Keith: "There's some nights I can't remember with friends I can't forget."

With his list of what a friend shouldn't be, Dylan's lines ("All I Really Want to Do") allow us to consider our expectations of a friendship: "I ain't looking to compete with you, beat, or cheat, or mistreat you…All I really want to do is, baby, be friends with you." Whereas these lines are a bit overheated—Dylan's need for a clever rhyme scheme here makes friendship seem anything short of outright abuse—his words do remind us of how much we expect our friends' undivided caring and loyalty. The problem, though, is that we often (unrealistically) expect friends to be constantly virtuous, unselfish, and supportive, almost without guile or flaws. We're surprised and hurt when friends are unreasonable, insensitive, and self-absorbed, as if our friends aren't allowed these very human failings. George Harrison's lines on this topic, which sound like something out of an old *Farmer's Almanac* or a Benjamin Franklin book of sayings, are worth savoring: "Scan not a friend with a microscopic glass, you know his faults, now let the foibles pass" ("The Answer's at the End").

Thus, like all intimate relationships in life (including marriage and parenthood), friendship includes behaviors and feelings that are complex, shameful, and often unacknowledged. Friendships are rarely, if ever, exclusively loving, mutually affirming, and free of hostility. Friends can, and often do, exhibit a remarkable range of behaviors, from the extremely loving to the extremely hateful. Dylan's words from "Positively 4th Street"—"You've got a lot of nerve to say you are a friend, when I was down you just stood there grinning"—are reminiscent of Mark Twains' famous observation (in his 1897 travel book, *Following the Equator*) about friendship: "It takes your enemy and your friend, working together, to hurt you to the heart; the one to slander you and the other to get the news to you."

But let's end this chapter on the positive note that friendship deserves. As the Dave Matthews Band ("Best of What's Around") put it: "Turns out, not where, but who you're with that really matters."

Chapter 2

LOVE

Help me, I think I'm falling in love too fast; it's got me hoping for the future and worrying about the past.

—Joni Mitchell, "Help Me"

Most songs, rock or otherwise, are about love. Of course, one could make the argument that most art, from fiction to painting to theater, focuses on the idea of love as secular salvation. As James Taylor noted (in "Carolina in My Mind"), "there ain't no doubt [in] no one's mind that love's the finest thing around." Similarly, Smokey Robinson ("My Girl") let us know that far more than "money, fortune or fame," being in love offered "all the riches…one man can claim." And, as the Dave Matthews Band ("#40") astutely observed, "A friend is always good to have, but a lover's kiss is better."

For most individuals, finding and holding onto love are seemingly the most important tasks in life, and failures in these ventures invariably cause inconsolable pain, longing, and self-doubt. Rock, like other art forms, explores several variations on these themes: When will I be loved? Will my fantasy of being with this person ever become reality? Has anyone else ever experienced a love so wonderful and overwhelming? Is this really the right person for me? Are the differences between us too great? Is there anything as painful as a love that is unrequited? Will our love last forever? How is it possible that our love has died? What did I do wrong and how can I make it up? Will I ever stop pining for him/her? Will I ever find someone new?

Early rock dealt mostly with love, but the lyrics to these songs were, for the most part, remarkably banal. The lyrics seemed to play endlessly and uncreatively on a few basic themes: Please love me; I miss you; I promise to love you forever. Or, to use real examples: "I want you, I need you, I love you" (in the Elvis Presley song with this title); "there goes my baby with someone new, she sure looks happy, I sure am blue" (The Everly Brothers, "Bye Bye Love"); "love love me do, you know I love you" (The Beatles, "Love Me Do"). But lyrics about love became more sophisticated in the mid to late 1960s as the political and social landscape began changing dramatically. Feminism became more powerful, sex and love took on different meanings, and songwriters became increasingly comfortable writing personally meaningful, introspective lyrics about relationships. Love, in life and songs, became more complicated, uncertain, and political. As Dylan noted with perfect irony in his (1967) song with the same title as this phrase, "love is just a 4-letter word."

According to Robert Sternberg (1988), a psychologist and former president of the American Psychological Association, this four-letter feeling consists of three primary components: intimacy, passion, and commitment. Intimacy refers to that warmth and closeness we experience with another. Passion can be experienced as love at first sight and often includes a strong sexual aspect. Commitment refers to that sense of forever in a relationship. Different combinations of these three basic ingredients lead to different kinds of love, seven in all. For example, passion, without significant doses of intimacy or commitment, adds up to infatuation; intimacy and commitment, without passion, is what Sternberg terms "companionate love." Intimacy, without passion or commitment, equates to friendship. It takes the combination of all three ingredients to produce "consummate love," that greatest experience of all and one which, according to Sternberg, is enormously difficult to sustain. Not surprisingly, rock songs have described each of these different forms of love, although without using these fancy labels. Many rock songs have also dealt with the terrible pain of losing love, and that subject is the focus of the next chapter.

Let's consider a trio of excellent Joni Mitchell lyrics to illustrate these three essential aspects of love. Intimacy is feeling close, sharing stories, finding time, caring deeply. Or, as Joni puts it in "All I Want": "All I really want our love to do, is to bring out the best in me and you too." What's lovely—and psychologically wise about this—is her simple acknowledgement that true intimacy is reciprocal. We both get to benefit. We each get to tell the other how we feel and what we need. There is considerable research to show that in equitable relationships both partners are especially content. For example, dating and marital relationships in which there is a high degree of disclosure of personal information (including thoughts and feelings) tend to last longer and feel more satisfying (Laurenceau, Feldman Barrett, & Pietromonaco, 1998).

On the other hand, loving relationships, including friendships, tend to go astray when one person invests or discloses more than the other in the relationship. In some relationships for example, one partner unilaterally takes on the helping role. While this can work for a while, more often than not it ultimately leads to resentment. During child-rearing years, when wives often do a disproportionate share of the housework and parenting (often while also holding down a part-time or full-time job), marital satisfaction tends to decline in both partners (Keith & Schafer, 1980). While one does not usually expect wise lyrics from the Monkees, these words from "I'm a Believer" (written by Neil Diamond) are spot on: "I thought love was more or less a giving thing, [but] it seems the more I gave the less I got." Despite protestations to the contrary, virtually every giver assumes that eventually his or her efforts will be reciprocated. Some individuals find it far more difficult to explicitly acknowledge needs or disclose deep feelings than to provide support; others are able to ask but their pleas for reciprocity are unheard. This then is the gift in true intimacy: each partner in a loving relationship is able and wants to both give and receive. The smart words of the contemporary supergroup, U2, are relevant in this regard: "We're one, but we're not the same/We get to carry each other" ("One").

Passion in love is that great intensity of body and soul, including that feeling of being obsessed with the other in that classic Barry White sense of "I can't get enough of your love, babe." Joni, though, said it with far more poetic flair in "Court and Spark": "Love came to my door with a sleeping roll and a madman's soul." It is an apt metaphor, this madman's soul, and one reminiscent of the frequent connection made throughout the ages between love and madness. "I am mad for you," we say. Or, "you drive me crazy." Love has been described in many ways, but perhaps its most distinctive characteristic is its intensity and power, especially its capacity during the early stages of a relationship to consume us. People in love are often irrational, exaggerating a lover's virtues, denying flaws, and feeling unable to focus on anything but the object of desire. "Love," sang U2 ("Miracle Drug"), "makes nonsense of space and time." Passion makes us lose our bearings. In fact, psychoanalysts believe that those in this state of love are incapable of being in effective therapy; such individuals are usually unable to invest their energies, thoughts, or feelings onto anyone or anything other than the loved object (Anna Freud, 1958). Research shows that clients who think about therapy and their therapists in between sessions tend to have better treatment outcomes (Geller & Farber, 1993); individuals in love tend only to think about their loved one, not about what happened in therapy.

One other aspect of passion needs to be noted—namely, that it may take multiple forms. An excellent illustration of this comes from Huey Lewis and the News ("The Power of Love"): "The power of love is a curious thing/Make a one man weep, make another man sing." Love's passion intensifies emotions, making us feel especially vibrant and especially vulnerable. Of course, where Huey and his group got it wrong was in their assumption that these two pathways are separate. For most people, they're intertwined; love makes them both weep and sing. A great lyric from a classic Motown song (Smokey Robinson's "I Second That Emotion") speaks to this two-sided nature of passion, though ultimately suggesting that the vulnerability in loving—the potential for loss— is even more intense than love itself: "Maybe you'd go away and never call, and a taste of honey is worse than none at all."

Finally, let's return to the Joni Mitchell lyrics that I began this chapter with to provide one last example of the dizzying and paradoxical effects of passion. She admits how falling in love "too fast" has got her "hoping for the future and worrying about the past." Psychologically speaking, what might she mean? I suspect that she's aware—quite wisely—that old patterns may yet come to haunt her present and future. In other words, I so want this love to last forever, and yet I'm also so fearful that I will make the same mistakes I have in the past that have sabotaged previous relationships. And she's right. We do play the same patterns out over and over again, a theme that's the subject of a later chapter in this book on "The Difficulty of Change."

And what of that last, and probably most difficult part of love—commitment? The number of rock songs with either the word *forever* or *always* in them is probably impossible to calculate. Pledges of forever often seem so real and meaningful while they're being said, and these sentiments flow easily into the narrative of romantically flavored songs. Here's Joni Mitchell's lovely take on these feelings (from "Morgantown"): "But the only thing I have to give…are all the mornings still to live." She offers her lover neither great passion nor understanding. And while both these qualities may well be in the relationship, it's clear to us that the gift she cherishes most, that which is deepest in her soul, is her wish and willingness to wake up next to her lover and spend each day of the rest of her life with him. Contrast this sentiment with that of Maroon 5 in their song, "Through with You": "Saying I love you has nothing to do with meaning it."

What else about love do wise lyrics teach us? That it is absolutely transformative. The words to "This Magic Moment" (originally sung by the Drifters in 1960, then later covered by Jay and the Americans) suggest this so very well: "This magic moment, so different and so new, was like any other until I met you." Jackson Browne's lyrics ("I Thought I Was a Child") also capture this quality beautifully: "I thought I was a child until you turned and smiled, I thought I knew where I was going until I heard your laughter flowing." My life can never be the same again. Another set of lines from this same singer conveys much the same sentiment ("I'll Do Anything"): "You hold a life there in your hands, you probably don't know; somehow your dreams became my plans, somewhere long ago." And once more, back to Joni Mitchell and some lines from a song ("Chelsea Morning") that speak to the magic of days spent with one's beloved: "Oh, won't you stay, we'll put on the day, and we'll wear it till the night comes." We'll create our own reality; we'll imagine the world as we need it to be. Not only is this a favorite song of mine, but it apparently inspired a fair number of baby boomer parents (including Bill and Hillary Clinton) when it came time to choose a name for their daughters.

Lyrics also suggest that love has the capacity to imbue time and place with enormous and enduring significance. A patient of mine speaks frequently, with great intensity and longing, of an image of an event that happened years ago: sweeping up his lover in his arms on a street in New York on a wintry day. To him, this was a moment of almost unbearable joy, a peak experience. Though they're no longer together, he cherishes the memory. The Beatles understood this feeling well ("In My Life"): "All these places have their moments with lovers and friends, I still can recall." In "Things We Said Today," they observe much the same phenomenon: "Someday when I'm lonely, wishing you weren't so far away, then I will remember things we said today." Memories of love are often indelible in a bittersweet way.

Rock lyrics have noted, too, that love both comforts and strengthens. Among my favorite songs that expound on this theme is James Taylor's "Something in the Way She Moves": "It isn't what she's got to say or how she thinks or where she's been; to me the words are nice the way they sound." The soothing presence of a loved one is something we often take for granted; that is, it's more often background than foreground and something we're aware of only when our lover is absent. James Taylor's words here are somewhat unique in his awareness of how his lover's voice quality provides this comfort for him. We might speculate that there's something about her voice that resonates with the soothing qualities of his mother's or other caretaker's voice, perhaps something about this woman's tone that now still evokes earlier feelings of being comforted.

A different kind of comforting, a somewhat more protective presence, is suggested by the lyrics of Elliot Smith, an "indie" folksinger of sorts who came to fame when his music was featured in the movie, *Good Will Hunting;* tragically, he committed suicide in 2003 at the age of 23. Here, in "Between the Bars," are some very psychologically savvy lyrics: "People you've been before, that you don't want around anymore, that push and shove and won't bend to your will—I'll keep them still." It would have been easy to have written "People you've seen before" in this phrase. The line still would have worked and would have made sense to everybody. "People you've been before," though, is far cleverer; assumably it refers to the fact that we all have multiple selves lurking within us. No, not (usually) the psychotic, multiple personalities type that screenwriters love, but rather different inner voices and emotional states that we experience at different times with different people—some of which we don't like very much. My appreciation of these words, then, is based on Elliot Smith's awareness of these multiple selves (or inner states), the especially intrusive nature of these selves to those who feel troubled, and of the desire for a lover to somehow be able to quiet these unwanted voices or feelings. And if this happens—if someone we love does comfort and soothe us—it may well leave us feeling strengthened and better able to negotiate what's often a hard world. Here I would invoke the words of Ben E. King in his 1960s hit, "Stand by Me." He first lays out a stark poetic vision, "When the night has come and the land is dark and the moon is the only light we see." But he adds: "I won't be afraid, no, I won't be afraid, just as long as you stand, stand by me."

A truth about love not often noted in rock lyrics is that for love to last, it takes endless negotiation and compromise. In teaching psychotherapy to my students, I often say that therapists' mistakes and misunderstandings are inevitable, and that the only real question is not *whether* these will occur but what one does when they do. (A good part of the answer is that the therapist must acknowledge his or her part in the misunderstanding or impasse). I love Roberta Flack's words in "The First Time Ever I Saw Your Face": "And I knew our joy would fill the earth, and last till the end of time." The problem is that they aren't likely to be true. These are words uttered in that great first flush of love, when it seems incomprehensible that the feelings and perfect harmony experienced in the moment will not last forever. Once again, Joni Mitchell's words ("Refuge of the Roads") reveal a more complicated truth: "He saw my complications and he mirrored me back simplified, and we laughed how our perfect world would always be denied."

An even darker line about this aspect of love comes from Ani DiFranco's "Small World": "I said skeletons are fine; your closet or mine?" She seems to be saying something on the order of, "Let's just acknowledge that we're imperfect, if not downright screwed up, and move on from there. We'll skip right over that part of the relationship where we tacitly agree to deny the existence of flaws in each other." Consistent with Roberta Flack's words, though, our expectations regarding love tend to be remarkably unrealistic—a problem that partially explains the high prevalence of divorce. Too often, we expect our lover to always be there, always take our side, always show a saintly amount of patience, and always yield to our needs: "Hold me when I'm here, love me when I'm wrong, hold me when I'm scared, and love me when I'm gone" (3 Doors Down, "When I'm Gone"). Sure, I'll do these things all the time—except when I've come home exhausted from work, or the baby has kept us up all night, or when the football game is on, or when you've taken your mother's side rather than mine.

Let's examine then what may be the most realistic rock lyrics ever written about love, the infamous words of Bruce Springsteen in "Thunder Road": "You ain't a beauty, but hey, you're all right." In this song, this is meant as a sincere proposal of sorts—we're not perfect, but we may be good enough for each other, and together we just might be able to make it out of here (a typical Springsteen dead-end, working-class town) to find a better life somewhere else. What's perhaps most striking about this line is its perfect failure to hew to the traditions of romantic songwriting and to the myths and assumptions surrounding romantic love. To call these words cynical is to miss the point; to call them gritty is insufficient. They feel real—the kind of stuff that men (and women) say to themselves in the privacy of their consciousness and sometimes even to their best friends and therapists. Springsteen's genius here lies in his willingness to give voice to this kind of rarely articulated thought, that which reflects not only optimism about love but also the limitations that we each bring to the task of loving.

Chapter 3

LOSING LOVE

The sting of reason, the splash of tears…Love emerges and it disappears.
—Paul Simon, "I Do It for Your Love"

As the previous chapter showed, there are some great lyrics describing the extraordinary, life-changing qualities of love. Given the blues tradition on which rock is based, it's not surprising that there are at least as many exceptionally smart and poignant lyrics about the loss of love.

The words used in these songs reflect a harsh reality about the fate of many relationships. Whereas the frequently cited statistic that "half of all marriages end in divorce" is probably overstated (Harris, 1987), the numbers of failed relationships are nonetheless dramatic. The percentage of marriages in the United States that ended in divorce reached a peak of slightly more than 40 percent in the early 1980s, and it now stands at slightly more than 30 percent (Hurley, 2005). Risk factors for marital breakups include getting married at a young age (before 20), having been raised in a one-parent household, dating for only a short period of time before marriage, working at a low-income job, and, perhaps surprisingly, cohabiting before marriage (Americans for Divorce Reform, 2006; DiCaro, 2005). The usual explanation for the last factor is that those who live together before marriage are often those who "know" they're better off not being married, and so if for whatever reason they do marry, they tend to be more likely to dissolve the relationship. In addition, differences in age, faith, or education raise the risk for divorce. It's also noteworthy that women are far more likely than men to file for divorce, especially among college-educated couples (Brinig & Allen, 2000).

Of course, marriage is not the only kind of relationship that sometimes ends badly. From adolescence onward, couples in all sorts of relationships struggle to stay together and keep each partner relatively happy. As the Beatles sang ("I'm Looking through You"): "Why, tell me why did you not treat me right? Love has a nasty habit of disappearing overnight." Well, maybe not quite overnight, but nevertheless often surprisingly, disappointingly, and hurtfully.

What causes marriages and other loving relationships to end? The old mantra was sex, money, and power—as in, I'm not getting enough, you (or we) are not making enough, and you are not treating me respectfully enough. It's a bit more complicated than this nowadays, in great measure because women's roles and their expectations around work and relationships have changed so dramatically in the last several decades. The great social transformations wrought in the 1960s and 1970s—the movement toward greater equality in jobs, education, and relationships—were surely needed and long overdue, but men and women are still struggling to incorporate these changes into new patterns of being and staying together. Dylan's words in the early 1960s that "the times they are a-changin'" were prophetic in many spheres of life (for example, politics and religion), and that has certainly been true of male-female relationships. Concerns related to "poor communication," equitably sharing household tasks, raising children, and balancing job and family demands are now very much in the mix of what causes relationships to fail (Pattison, 2001). Namely, you don't tell me anything, you don't do anything (around the house), you don't know anything (about raising children), and you don't have time for anything (other than work). Relationships have become far more complicated as gender roles have become more complex and interchangeable. This is probably as true for gay relationships as it is for heterosexual ones.

We also need to include the fact that many relationships end as a result of infidelity. In the words of ZZ Top (those guys with the great, long beards): "Somebody else been shakin' your tree/Supposed to be saving all that stuff for me" ("Somebody Else Been Shakin' Your Tree"). Sometimes what starts out as a casual fling becomes far more and far more dangerous to the integrity of an ongoing partnership. Elvin Bishop confessed as much in his song, "[I] fooled around and fell in love." In "Cautious Man," Springsteen hypothesized that it's the loss of love that opens the door to affairs: "in a restless heart the seed of betrayal lay." But sometimes it's despair or the loss of passion that fuels affairs, sometimes a partner's inattentiveness, sometimes lust, and sometimes it's impossible to disentangle these motives. Neil Young's words ("Shots") suggest all these possibilities: "Lust comes creeping through the night to feed on hearts of suburban wives who learned to pretend when they met their dreams end." And, of course, ultimately, it barely matters. Regardless of reasons, affairs hurt and often end relationships.

Notably, too, affairs of the heart can be every bit as destructive as sexual affairs. Sometimes, however, a lover will try to hold onto the relationship even in the aftermath of being very hurt. In this regard, Rod Stewart made famous these plaintive words of Tim Hardin ("Reason to Believe"): "Knowing that you lied straight-faced while I cried, still I look to find a reason to believe." On a more desperate note, Dido ("White Flag") sang of an unwillingness to let go in the face of a dissolving relationship, "I will go down with the ship."

Researchers investigating relationships and their dissolution have also shown that it may not be what couples argue about but how they argue that most determines whether they'll stay together (Gottman, 2001). Couples who fight fair, who don't insult or blame or constantly bring up past grievances, are those who are most likely to resolve their inevitable conflicts. Marital and family therapists are aware of how important it is for partners to replace criticism, or at least tone it down considerably, by owning up to their own flaws and attempting to see the other's point of view. In fact, a good deal of the work in marital therapy is teaching partners to hear, and acknowledge, what the other is saying. Still, our narcissism, our need to be right, so often gets in the way. We struggle to admit our mistakes, even though we know we must. Tracy Chapman ("Baby Can I Hold You") got this exactly right: "Words don't come easily, like forgive me, forgive me."

Whatever the reasons for a relationship ending, lovers often try to find a way to make sense of what happened. Some of the most poignant lyrics in rock history have come from this painful place. Some songwriters have seen the loss of love as inevitable. The lyrics of Paul Simon with which I started this chapter suggest as much: "love emerges and it disappears." Similarly, though more metaphorically, the late folk singer Phil Ochs in his beautiful song "Changes," professed that "passions will part to a strange melody, as fires will sometimes turn cold."

More often, though, songwriters have attempted more personal explanations. Here are four of the more compelling reasons offered for why a loving relationship has ended. Let's start with Carole King's sense, in "It's Too Late," that love dies as a result of a lack of commitment to making the relationship last: "there's something wrong here, there can be no denying; one of us is changing, or maybe we've just stopped trying." This lack of trying often takes the form of no longer hearing or caring to fulfill the other's needs. Whereas loving, mutual affirmations tend to mark the beginning of most relationships, they also tend to fade—too often, we do stop trying. Jackson Browne ("Fountain of Sorrow") gets high marks for being aware of this very human tendency and for finding the right words to express it: "when you see through love's illusions, there lies the danger; and your perfect lover just looks like a perfect fool." The hard work of a relationship starts after the honeymoon period, and many relationships do not pass the test. Another set of superb lyrics on this theme of losing our commitment to our partner's needs or happiness comes from Ani DiFranco ("Both Hands"): "And in each other's shadows, we grew less and less tall, and suddenly our theories couldn't explain it all."

These lyrics imply that, over time, lovers become less likely to be affirming and more likely to be critical, and this is what drives relationships apart. It's an excellent hypothesis. Despite the fact that no one likes being criticized, we all can tolerate it—but only up to a limit. John Gottman, a prominent researcher in this area, concluded that healthy marriages were marked by the ability of partners to balance criticism with compliments and affection. He found that in successful marriages, positive interactions (including smiling, complimenting, laughing, and touching) occur five times as often as negative interactions (such as disapproval, insults, and sarcasm). Unsuccessful marriages feature a far less favorable ratio of positive to negative interactions, a fact that J. D. Souther ("Simple Dream") seemed to have intuitively known in composing these lyrics: "Well in some ways I am like a child, you never seemed to know it; and if a kind word ever crossed your mind, you never tried to show it." We expect a lover to accept us—flaws, quirks, and all—and to affirm those parts of ourselves that we like best. (For men, these are likely to be the childlike or adolescent-like parts of their persona.) And we expect a lover to mostly overlook our flaws, or at least begrudgingly accept them. Souther's lyrics, then, point to one of the more frequently observed complaints in marital therapy: "My partner is too critical. He or she is so much more aware of what I do wrong than what I do right."

A second explanation for failed relationships is somewhat of a variation on this first theme. Here, though, lyrics emphasize lovers' inability to negotiate mutually satisfying roles, or even to accept the other's point of view. Lovers in these songs find themselves at terrible impasses when they need to compromise on issues of power or influence. Here's the Eagles' wise take on this in "Best of My Love": "You see it your way, and I see it mine, but we both see it slippin' away."

A third reason offered for breakups is that they are the result of each partner promising too much too soon in the relationship. "Unsettled hearts," sang Tracy Chapman ("Speak the Word"), "promise what they can't deliver." And David Gray, a contemporary singer recommended to me by many of my graduate students, offered these astute words in "Say Hello, Wave Goodbye": "Take a look in my face for the last time/I never knew you, you never knew me." Although there are many moving stories of long-term relationships that individuals committed to after but a few weeks or months of dating, there are probably far more stories of failed relationships that began with rapid infatuation and mutual pledges of forevermore.

The final perspective on why love doesn't last comes from Dylan. In some ways these lines from "Don't Think Twice, It's All Right" overlap with some of what has already been cited. In other ways, though, they represent another layer of complexity to the enduring problem of why men and women don't see eye-to-eye. Here Dylan suggests, rather brilliantly I think, that the problem revolves around fundamental differences between men and women in what constitutes love: "I once loved a woman, a child I'm told/I gave her my heart but she wanted my soul." Love, at least enduring love, is so difficult when one person is giving all he or she can, and the other still wants more, or at least something different. Similarly embedded in these lyrics is the frustration of a lover wanting to have or know a part of her partner—the deepest, innermost part—that he cannot or will not give. It's too precious, too private, or perhaps too fragile to share, even with the person he loves. And so they part.

And what happens next? Psychologists have found a predictable sequence of reactions to breakups, beginning with preoccupation with the lost partner, followed by sadness and distress, and moving finally to a state of emotional detachment, resigned acceptance of what occurred, and awareness of the need to move on (Hazan & Shaver, 1994). Rock songs have understood well each of these stages. As examples of preoccupation, we can start with the Rolling Stones' line in "Honky Tonk Woman": "I just can't seem to drink you off my mind." Paul Simon ("Kathy's Song") cannot find another satisfying way of being in the world now that his love is gone: "I stand alone without beliefs, the only truth I know is you." The Indigo Girls ("Ghost") sang wistfully of a lost love ("I'm in love with your ghost") and being unable to "swim free, the river is too deep." The singer here can't or won't let go; she continues to be haunted by bittersweet memories, tormented by incessant thoughts of her old lover.

Even more than preoccupation, however, rock songs emphasize feelings of sadness following breakups. Some early Dylan lyrics ("Tomorrow Is a Long Time") hint at depression: "I can't see my reflection in the waters, I can't speak the sounds that show no pain." There's no escaping from the awareness of such a terrible loss; there's no conceivable way of recovering normal functioning. There's also a vivid sense of sadness and resignation in Bonnie Raitt's poignant lyrics in "I Can't Make You Love Me": "I can't make you love me if you don't/ You can't make your heart feel something it won't." Still, my own favorite set of lyrics on this theme—because they are enormously clever and also powerful and moving—are those of Bonnie Tyler, "Total Eclipse of the Heart": "Once upon a time I was falling in love, now I'm only falling apart."

Related to sadness are feelings of disillusionment, regret, and bitterness. The sense of disillusionment is well represented in the pained words of Fiona Apple ("Shadow Boxer"): "Once my lover, now my friend. What a cruel thing to pretend." Ex-lovers so often promise that they will always be friends, and yet this so rarely occurs for any significant length of time. For the spurned partner, accepting so different a role is a painfully difficult task under the best of circumstances, and one made nearly impossible when the partner who wanted out has found someone new. Moreover, as Fiona Apple understood, the promise of friendship is often an illusory gift, one perhaps partially born of sincerity but mostly born of a need to alleviate guilt.

The state of regret brings to mind the words of a classic Simon and Garfunkel song, "I Am a Rock": "If I never loved, I never would have cried." Intense ambivalence so often follows the dissolution of a love affair. Not uncommonly, even as the relationship is ending, partners will simultaneously hold onto feelings of gratitude for "giving me the best days of my life" (Dido, "Thank You") and feelings of deep and overwhelming anger and regret for ever having begun the relationship.

For bitterness tinged with cynicism, there are no better lyrics than Joni Mitchell's in "A Case of You": "Just before our love got lost you said, 'I am as constant as a northern star.' And I said, 'Constantly in the darkness'." The second part of the first sentence ("I am as constant...") is actually from Shakespeare's *Julius Caesar*, but it's her put-down pun in the second sentence that really gives these lyrics their punch. In this same vein and almost as good is Elvis Costello's parting shot to his lover in "Love Went Mad": "I wish you luck with a capital F."

The last stage of getting over a love affair is that of acceptance, the emerging belief that despite being hurt, I can and will go on. Or, in the famous words of Gloria Gaynor, "I will survive." I'll end this chapter with what I think are especially moving lyrics from Billy Joel ("And So It Goes") about this bittersweet part of life that nearly all of us have experienced: "In every heart there is a room, a sanctuary safe and strong, to heal the wounds of lovers past, until a new one comes along."

Chapter 4

FREEDOM AND COMMITMENT

Freedom's just another word for nothing left to lose.
—Janis Joplin, "Me and Bobby McGee"
(Written by Kris Kristofferson and Fred Foster)

Freedom invokes many images—from the powerful desire of people to be liberated from slavery, or of nations to be free of outside rule, to the need of individuals to be unencumbered by obligations or committed relationships, to the lure and possibilities of the open road. Think Richie Havens' heartfelt, politically charged plea on behalf of the oppressed ("Freedom"); think Bruce Springsteen's recurrent images of fast cars heading nowhere in particular except out of here; think Jackson Browne (and the Eagles) running down the road trying to loosen their load ("Take It Easy").

The study of psychology reveals many tensions in life, including independence versus dependence, selfishness versus selflessness, cooperation versus competition, intimacy versus isolation, disclosure versus privacy, and change versus status quo. Although these may be seen as opposing forces, one side usually doesn't win outright. Rather, people find ways to live so that the needs of both positions are somewhat fulfilled. Billy Joel understood this particularly well ("Summer, Highland Falls"): "Our reason coexists with our insanity." Thus, we tend to be both selfish and selfless, private and revealing, rational and irrational. We may have a basic inclination to be closer to one pole or the other, for example, to be more selfish than selfless, but our actual behavior may also change as a result of how we feel on any given day and the circumstances we're in.

One of the more intriguing tensions in life is that between the need to be free and the need to belong—to have limitless possibilities and no restrictions on one hand, and to be fully committed to a person, a job, or an idea on the other. How to reconcile these two forces is a formidable task that often must be negotiated multiple times over a lifetime. Freedom from responsibilities or commitment can be exhilarating. Joni Mitchell's words express this notion in a particularly vivid fashion: "I was a free man in Paris, I felt unfettered and alive" ("Free Man in Paris"). This sense of freedom is one reason that college and those immediate postcollege years are remembered by many as such an extraordinary time. During late adolescence and young adulthood, we may well feel a pull toward committing forever to that person we love, but most of us, at least nowadays, resist. Sometimes this resistance is even abetted by advice from family members. I'm thinking of Smokey Robinson's first big hit for the Miracles, "Shop Around," and these words: "keep your freedom for as long as you can; my mama told me, 'you better shop around'." Joni Mitchell's words in "Help Me"—"we love our lovin', but not like we love our freedom"—also seem particularly appropriate here. Commitment seems too closely connected with "being tied down," while freedom seems to possess the grandeur of a life fully experienced.

The rock star who has most consistently pursued the theme of freedom in his songs is Bruce Springsteen. Among his better lines: "Got a wife and kids in Baltimore, Jack/I went out for a ride and I never went back" ("Hungry Heart"); "Grab your ticket and your suitcase, thunder's rollin' down this track/ You don't know where you're goin', but you know you won't be back ("Land of Hope and Dreams"); and "Take a right at the light, keep going straight until night" ("Blinded by the Light"). To be fair, Springsteen doesn't simply extol the virtues of hedonism or total freedom. Rather, his notion of freedom is more along the line of the need to escape from impossible circumstances. Moreover, he seems to understand that there's a price to pay for this brand of freedom. In one song ("The New Timer"), he asks whether his kid misses his old man and whether this child wonders "where I am." In "Thunder Road," a song filled with consistently vivid images, Springsteen's plea to his girlfriend to go away with him is tempered with his wise warning that "the door is open but the ride ain't free."

Even more sharply, the Eagles sagely note that the price of absolute freedom is often loneliness: "An' freedom, oh freedom, well that's just some people talking/Your prison is walking through this world all alone." These lines, of course, are from "Desperado," one of those great, haunting, sing-along songs and one in which the usually romantic image of the fiercely independent cowboy is played out in an unexpected, though far more realistic way: the loner here pays a heavy price for his unwillingness to commit.

Even in childhood, there are opposing forces between the need for exploration and the need for security. In fact, the relationship between these two needs is an interesting one. For the most part, the young child must feel sufficiently attached or connected to parents in order to readily explore his or her environment. However, if the child's exploration extends too far, he or she will usually need to return to a parent as a "safe base" (Bowlby, 1969). There, the child can emotionally refuel and then begin exploring again. The child needs to feel part of a unit before he or she can feel safely alone. Some kids, a bit hesitant to venture into the world (perhaps because security feels so good), may need a gentle push toward independence from their parents. While connection and freedom may seem like opposing states, they are complementary parts within a system.

In adulthood, we still have needs for both security and freedom. Often, when we feel too connected we yearn for freedom, and when we feel too free and alone, we yearn for commitment. Married and single people often envy each other's lifestyles. These two poles are well represented in rock lyrics. Contrast, for example, Steppenwolf's invocation in "Born to Be Wild"—"get your motor running, head out on the highway, looking for adventure in whatever comes our way"—with the urging of Jackson Browne (or the Eagles) in "Take It Easy" to "find a place to make your stand."

For many people, the tension between these forces is resolved when, after a period of adventure or "sowing one's wild oats," they fall in love and commit to a life with one person. Indeed, most adults have acted in accord with Springsteen's observation in "Two Hearts": "Someday the childish dreams must end…Now I believe in the end, two hearts are better than one." The dreams and wishes for adventure yield to different dreams, to those that involve the creation of new realities—that is, of plans and dreams that include the commitment of two people to a shared life. Sometimes, too, the struggle to commit involves less a sense of relinquishing freedom than it does giving up a long-held need to be left alone. Not surprisingly, Paul Simon ("Something So Right") penned sensitive words about this very conflict: "I've got a wall around me you can't even see/It took a little time to get next to me."

For some, though, relinquishing a sense of personal freedom or independence or autonomy is just too hard. Some cannot or will not compromise their own needs even for the sake of a loving relationship. The excitement of the open road, the possibilities for new partners and experiences, the romantic vision of rugged individualism—all are part of the American landscape and serve as powerful lures. As the 1960s group, the Mamas and The Papas sang "You gotta go where you wanna go, do what you want to do, with whoever you want to do it with."

Moreover, commitment is risky and may feel like a bad deal—giving up too much for an elusive ideal. For those who've witnessed firsthand an abusive or even distant parental relationship, or experienced the breakup of their parents' partnership, commitment may seem particularly troublesome. Some consciously avoid commitments their whole lives, some escape the turmoil of parental or family discord by making an early (often premature) commitment to another, and some make multiple commitments in their lives, a pattern sometimes referred to as serial monogamy. Some claim (justifiably) that they're just not ready at this particular moment, a notion made popular many years ago by Linda Ronstadt and the Stone Ponies ("Different Drum"): "All I'm sayin' is I'm not ready for any person, place or thing to try and pull the reins in on me." And some claim to desperately want a committed relationship but need to be so sure that they're not making a mistake that they wait and wait, in the process giving off signals that no one will ever be good enough. They are afraid, and although their fear "makes sense," they pay a price. The lyrics of "The Rose" (a big hit for Bette Midler) poignantly describe the consequences of this fear: "It's the heart afraid of breaking that never learns to dance/It's the dream afraid of waking that never takes the chance."

Not surprisingly, those who avoid commitment often attempt to convince themselves of the wisdom of their decision. However, this kind of freedom often comes with more illusions than pleasures. In the smart words of the song that I began this chapter with, "Me and Bobby McGee" (written by Kris Kristofferson and Fred Foster, but popularized by Janis Joplin), "freedom's just another word for nothing left to lose." To be without commitments is the stuff of stress-induced fantasy; in real adult life, it almost invariably leads to anxiety and depression. Sometimes, too, those who are averse to commitment claim they are available for the so-called right one—but, in fact, the righter the person or the stronger the emerging feelings, the more they avoid the possibility of engagement and commitment. As Billy Joel so well put it ("Innocent Man"), "Some people stay far away from the door if there's a chance of it opening up." Similarly, the Eagles ("Desperado") got it just right in noting the self-deception involved in this process—that despite the many goodies offered, some only seem to want just what they can't get.

Still, most people, even those who do commit to a partner or a particular lifestyle, vacillate throughout their lives between a need for independence and a need for connection. We like the occasional night out (or fishing trip with the boys, or shopping with the girls), even as we enjoy the familiarity of our homes and family; we wonder what it would be like to start anew, even as we enjoy the security of our long-term job or relationship. Some, of course, do more than wonder, engaging in other relationships in the midst of an apparent commitment. Leonard Cohen (in "Everybody Knows") found a wonderfully cynical way of describing this: "Everybody knows you love me baby, everybody knows you really do; everybody knows that you've been faithful, give or take a night or two." For others, the only way to sustain a loving, committed relationship is to keep a safe distance, a paradox beautifully described by John Hartford in a song ("Gentle on My Mind") made popular in the 1960s by Glen Campbell. Here, the singer feels close to his lover as a result of knowing that her "door is always open" and knowing too he is not "shackled by forgotten words and bonds and the ink stains that have dried up on some lines." And for still others, the lure of adventure or of leaving a relationship is quickly undone by an awareness of what one would be losing. As an example, I like these quirky, alliterative lines from Crosby, Stills, and Nash ("Helplessly Hoping"): "Gasping at glimpses of gentle true spirit he runs, wishing he could fly, only to trip at the sound of good-bye."

Yet another means to resolve the tension between freedom and commitment is for both partners to agree to live adventurous lives together. While this can work, especially if being adventurous essentially translates to doing new and creative things together, more often than not it leads to misery. A good twentieth-century example is how the existentialist philosophers and writers Jean Paul Sartre and Simone de Beauvoir, after acknowledging the restrictions of what he called "bourgeois marriage," made each other's lives hell by the practice of unalloyed sexual freedom. They both experienced great bouts of depression, envy, and resentment. The rock equivalent? How about Jackson Browne's words in "Two of Me, Two of You"—ironically written for the album *I'm Free:* "together we went crashing through every bond and vow and faith we knew." Being able to make a commitment is vital to a long-lasting healthy relationship, as psychologist Judy Kuriansky (2004) has shown.

Men are usually thought of as having an especially strong need for freedom and a fear of commitment, and many of the rock lyrics expressing these feelings have been penned by men. But there are some notable exceptions. There's a set of lines written by Joni Mitchell that astutely depicts how our society struggles to allow women the same options it typically affords men: "My gentle relations have names they must call me for loving the freedom of all flying things" ("Song to a Seagull"). And then there's Laura Nyro's classic plea in the song "And When I Die" (made popular by Blood, Sweat, and Tears): "Give me my freedom for as long as I be, all I ask of living is to have no chains on me."

Despite these exceptions, commitment does appear to be harder for men than for women. There is some consensus among psychologists and neurologists that certain behaviors are hard-wired. That is, men and women may well be programmed to have different needs, abilities, and goals that, taken together, ensure the perpetuation of the species. Men seem to be somewhat more autonomous and more driven to activity; women seem to be more relational, better able to understand and give to others. Although there is much overlap in these behaviors—both men and women are obviously capable of productive work, empathic understanding, and raising children—there also may be inborn tendencies (more pronounced in some individuals than others) that are difficult to change. Or, in the oft-sung words of Lynyrd Skynrd, "I'm as free as a bird now, and this bird you cannot change" ("Free Bird"). Dire Straits ("Heavy Fuel") also found a perceptive, if somewhat stereotypical way of explaining male motivation: "My life makes perfect sense/lust and food and violence." This view of what drives men is right out of Freud.

In addition, as a host of psychologists have pointed out in the last few decades—most notably Nancy Chodorow (1975) and Carol Gilligan (1982)—girls and boys have quite different tasks in growing up and separating from mom: to gain their sense of self, girls need to identify with mom; by contrast, in order to gain their sense of identity, boys need to separate from mom. According to this theory, this process leads girls to become relationship-oriented early in life and boys to become focused on independence and autonomy. Thus, there may always be tension between the sexes on these issues, and words like those sung by Fleetwood Mac's ("Dreams")—assumedly from a woman to a man—are likely to be heard for generations to come: "Now here you go again, You say you want your freedom." The final words of this verse, though, are much like the warning in "Desperado." Stevie Nicks of Fleetwood Mac suggests to her lover that while she understands his need to follow his feelings, he might ultimately have to "listen carefully to the sound" of his own loneliness.

Part II

ON PAIN, UNCERTAINTY, AND DESPAIR

The first section featured lyrics that concerned interpersonal issues, especially the rewards and pains of friendship and romantic relationships. This section focuses instead on intrapersonal issues—those that play out primarily within our own bodies, minds, and souls. The songs and lyrics within these next three chapters illuminate three distinct types of stress that many of us confront during the course of a lifetime.

Depression (Chapter 5) is a condition that a sizable percentage of the adult population in this country has or will have to face. The lyrics in this chapter (especially those of Paul Simon) are surprisingly accurate regarding the causes and symptoms of this disorder, though they tend to concentrate on feelings of loss or alienation. In this regard, they have much in common with the blues tradition that predated and influenced rock music.

The theme of Chapter 6 is the search for a personal identity. Here, some wise lyrics attempt answers to the age-old question, "Who am I?" These lyrics are especially astute in recognizing that our identities are often comprised of multiple, and even contradictory, components. Artists as diverse as Alanis Morissette, the Beatles, and the Grateful Dead have had smart things to say about the challenges of this quest.

The last chapter of this part (Chapter 7) is about significant emotional distress, the kind that sometimes manifests in psychotic conditions (like schizophrenia) but more commonly results in what is technically called borderline personality disorganization. Artists ranging from Tory Amos to Billy Joel to the Indigo

Girls have written remarkably accurate lines about the debilitating, seemingly intractable nature of such serious disorders. They've also managed to convey the idea that while relatively few individuals are chronically unstable or self-injurious, many of us have, at least occasionally, experienced terrible bouts of uncertainty or confusion.

Chapter 5

DEPRESSION

Smiling faces I can see, but not for me / I sit and watch as tears go by.
— The Rolling Stones, "As Tears Go By"

Singing the blues can be traced back to the inglorious days of American slavery. Moreover, the tone and style of the songs that emanated from this tradition have shaped some of the most influential musicians of our time. Ray Charles ("Born to Lose") sang "all my life, I've always been so blue"; before him, the great blues musician John Lee Hooker (who's a member of The Rock and Roll Hall of Fame) sang "I have the blues before sunrise, tears standing in my eyes" ("Blues before Sunrise"). Big Mama Thornton wrote the words to "Ball and Chain" ("why does every little single thing I hold onto go wrong?"), a song made famous when Janis Joplin covered it years later.

Given that the blues is a root source of rock 'n' roll, and given, too, the fact that many rock songwriters and singers have acknowledged being depressed or even succumbed to suicide (most notably in recent years, Kurt Cobain), it's hardly surprising that many rock songs have been about sadness and depression. Moreover, it's likely that virtually every listener of rock music either understands from personal experience what depression feels like or knows someone who's gone through some awful times.

Nearly 10 percent of American adults—over 20 million in all—suffer from depression in any given year (Kessler, Chiu, Demler, & Walters, 2005). Depressive disorders constitute the second most common group of emotional problems encountered by adults (only anxiety disorders are more common).

According to the World Health Organization, depression is the leading cause of disability worldwide. As Paul Simon ("American Tune") noted, "I don't know a soul who's not been battered, I don't have a friend who feels at ease." Indeed, Paul Simon's music, perhaps more than that of any other major pop singer, has consistently been infused with themes of alienation, loneliness, sadness, and depression. In the song, "America," he acknowledges being lost, announcing to his sleeping girlfriend, "I'm empty and aching and I don't why." Much later in his career, in one of the songs for his Broadway show, *Capeman*, he declares that "time is an ocean of endless tears." One could learn a great deal of what depression is like simply from listening to the music he's written over the past four decades.

What may not be obvious, though, from listening to rock lyrics is that depression comes in many forms and degrees of severity. It ranges from temporary states of feeling blue, to the deep sadness that so often follows losing love or loved ones, to the recurrent lows that are part of bipolar (manic-depressive) disorder, to major depressive episodes that often include feelings of suicidality. There's also low-grade, chronic depression that's technically called dysthymia, the essence of which has been described fairly accurately by Springsteen in "State Trooper": "Maybe you got a kid, maybe you got a pretty wife/The only thing I got's been bothering me my whole life." Individuals with dysthymia may function reasonably well on a day-to-day basis but just never seem particularly happy, lively, or hopeful. Being down seems almost a permanent part of who they are.

Some psychologists even consider overt displays of anger and aggression to be forms of masked depression. The assumption here is that these kinds of acting-out behaviors, most often seen in adolescence, mask a deep inner sadness and emptiness. The anger, according to this theory, is a way of channeling the feeling of not being given very much in life: not been held enough, nurtured, or loved. Because sadness is far too vulnerable a feeling for many adolescents (especially males) to express, the pain gets transformed to anger, resentment, and aggression toward others. Because masked depression is often found in tough, urban environments, it's not surprising that a hard rock/rap band would get it right. Here are the insightful and powerful words of Rage Against the Machine ("Settle for Nothing Else"): "A world of violent rage, but it's one that I can recognize having never seen the color of my father's eyes." Thought of this way, perhaps it's not surprising that there is so much simmering depression in urban neighborhoods.

Depression can occur in reaction to a tragic life event, the unremitting pressure of terrible circumstances, or the absence of loving people in one's life. These depressions seem to have identifiable precipitants (causes) and therefore have the feel of a psychologically based disorder. Sometimes anniversary events, such as the date of a loved one's death or of one's divorce or a milestone birthday, can trigger transient depressions. On the other hand, depression sometimes begins in childhood, recurs throughout a lifetime, has no readily identifiable precipitants, and has the feel of a biological disorder. For the most part, however, depression (like most mental health disorders) is typically viewed as a combination of biological/genetic vulnerabilities and environmental stressors—the interaction of both nature and nurture, of what one is born with and what one is exposed to in life. An environmental stress sufficient to trigger a depression in one person may be experienced as relatively benign, or at least manageable, by another. Stated more simply, everyone's got a different breaking point. But when depression does hit, regardless of its exact origins or form, it is debilitating and hurts deeply. As the Band ("The Weight") sang, it is often like feeling "half-past dead."

Different types of depression have somewhat different symptoms. Nevertheless, what seem to be fairly constant across types are feelings of helplessness and hopelessness, often termed *H & H* by mental health professionals. These are feelings that reflect a sense of "I can't do this" or "I can't get out of this funk" and "I'll never be able to do this" or "It'll never get better." Of course, rock songs have echoed these feelings in a far more poetic way. One example is Jimmy Cliff's "Many Rivers to Cross": "Many rivers to cross, but I can't seem to find my way over." Or, consider the words of Phish ("Maze"): "The torrent of helplessness swept me away, to the cavern of shame and the hall of dismay." One of the first tasks of psychotherapists in working with individuals who are depressed is to attempt to combat these feelings, to try to instill hope in those who have lost the capacity to believe that their lives can ever be different. Jerome Frank, author of one of the most influential psychotherapy books ever published, *Persuasion and Healing* (1974), calls this the process of remoralization. For him, the essence of psychotherapy is attempting to restore hope in those who seem to have lost it.

This is no easy task. Individuals who are depressed often suffer from what's been called learned helplessness (Peterson, Maier, & Seligman, 1995). Imagine the following, admittedly somewhat gruesome scenario (based on actual research): there's a cat in a special cage. A light goes on when the cat is about to get (mildly) shocked. The cat eventually learns how to avoid getting shocked by pressing a lever in the cage. At some point, however, this procedure is changed, and the cat's adaptive response no longer works—that is, regardless of how insistently the cat pushes the lever, he still gets shocked. The experimenter, though, now reinstates the original condition—the cat can avoid getting shocked by pressing the lever. Sadly, however, the cat never does so. He's come to believe that there's nothing he can do to avoid his painful fate. This is learned helplessness, a condition that several songwriters have described in more human terms. For example, Cynthia Weil and Barry Mann, a prolific songwriting team, wrote the following words for the Animals ("We Gotta Get out of This Place"): "in this dirty old part of the city where the sun refused to shine, people tell me there ain't no use in tryin'." Or, as Neil Diamond wrote and the Monkees sang, "What's the use in tryin', all you get is pain" ("I'm a Believer"). In a more subtle vein, Sarah McLachlan, wrote the following words for her haunting song, "Angel": "There's always one reason to feel not good enough." Many therapists believe that they must help their depressed patients find at least one reason to feel good enough to keep trying.

Mental health workers use a technical manual to help with diagnosis: *The Diagnostic and Statistical Manual of Mental Disorders: Fourth Edition, Text Revision* (DSM-IV-TR; American Psychiatric Association, 2000). It's a rather unwieldy volume at nearly 900 pages, but it's also useful and often necessary, especially in those cases where subtle distinctions exist among overlapping conditions. According to the DSM-IV-TR, to be diagnosed with a major depressive disorder a person must, for starters, either feel depressed most of the day nearly every day for at least two weeks, or lose interest (or pleasure) in all or most activities for at least a two-week period. There is no shortage of rock songs that have described such experiences. "Still I'm on the dark side of the moon," sang James Taylor ("Carolina in My Mind"), "and it seems like it goes on like this forever." "Hello darkness my old friend, I've come to talk with you again" (Simon and Garfunkel, "The Sound of Silence"). "Pleasure moves on too early, and trouble leaves too slow" (Joni Mitchell, "Down to You"). A major depression does seem like it will go on forever, feels far too familiar and consistent with one's self-image, and is associated with the thought that life will never again be pleasurable. Aaron Beck, founder of the very popular and influential cognitive therapy, contends that depression results from the tendency of individuals to view themselves, the world, and the future in negative ways (Beck, Rush, Shaw, & Emery, 1987). He calls this kind of distorted thinking the negative triad.

Other symptoms of depression have also been described in accurate terms by rock songs. Insomnia is one such common symptom, and Crosby, Stills, and Nash ("4 + 20") provided an apt description of this behavior and the feeling that often accompanies it: "night after sleepless night I walk the floor and I want to know, why am I so alone?" This song also provides one of the most explicit and moving accounts of a major depressive episode in the pantheon of rock music, including a wrenching line about the allure of suicide—a line that concludes with the words, "and I find myself just wishing that my life would simply cease."

Fatigue or loss of energy is another typical symptom of depression. A line from Dylan's "Mr. Tambourine Man" expresses this well: "My weariness amazes me, I'm branded on my feet." This song, while often thought of as an ode to mind-altering drugs (and it may well be that), nevertheless offers some imaginative descriptions of the numbness and deadness so frequently found in depression. Carole King's "(You make me feel like) A Natural Woman" (popularized by Aretha Franklin) also offers lyrics that are suggestive of this kind of deep-seated fatigue: "Looking out on the morning rain, I used to feel uninspired, and when I knew I'd have to face another day, Lord, it made me feel so tired." Lastly, a great metaphor from a classic Kris Kristofferson song ("Me and Bobby McGee"): "I was feeling 'bout as faded as my jeans." This line worked in the 1960s and it still works now. Although the deadness described by these songwriters (and Springsteen, too, in "Dancing in the Dark") is characteristic of depression, there's an opposite behavior, that of incessant nervous energy, that can also be part of the symptom picture of depression. Picture someone pacing around a room with racing thoughts and you get a good sense of the idea of agitated depression, a disorder that has the feel of depression combined with high levels of anxiety. "My mind is rambling rambling," sang James Taylor ("The Blues Is Just a Bad Dream"), "it's just like some rolling stone since that nightmare's come to stay."

Another symptom of depression should be noted before discussing that ultimate set of symptoms, suicidal thoughts or feelings. Depressed people, as psychiatrist Aaron Beck noted, are often full of negative feelings toward themselves; they believe they are essentially worthless. This is captured well in Jackson Browne's classic 60's song, "These Days." The image conveyed is of the singer sitting on steps, counting the time "in quartertones to ten." Then, almost abruptly, these words follow: "Please don't confront me with my failures, I had not forgotten them." More simply, but equally accurately, the contemporary hard rockers Papa Roach declare the following in the well-named song "Black Clouds": "Confession of depression, this life I'm second-guessing." Even more simply, Tori Amos ("Crucify") wonders, "Why do we crucify ourselves?" By itself, a lack of self-esteem does not qualify for a diagnosis of depression. The problem is that this characteristic can easily lead to behaviors that make it hard for a person to get sufficient rewards in the world, including friends, lovers, a good job, and various other pleasures. In turn, this person may protect him or herself from the pain of real or anticipated rejection; he or she may, in Simon and Garfunkel's words ("I Am a Rock"), "build walls, a fortress deep and mighty that none may penetrate." Then, other symptoms of depression may follow.

Early in my professional career, I studied therapists' perceptions of stressful patient behaviors (Farber, 1983). What I found was that no behavior feels more stressful to a therapist than a patient's suicidal thoughts. This was ranked highest among 25 behaviors listed in a survey; 85 percent of the therapists in this study found this behavior at least moderately stressful. It may surprise some readers, but suicidal thoughts or feelings are often not especially stressful to patients themselves. For many depressed patients, such feelings serve as a useful "bottom line." They say to themselves, if things get worse (or even stay the same), I have a way out. It's a comforting thought—in fact, often too comforting. Thus, even as it intensifies the anxiety of therapists, it may soothe the anxiety and attenuate the depression of patients themselves. Quoting the contemporary songwriter Gary Jules ("Mad World"): "I find it kind of funny, I find it kind of sad/the dreams in which I'm dying are the best I've ever had." Because it works to alleviate their pain, some patients recurrently evoke suicidal thoughts or feelings. Even worse, of course, some patients do resort to suicidal gestures or actually succeed in committing suicide. This is every therapist's worst nightmare.

What makes patients suicidal? Although it may feel a bit incongruous to use rock lyrics to illustrate suicide, in fact some songs have portrayed quite accurately the feelings that typically accompany suicidal thoughts or precede suicide attempts. Consider these lines by Counting Crows in "Black and Blue": "Tell yourself we'll read a note that says, I'm sorry everyone, I'm tired of feeling nothing, goodbye." Words sung by the Dave Matthews Band ("Dancing Nancies") emphasize both a sense of overwhelming tiredness and a terrible lack of self-esteem: "Twenty-three I'm so tired of life, such a shame to throw it all away…could I have been anyone other than me." And then there's the hopelessness embodied in these famous lines sung by Otis Redding in "(Sittin' on) the Dock of the Bay": "I have nothing to live for, looks like nothing gonna come my way."

There is a remarkable, counterintuitive fact about depression. It's that depressed people actually view their abilities more realistically than do nondepressed people. Depressed people tend to be quite accurate about their attributes and skills; they tend not to exaggerate upward (like nondepressed people do) their intelligence, or looks, or driving ability. If Lake Woebegone was populated with depressed people, everyone there would not see themselves as above average. The point is this: small amounts of denial, or what psychologists call positive illusions, tend to be quite adaptive. The ability to see oneself as more skilled or competent than one really is, or to think one can control his/her world more than is realistically possible, tends to ward off depression. Depressed people can't seem to do this very effectively; they take in the negativity and bad stuff all too well and can't seem to sugarcoat experiences the way that nondepressed people do. Shelley Taylor, a psychologist at the University of California at Berkeley who has studied this phenomenon, has shown that depressed people suffer from a deficit in positive illusions (Taylor & Brown, 1988). Don Henley (a member of the Eagles) seems to have understood this general concept when he wrote these lines for "New York Minute": "One day he crossed some line, and he was too much in this world."

What needs to be remembered, though, is that depression is a treatable disorder. Sometimes, depressed individuals need to make significant changes in their environment, with the expectation that a different job, place to live, lover, or group of friends, will provide a less stressful, more rewarding way of life. "We gotta make a decision," Tracy Chapman declared, "we leave tonight or live and die this way" ("Fast Car"). A change of circumstances can make a difference. In a related vein, depressed individuals—often suffering from a lack of positive strokes from the environment—may need more caring and affirmation from others. "When all the joy inside you dies, don't you want somebody to love?" (Jefferson Airplane, "Somebody to Love"). The problem is that depressed people often struggle to change their life circumstances and find it difficult to find an intimate partner, precisely because of their depression. Their way of thinking about themselves and the world, their lethargy, their lack of self-esteem, their hopelessness, and so on, make such changes far harder than most others realize. And so mental health workers are often consulted.

Increasingly, individuals are turning to medication for relief of depressive symptoms, usually Prozac or a similarly acting antidepressant. These medications (technically called SSRIs, Selective Serotonin Reuptake Inhibitors) facilitate the work of our neurotransmitters, chemicals in our body that affect our emotions. The use of antidepressant medications in this country tripled in the decade between 1994 and 2004. Although we're finding that these pills are not quite as magical as we once thought—they do have side effects (sexual dysfunction is a particularly nasty one), they can be habituating (over time, more pills are needed to achieve the same effect), and they don't work for everyone (about one-third of those suffering from depression get little or no relief)—they are nonetheless effective for many individuals who remark on the ability of these pills to ease their troubled minds. Satisfied users swear that these pills make it easier to cope with the inevitable stresses of life.

The prevalent use of SSRIs, especially among women, brings to mind the somewhat cynical words of the Rolling Stones about women "running to the shelter of a mother's little helper" ("Mother's Little Helper"). Back then (1966), Mick et al. were assumably singing about antianxiety agents like Valium and Librium, but their disparagement of the need for women to have something that "helps her on her way…through her busy day" is eerily similar to current criticism of the proliferation of antidepressant medication. A new experimental method of treating seemingly intractable depressions (those resistant to medication, shock therapy, and talk therapy) is likely to be quite controversial as well. This treatment entails implanting a small generator in the chest that transmits electronic pulses to a nerve pathway in the neck. Preliminary studies of the effects of this device have yielded positive results, but the Federal Drug Administration has nonetheless withheld official approval (Feder, 2006). What comes to mind here are the prophetic words sung by Simon and Garfunkel about 40 years ago in "The Big Bright Green Pleasure Machine": "We'll eliminate your pain, We can neutralize your brain."

But some depressed people don't like taking medication, much less getting electric shocks or having electrodes planted in their chest. Instead, they want or need to talk to someone about psychological ways of coping with their depression. Thankfully, psychotherapy, the so-called talking cure, has generally been shown to work as effectively as antidepressant medications in the treatment of chronic depression (Nemeroff et al., 2005). Psychodynamically oriented therapy helps patients understand and work through their belief in their essential unlovableness and their pattern of expecting rejection from others. Cognitive-behavior therapy works by teaching depressed individuals to curb their tendencies to see the world in primarily negative terms; therapists working in this tradition strive to increase the frequency of their clients' positive self-statements and decrease the frequency of their self-defeating or self-deprecating thoughts. As Joni Mitchell said in her haunting song, "Blue," "You've got to keep thinking you can make it through these waves."

Chapter 6

IDENTITY

I don't know who I am, but you know life is for learning.
—Joni Mitchell, "Woodstock"

"Who am I?" is one of the great questions of life, pondered by philosophers, writers, artists, psychologists, and yes, songwriters. It becomes an especially meaningful question in adolescence, as we begin thinking about ourselves in a more abstract, thoughtful, and future-oriented way. We also begin wondering how others see us; indeed, our identities are often a reflection of the appraisals of important others in our lives. But questions about ourselves neither begin nor end during this period of life. Well before adolescence we may begin to wonder, "What will I be?" And one of the greatest of all psychological theorists, Carl Jung, believed that profound questions about ourselves are best answered during the second half of life, when one is better prepared to contemplate issues of one's purpose and identity.

Many lyrics have echoed these timeless questions about identity and self-expression and probably provided ideas and solutions that some listeners have taken quite seriously. At a minimum, rock lyrics have allowed fans, especially those of high school and college age, to realize that their concerns about who they are and how they feel are widely shared. Although Meatloaf ("Everything Louder Than Everything Else") made fun of such existential questions, he also noted implicitly that these are just the kind of things that many think about a good deal: "Who am I, why am I here? Forget the question, someone give me another beer." It's also possible to view these lyrics as speaking to the inherent pain of asking such questions, and the subsequent need to numb this away through alcohol.

Here's what most psychologists learned in their training: We should all strive to attain a single, coherent identity. We should try on multiple identities, especially in adolescence, but by the time we reach early adulthood, we really should be pretty clear about who we are, what we want to do in life, what roles we want to play, and how we prefer to interact with others. We should be more or less consistent in our thoughts, feelings, and actions. We should have an identifiable style. Our identities—our sense of self, others' sense of us—should be solid and stable. Identity, according to Erik Erikson, the psychologist who popularized the study of this concept, has to do with "personal sameness and continuity." Moreover, said Erikson (1968), individuals will experience a so-called identity crisis if they fail to achieve, or lose, this sense of personal sameness. They will feel anxious and unsure of themselves and their place in the world. Or, as the Byrds noted ("Eight Miles High"), "Nowhere is there warmth to be found among those afraid of losing their ground."

Much of this thinking came out of the '60s. Interspersed with all the excesses of that era, there was a newfound appreciation for the idea of human growth and human potential. The emphasis, though, was not just on love and understanding others, but also on loving and understanding oneself. From that quintessential '60s musical, *Hair*—"Where is the something, where is the someone that tells me why I live and die?" ("Where Do I Go?")—the question of identity, of "Who am I?" became part of the cultural and social landscape. Self-understanding—whether achieved through encounter groups, meditation, various forms of traditional and nontraditional therapy, gurus, psychedelic drugs, or otherwise—was an essential goal. It was also about that time that even traditional forms of psychotherapy began to dramatically change focus. Therapy was no longer just for individuals with serious and significant mental health problems; increasingly, therapists worked with relatively healthy individuals (the so-called worried well) to further their self-understanding, self-acceptance, and ability to form satisfying relationships.

Self-expression also became important in the '60s, and much thinking went into styles of clothing and hair. How one looked became a political statement and very much a part of one's identity. "Almost cut my hair," sang Crosby, Stills, and Nash on their first, best-selling album, but ultimately I had to "let my freak flag fly." Apart from the whimsical alliteration in this phrase, we can hear how much long hair meant to the songwriter's self-concept and political sensibilities. Almost identically—and one wonders whether he was consciously paying homage to Crosby, Stills, and Nash—Jimi Hendrix in "If Six Was Nine," sang: "They're hoping my kind will drop and die, but I'm going to let my freak flag fly." Identity became something one actively thought about and worked toward. The goal was to find oneself. "Forget what life used to be," Jackson Browne suggested, "you are what you choose to be" ("The Fuse"). Despite the paradox of extensive stylistic conformity among young people— or at least among those who saw themselves as part of the so-called counter- culture—there was still a sense that forming a distinct identity was of great importance. Almost nothing was considered worse than selling out and losing one's individuality, for example by being a "well-respected man about town," getting to work at 9, "coming home at 5:30, catching the same train every time" (the Kinks, "A Well-Respected Man"). Conformity, as stereotyped by the 1950s man in the gray flannel suit (or "well-respected man about town"), was to be absolutely avoided.

All this sounds fine, and right, and existentially important. Although it's easy to criticize the '60s as a time of obsessive dedication to the pursuit of self—a "culture of narcissism" in the words of the social critic Christopher Lasch (1979)—questions of identity ("Who am I?") are an essential aspect of being human, ranking equal in importance to that other great existential question, that of intimacy ("Will I love and be loved?"). Joni Mitchell's philo- sophical words from "Woodstock"—"I don't know who I am, but life is for learning"—ring true. It turns out, though, that this quest for identity isn't all that easy. There are lots of roadblocks along the way, some of which explain why so many of those ex-radical activists turned out be the lawyers or stock- brokers that their parents wanted them to be. "You know that man that you hate? You look more like him every day" (Jane's Addiction, "Idiots Rule"). Let's go to some psychological theory and research to find out why identity achievement is just one of several possible outcomes of this journey.

According to Erikson and other psychologists, one needs to have experi- enced a significant period of exploration—of sifting through alternate ways of being in the world—before committing to a more-or-less stable identity. Commitment provides a person with a sense of purpose and continuity. It also alleviates any drift toward identity confusion. But different combinations of exploration and commitment produce very different kinds of identity, a line of research that psychologist James Marcia (1966) has pursued for decades. There are those individuals who are "identity diffused": they have neither explored their options very much, nor have they committed to a particular identity. They are drifters, not sure of who they are, not sure of where they want to be, and not especially interested in doing the work to find out. They're not intro- spective, they're usually not in therapy, and they usually don't care very much that others see them as lost. "Doesn't have a point of view, knows not where he's going to" sang the Beatles ("Nowhere Man"). Or, as one of the Beatles (George Harrison) sang in "Any Road," "If you don't know where you're going, any road will take you there." One has to both actively explore options and commit to one in order to have a firm, achieved identity. These tasks are typically accomplished in late adolescence and early adulthood.

Then there are individuals who haven't done a whole lot of exploration or soul-searching but who have nevertheless committed themselves to an identity, most often one that resembles that of one or both of their parents. These individuals are "identity foreclosed": they've decided early in life—or it's been decided for them—what their path will be. This is essentially the opposite of the words that Alanis Morissette wrote for "Precious Illusions": " Once I know who I'm not, then I'll know who I am." Foreclosed individuals instead follow the mantra, "once I know who my parents are—their values, their needs—then I'll know who I must be." Individuals from extremely religious backgrounds are often foreclosed in their identities. There's been no possibility, and sometimes no real temptation, to think about or explore other kinds of lives. This does not mean that these individuals cannot live happy, satisfied lives. Indeed, they can and do. But from this psychological perspective, they have not explored multiple ways of being in the world, and so they are not considered to be identity achieved.

The last identity status is called moratorium. These are individuals who are actively exploring their options but have not yet come to any firm decisions about where, how, or what they'll be. Some are perpetual seekers or perpetual students switching majors and careers. Some have extended their adolescence well past their 20s. The essence of this moratorium status can be found in the words of U2: "I still haven't found what I'm looking for" and "well, yes, I'm still running" ("I Still Haven't Found What I'm Looking For"). Here's another good phrase to describe moratorium, this sung by Simon and Garfunkel ("A Hazy Shade of Winter"): "Time, time, time, see what's become of me, while I looked around for my possibilities." A prolonged moratorium period is quite likely to greatly frustrate parents or significant others. And although the Allman Brothers Band was singing about the need to find that one special girl, the words in "Melissa" accurately portray both the ongoing excitement and frustration of those who keep looking but just can't seem to commit: "Knowing many, loving none, bearing sorrow, having fun."

Like many classification systems that force individuals into a small number of categories, this one on identity status has significant limitations. For example, it seems to give some moral advantage to those who have an introspective, questioning style; they are the ones who actively seek out alternatives before they commit to an achieved identity. But the primary problem is that most of us don't neatly fit into one category. The line I left out before in quoting the Beatles' "Nowhere Man" was "Isn't he a bit like you and me?" Most of us tend to fit, at least somewhat, into each of these categories. Sometimes we're fairly certain that we've created our own unique path in life, and sometimes it feels like we're mostly following the footsteps and adhering to the values of our parents and grandparents; at other times, it feels like we're still searching for our identities; and, at still other times, we feel lost and somewhat diffuse. Identity is more fluid than these categories of identity status imply. Sometimes we're sure of where we are and who we are, and sometimes it all tends to get pretty jumbled. The Grateful Dead seemed to have understood this well in writing the words for "Truckin'": "Sometimes the light's all shining on me, other times I can barely see."

Identity, then, is a complicated concept. But it's been made even more so in recent years though the introduction of postmodernist thinking—the idea that truth is elusive, that reality is a matter of perspective (or even an illusion), that objectivity is impossible, and that logical, linear thinking is a convenient fiction. Postmodernist thinking is reflected in such movies as *Eternal Sunshine of the Spotless Mind* and *The Matrix*. And, though it wasn't called postmodern back in 1967 when this song was released, the words of the Beatles' "Penny Lane" are consistent with this concept: "A pretty nurse is selling poppies from a tray and tho she feels as if she's in a play, she is anyway." So, whereas psychological thinking once held that maturity should bring a sense of consistency to who we are and how we think of ourselves, there is now a burgeoning belief among some psychologists, philosophers, cultural theorists, artists, writers, and filmmakers that the world just isn't that simple anymore—if it ever was.

This new perspective assumes that having one consistent self is an impossibility. We are different and change constantly in reaction to myriad circumstances and people and moods. What I am now I was not a moment ago. Joni Mitchell's words in "Both Sides Now" come close to expressing this new set of beliefs about identity: "There's something lost and something gained in living every day." Actually, this new way of understanding identity goes even further than this. It's not just that life events change daily and that we learn and change as a consequence. It's more that life is constantly shifting and that it should be considered neither regrettable nor pathological that we shift too. Donovan, a '60s English folksinger once considered the next Bob Dylan, wrote these words for his song, "Season of the Witch": "When I look out my window, many sights to see, and when I look in my window, so many different people to be."

Somewhere between the traditional belief in the possibility of achieving a firm, coherent identity and these newer, radical postmodernist ideas is the notion of multiple selves. This concept assumes the following: even as we have one central voice, one fairly consistent set of beliefs about ourselves, we may still experience dramatic shifts in our feelings and thoughts about ourselves and others (Mitchell, 1993). For example, we may shift from essentially believing in ourselves to seriously doubting ourselves. We may feel absolutely in control of our lives and confident that the future is rosy and then—even just a few hours later—believe that the world is crashing down upon us. According to this perspective, then, it's normal to feel and act very differently at different times, even to hold seemingly contradictory attitudes toward ourselves or others. The Academy-award-winning movie *Crash* (2004) offered a splendid example of this: one of the main characters, a policeman played by Matt Dillon, heroically saves a passenger from a burning car—the very same person whom he had sexually abused earlier. In great measure, the movie's power stems from its awareness of the universality of these kinds of shifts. We like ourselves, we don't; we feel wonderful, we feel miserable. We may be "frequently kind and...suddenly cruel" (Billy Joel, "She's Always a Woman"). Phoebe Snow's great voice also gave expression to these sentiments in her song "Either or Both": "What I want to know from you, when you hear my plea, do you like or love either or both of me?" My favorite words on this theme, though, are those of Dylan's in "Just Like a Woman": "She takes just like a woman, she makes love just like a woman, and she aches just like a woman, but she breaks just like a little girl." Almost all of us revert, at least at times, to some piece of ourselves from way back when.

The value of this compromise position is that it recognizes that we are far more inconsistent in our attitudes and behavior than we may realize (though some good lyricists are aware of this). Moreover, changes and ambivalence in our sense of self do not, as earlier generations of psychologists thought, render us psychologically immature. We are quite capable of experiencing conflicting feelings. We can, and do, hold multiple perspectives on who we are and how see ourselves in relationship to others.

Can this go too far? Yes, of course. Even farther than "her name was McGill but she called herself Lil, but everyone knew her as Nancy" (The Beatles, "Rocky Raccoon"). At the very far end of this continuum are people who have several discrete personalities—separate selves with different voices, characteristics, memories, needs, emotions, and even blood pressure. These individuals, once diagnosed with multiple personality disorder, are now technically described by the term Dissociative Identity Disorder. Though rare, they do exist, and their disorder is most often the terrible result of having been severely abused as children. Their lives tend to be terribly painful, and their shifts in perception are not merely a reflection of flexible thinking. Rather, these dramatic shifts from one personality to another are drastic, and almost always unsuccessful, attempts to find an adaptive solution to being in the world. Most of us, though, are not multiple personalities, à la that old movie, *Three Faces of Eve*, or that somewhat newer one, *Sybil* (which, by the way, was essentially fiction). Closer to the truth, or at least the current thinking in the field, is what Ani DiFranco ("Light of Some Kind") alluded to so wisely: "there's a crowd of people harbored in every person, there are so many roles that we play." We do play out multiple roles; we can even feel very different to ourselves in different contexts with different people. Still, as noted above, we generally have one central ego, one central voice, through which all these experiences are channeled.

And so, I am different, sometimes dramatically so, with my patients than I am with my family, friends, or students. For one, I am far more serious with my patients. Although I retain a sense of humor when I am doing psychotherapy and can sometimes even be playful, I am not as loose. I suspect that some very old friends of mine, knowing me as the person who likes to sing and pun and kid and laugh, and even as the person who can zone out quickly if there's a football game on, wonder how I can sustain serious attention with patients. But I do. It's a different part of me, one that friends, even good friends, may not see (or even have trouble imagining), but one that is clearly part of who I am. As Billy Joel insightfully noted ("Summer, Highland Falls"): "we are always what our situations hand us."

Many individuals like to drink or otherwise get high in order to access parts of themselves that aren't so available when they are sober—sexiness perhaps, or maybe even sadness. A sense of self is comprised of many parts, some of which are quite different than others and emerge at very different times. This diverse presentation is neither a case of manipulation nor hypocrisy; it's just the complex nature of the self in a complex world. In "Both Sides Now," when Joni Mitchell sang "it's life's illusions I recall," she may have been referring not just to the sense of unreality that life sometimes hits us with, but rather the constancy of change in the world. The basic illusion may be that of stability. And thus, "in a world that's constantly changing" (The Young Rascals, "How Can I Be Sure?"), the question, "Who am I?" may be answered in a somewhat different way on an almost constant basis.

Chapter 7

SERIOUS EMOTIONAL DISTRESS

All day, staring at the ceiling, making friends with shadows on my wall.
—Matchbox 20, "Unwell"

Some things in the world are so very frightening. High on the list is the sense of losing one's sanity, a feeling that may manifest in various ways. Not being sure of what is real, or even if one's self is real. Hearing voices and not being sure whether they really exist, or seeing things and not being sure whether they're really there. Speaking incoherently or illogically. Having persistent, intrusive thoughts of the world or loved ones being destroyed. Feeling so out of sorts that one can't find a comfortable emotional place. Feeling as if one doesn't quite belong to the human race or understand the rules for living effectively in the world. Feeling out of control with racing thoughts or urges to overeat or self-mutilate. Feeling that the world is overwhelming and incomprehensible. Feeling constantly anxious with no apparent reason. Or simply feeling that one's mind is not working right or that one's sense of self is too fragmented. Just reading this list is likely to make many individuals a bit shaky. The fear of being out of one's mind or going insane (feeling crazy) is fairly common, fueled in part by the fact that almost everyone has experienced some mild degree of some of these feelings at one time or another.

Some of the symptoms noted above, like hallucinations and delusions, may be indications of a serious mental disorder—that state of true out-of-touchness with reality that is technically called psychosis. "Making friends with shadows on my walls" is a statement that, as a psychologist, I'd take very seriously and one that would prompt me to ask a series of questions about the speaker's history, state of mind, present circumstances, and ability to differentiate reality from fantasy. I'd do the same with someone who presented with the delusion of being Superman: "Believing I had supernatural powers, I slammed into a brick wall" (Paul Simon, "Gumboots"). Similarly, I'd have to consider seriously a diagnosis of psychosis for someone who acknowledged "seeing faces come out of the rain" (The Doors, "People Are Strange"). It also bears noting, though, that while these kinds of perceptual distortions are often an indication of a psychotic condition like schizophrenia, they also may be induced by certain medical disorders, medications, or illicit drugs. Hallucinogenic drugs, including marijuana, hashish, peyote, and LSD, can all cause significant distortions in the way we see the world: "Eight miles high and when you touch down, you'll find that it's stranger than known" (The Byrds, "Eight Miles High"). The same idea was whimsically portrayed in Simon and Garfunkel's "59th Street Bridge Song": "Hello, lamppost, whatcha knowin'? I've come to watch your flowers growin'." Feeling that groovy can make you distort reality.

Although there is no definitive laboratory evidence, like blood tests or CAT scans, that can be used to positively diagnosis schizophrenia, contemporary researchers believe that this form of psychosis is genetically transmitted. Somehow, then, the Who ("The Real Me") got it right: "I went back to my mother, I said I'm crazy ma, help me. She said, I know how you feel son, cause it runs in the family." There's about a 10-fold risk of being schizophrenic if one has a close biological relative with this disorder—so, yes, schizophrenia does run in families (American Psychiatric Association, 2000). Nevertheless, schizophrenia, which usually hits for the first time when an individual is in his or her late teens or early 20s, is not entirely due to biological or genetic or neurological factors. There's something about an individual's environment that can influence the onset and course of this terribly debilitating disorder. Although he was not singing about schizophrenia per se, Elton John ("Goodbye Marlon Brando") clearly understood how stress can affect our psychological equilibrium: "This overload is edging me further out to sea, I need to put some distance between overkill and me." Hardly anyone still believes that "lousy parenting" or a terribly stressful environment can, by itself, can cause schizophrenia, but most mental health professionals do believe that these kinds of risk factors can influence in-born tendencies toward developing this disorder in a full-blown fashion.

But just as there is no firm demarcation between depression and nondepression, or having a coherent sense of self and a fragile sense of self, the boundary between sanity and insanity is not always clearly defined. Having hallucinations (hearing or seeing things that aren't there) or delusions (imagining things that aren't real) are usually signs of a psychotic disorder like schizophrenia. But diagnosis gets tricky below the level of outright psychosis—and only about 1 percent of people are truly psychotic. As noted in the song "Maniac" (from the movie, *Flashdance*), "The ice blue line of insanity is a place most never see." We can be thankful for this. Nevertheless, many people do have occasional symptoms that leave them fairly shaken and wondering about their level of sanity. To quote James Taylor ("Something in the Way She Moves"), "every now and then the things I lean on lose their meaning and I find myself careening in places where I should not let me go." Just as virtually all of us have felt somewhat depressed at some point in our lives, most of us have also had times when we've felt scared about not being anchored sufficiently well in the world. "I'm losing it" is a common expression of this experience.

Moreover, some people live almost constantly at a level somewhere between mildly neurotic and essentially psychotic, an in-between state that mental health professionals call borderline or, more technically, borderline personality disorder. These individuals tend to be quite needy and very difficult—their emotions and behaviors change quickly and seemingly without much cause—but they also can be quite engaging and even charismatic. "I'd rather stay here with all the madmen than perish with the sadmen roaming free," claimed David Bowie ("All the Madmen"). And Billy Joel may well have been referring to a borderline person when he wrote these words: "You may be right, I may be crazy, but it just may be a lunatic you're looking for" ("You May Be Right"). We all know individuals who are especially creative, charming, and fun to be with, but who are also thoroughly maddening and frustrating. Many hold responsible jobs in the world, even as they seem to be impossible to deal with and chronically unstable.

Some people diagnosed as borderline are able, for surprisingly long periods, to mask their considerable inner turmoil. But, as Bonnie Raitt once observed ("All at Once"), "Looks to me there's lots more broken than anyone can really see." A fair number of celebrities, including rock stars, actors, and models, seem to fit in this mold: successful and engaging, but also unreasonably demanding and terribly erratic in their behavior (for example, trashing hotel rooms, or acting abusively toward significant others or members of their entourage).

Borderline individuals may be fundamentally uncertain about who they are. Their identity may be diffuse and confusing to both themselves and others. "My thoughts are scattered and they're cloudy," sang Simon and Garfunkel ("Cloudy"), "they have no borders, no boundaries." Some may doubt their very existence: "If I'm alive then there's so much I've missed. How do I know I exist?" (Harry Chapin, "Sniper"). Similarly, some may experience great difficulty believing that things around them are real: "What if everything around you wasn't quite as it seems? What if all the world you think you know is an elaborate dream?" (Nine Inch Nails, "Right Where It Belongs"). As I noted in the previous chapter, these feelings of uncertainty, bordering on paranoia, are reflected in many aspects of popular culture, including many recent movies. *Girl, Interrupted* is a particularly good example of a movie (and book, by Susanna

Kaysen, 1994) that accurately depicts the personal agonies of borderline personality disorder.

Individuals with borderline personality disorder also tend be anxious without knowing exactly why, though it's often linked to their sense that the world just isn't a safe place: "At night I wake up with my sheets soaking wet and a freight train running through the middle of my head" (Bruce Springsteen, "I'm on Fire"). Dylan, too, understood this awful place ("Everything Is Broken"): "broken voices on broken phones, take a deep breath, feel like you're chokin', everything is broken." The other side of this anxiety is the feeling of not being well-connected to others or the world, not feeling fully a part of the human race. As Elvis Costello ("Lipstick Vogue") sang, "Sometimes I almost feel just like a human being."

Borderline individuals often make life miserable for themselves and others. They struggle to believe that they will be cared for, and often manipulate others to get some desperately sought-after satisfaction and attention. Their needs often feel insatiable. Black Sabbath ("Paranoid") understood such feelings remarkably well: "All day long I think of things but nothing seems to satisfy/ Think I'll lose my mind if I don't find something to pacify." It's often said that if a hospital's psychiatric unit feels chaotic, it's not because of the presence of overtly psychotic individuals but because there are more borderline patients there than usual. To paraphrase both the Doors ("When the Music's Over") and the Ramones ("We Want the Airwaves"), the attitude and behavior of borderline people often reflects a sense of "I want it all, and I want it now." Individuals with this disorder have low levels of frustration tolerance and are often impulsive. They get into fights. They don't know how to contain all their inner rage. Here, Paul Simon's famous lines ("Still Crazy after All These Years") are instructive: "Now I sit by my window and I watch the cars, I fear I'll do some damage one fine day."

To alleviate their chronic feelings of emptiness, they may try to fill themselves up with great amounts of alcohol, prescription medications, street drugs, food, or sex; rarely do any of these offer anything other than a quick fix." The Dave Matthews Band, in "Grey Street," offers a perfect description of such behavior: "There's an emptiness inside her, and she'd do anything to fill it in." In a similar vein, Tori Amos ("Crucify") understood well how anonymous sex can sometimes be used in the service of this urgent need to feel filled up: "I've been looking for a savior in these dirty streets, looking for a savior beneath these dirty sheets."

For the same reasons, borderline individuals often have a history of intense but unstable relationships. They desperately need others and so invest a great deal in the beginning stages of relationships, hoping and believing that "this is the one." Unfortunately, they almost inevitably feel disappointed when they become aware of the other's flaws or needs. More generally, those who fit the borderline picture fluctuate between idealizing and devaluing others; this is an aspect of their tendency to view the entire world in black-and-white terms. Psychotherapists call this splitting. Everything seems to be one side or the other, never an integration of good and bad. It's either my way or your way, not a compromise; it's either now or never, not eventually. You are either wonderful or awful, not a combination of the two; and I am either bad or good, not a combination of the two. Billy Joel's words in "I Go to Extremes" offer a great example of this concept: "I don't why I go to extremes/Too high or too low, there ain't no in betweens." Or, as Rush ("Double Agent") noted: "My angels and demons at war, which one will lose depends on what I choose, or maybe which voice I ignore." Therapy with such individuals is often aimed at helping them tolerate ambiguity and accept shades of gray in their world. Meatloaf ("I'd Do Anything for Love") seems to have understood this goal extremely well: "Can you colorize my life, I'm so sick of black and white?"

In response to the frustration of not getting what they believe they desperately need, borderline individuals may become rageful, self-hating, or even self-mutilating. There are several theories as to why some people would cut or burn or otherwise mistreat themselves. One idea is that they feel they are terrible individuals and deserve it: "I'm sorry to myself, for treating me worse than I would anybody else" sang Alanis Morissette, in "Sorry to Myself." That is, they treat themselves as they have been (mis)treated by others in their lives. A related idea is that they cannot tolerate the burdens of feeling good enough; if they did, they would inevitably disappoint themselves or others. Lou Reed ("Downtown Dirt") expressed this thought quite concisely and accurately: "Psychologically, it's better that I think that I'm dirt." Yet another theory is that self-mutilation is a physical release, a way of doing something (anything) to escape intolerable inner turmoil. There's even some evidence to suggest that cutting oneself releases endorphins in the brain, the body's natural pain-killing substance. And then there's the theory that's perfectly well stated by Nine Inch Nails in their song "Hurt": "I hurt myself today, to see if I still feel. I focus on the pain, the only thing that's real." When it all becomes too much—too much anxiety, too much negative thinking, too much self-blame—finding a physical focus for one's pain is almost a relief. About 8–10 percent of borderline patients go beyond self-mutilation and successfully commit suicide; many more have a history of multiple suicide attempts or suicidal gestures aimed at convincing others that their pain is intolerable. The words of the Indigo Girls ("Blood and Fire") provide a vivid summary of the tendency of these individuals to seek desperate solutions to what often feels like a lifetime of emotional pain: "Well I have spent nights with matches and knives, leaning over ledges only two flights up."

So, in general, rock lyrics have been remarkably accurate about this terribly debilitating state called borderline pathology. Or, stated somewhat differently, many lyricists seem to have a very personal knowledge of feeling somewhat borderline. They also seem to have a good understanding of the origins of this disorder. Most often, it is caused by trauma in childhood—typically, physical, sexual, or emotional abuse at the hands of parents (many of whom were abused themselves). "How can I have feelings," John Lennon asked in "How," "when my feelings have always been denied?" In other words, how can I care about myself and others when I've never been given care, understanding, or love? A similar thought was put forward by Cat Stevens ("Father and Son"): "From the moment I could talk, I was ordered to listen." In other words, how can I believe in myself and my abilities when I've never been cared about and when my needs have never been considered? Those who have been abused as children do not learn to trust the world to provide for them; they become unable to cope with even small frustrations (Pine, 1986). They have, in the words of the Rolling Stones ("19th Nervous Breakdown"), "seen too much in too few years." A bit more accurately: they've experienced too much too early in life.

Those who have been abused also struggle mightily, sometimes their whole lives, to make sense of what happened. This is particularly true when abuse occurs at the hands of a parent. As children, they sense that a parent is doing something unspeakably awful but they mostly cannot bear to blame mom or dad for the abuse—they still depend too much on this parent for the occasional love they receive. "She holds the hand that holds her down" (Pearl Jam, "Daughter") is a remarkably astute line, speaking to the terrible need to hold on tightly to that person who has caused pain, shame, and self-hatred.

In "Daniel," Elton John both poses a question and offers a powerful insight about the consequences of abuse: "Do you still feel the pain of the scars that won't heal/your eyes have died but you see more than I." If this interpretation is correct—that this song is about abuse—he's right on both counts. Traumatized children, many of whom grow up to be troubled adults with a borderline diagnosis, continue to feel the pain of being terribly hurt by those who were supposed to love them. And although a part of them—a trust-in-the-world part—seems to have died in childhood, most remain acutely sensitive to their own pain and remarkably perceptive about the needs and vulnerabilities of others. As children, they needed to scan the environment constantly to try to protect themselves, and as adults they continue to be aware of even the smallest changes in their environment. It also bears noting, though, that not everyone who has experienced an awful childhood develops the symptoms I'm describing here. Some manage to cope remarkably well in the face of a great deal of adversity and become well-functioning adults. As sagely observed by the group Tears for Fears ("I Believe"), "You just can't see the shaping of a life."

By far, my most difficult patients are those who would be diagnosed as borderline. But these are also the people whom I often feel most deeply about, for almost invariably I come to admire their courage in trying to find a way to have a good life for themselves. The words of Jackson Browne ("Alive in the World") embodies this often desperate but sincere hope: "I want to live in the world, not behind some wall/I want to live in the world, where I will hear if another voice should call."

Part III

ON SEX, DRUGS, AND MONEY

This section contains three chapters, each of which deals with a powerful need that sometimes ends up ruling our lives. Each of these needs or wants (sex, drugs, and money) has been sung about a great deal in the history of rock 'n' roll. Sex (Chapter 8) is a biological imperative for all species; without it, there's no propagation of our genes. But, of course, sex is far more than an innate drive. It has enormous psychological significance, a fact that a great many songwriters have acknowledged. From Marvin Gaye to Aerosmith to Meatloaf, wise lyricists have found poetic, and sometimes even humorous words to represent the ongoing struggle between the forces of sexual expression and repression, or of passion and propriety. Rock 'n' roll has always been about sexuality, and the many lyrics in this chapter provide ample evidence that many songwriters have understood how profound, complex, and confusing the topic of sex is to so many individuals, from childhood on.

The second chapter of this section (Chapter 9) focuses on a different type of need, one that is, strictly speaking, not a need at all. But drug and alcohol use can become addictive and can feel biologically and psychologically necessary. Moreover, drug and alcohol use can and must be addressed not just as a potential addiction, but, like sex, as a recreational activity. Whereas most of the rock lyrics of the 1960s and 1970s that addressed this topic, including those of the Beatles, emphasized the fun part of getting high, many recent lyrics have been far more cautionary—and wise—about drug use.

The last chapter of this section (Chapter 10) is about the pursuit of money. As in Chapter 9, lyrics here reflect both sides of an equation: the words of some groups, like Pink Floyd, have extolled the need for and virtues of money; the words of other groups, like the Eagles, have warned against the corrupting nature of money, especially its power to blind us to other needs.

Chapter 8

SEX AND PASSION

Could it be the devil in me or is this the way that love's supposed to be?
—Martha and the Vandellas, "Heat Wave"
(Written by Eddie Holland,
Brian Holland, and Lamont Dozier)

Given the attention paid to sex in books, magazines, television, and movies, it's hardly a surprise that there's a good deal of it in music. And much like in the movies, the content of these sexually tinged song lyrics ranges from the PG level in much of soft rock (for example, Roberta Flack's "Feel Like Making Love" or Van Morrison's memories in "Brown-Eyed Girl" of "making love in the green grass behind the stadium") to R-rated stuff (for example, Donna Summer's rendition of "Love to Love You Baby," complete with moaning) to the blatant and explicit X-rated level found in a good deal of heavy metal and rap music (for example, R. Kelly's "Sex in the Kitchen," featuring an explicit description of tabletop lovemaking).

It was, in fact, the supposedly high levels of drug and sex-related lyrics in rock music that led Tipper Gore to establish the Parents Music Resource Center (PMRC) and testify before a senate panel in 1985 to urge the introduction of warning labels on record albums. An example of what our former vice resident's wife thought of as an offending lyric (from Motley Crue's "Tonight"): "Slide down my knees, taste my sword." She probably wouldn't have much liked the lyrics in Jefferson Starship's "Miracles" either, and these are some of the more printable ones: "When I pluck your body like a string, when I start dancing inside ya…you make me wanna sing."

Mrs. Gore claimed that explicit lyrics were in part to blame for increases in rape, teenage pregnancy, and suicide. She ended up writing a book in 1987 (now out of print) called *Raising PG-Kids in an X-Rated Society* in which she made extensive use of lyrics from Prince, AC/DC, Motley Crue, and others to further her crusade against what she called "porn rock." The outcome of those contentious hearings (in which, among others, Dee Snyder of Twisted Sister and Frank Zappa, testified) was that major record labels agreed to put the phrase "Parental Advisory: Explicit Lyrics" on selected releases. The label became known as the Tipper Sticker and, as many psychologists would have undoubtedly predicted, led to higher sales of many so-designated albums. Forbidden fruit, as we all know, often tastes better. As Ice-T ("Freedom of Speech") so unsubtly noted: "Hey PMRC, you stupid f…assholes, the sticker on the record is what makes 'em sell gold." Needless to say, the *f* word was quite explicitly pronounced in the song. Moreover, independent record labels, frequently the source of rap and hip-hop lyrics, never agreed to use the infamous sticker. So, there are still plenty of sexually explicit lyrics in the contemporary music scene. Of course, *explicit* doesn't necessarily translate to *wise* or *smart*, and many of the sexually-oriented lyrics in rap are neither. The same can be said of many of the lyrics in the songs of Madonna, Sade, or Prince. They're frequently blatant, but rarely clever or creative.

Another historical note: there's always been sex in rock music. The very name "rock 'n' roll" is often thought to be a euphemism for sex. In the very early days of rock, well before PMRC but still a time when censorship and even arrest could too easily happen (especially to black performers), singers and songwriters disguised the sexual nature of their music. Although it now seems absurd that no one seems to have noticed back then, the words of many early rock songs are clearly sexual. In 1956 Fats Domino sang "I found my thrill on Blueberry Hill," and in 1958 Little Richard belted out "Good golly, Miss Molly, you sure like to ball."

Most every serious or even semiserious discussion of sex has got to include Freud (1959). It's very easy to mock Freud's supposed obsession with sex, but it was he who insisted on the scientific need to investigate the role of sexuality throughout the life span (including childhood), especially the relationship of repressed sexual feelings and needs to personality development and psychopathology. Repression, thought Freud, was sure to create problems; mental health rested on the need for healthy expression of sexual urges. These thoughts have been unambiguously endorsed in contemporary times by Marvin Gaye both in the song "Let's Get It On" and in his other well-titled song, "Sexual Healing": "Makes me feel so fine, it's such a rush/helps to relieve the mind, and it's good for us." (Paradoxically, it was also Marvin Gaye who was shot to death by his father. Reportedly, the father, a Baptism minister, could not tolerate the extent of sexuality in his son's music. Freud surely would have had a field day with this, speculating about the father's own ambivalence toward sexuality, and wondering too about unresolved issues of sexual rivalry between father and son that are essential aspects of the boyhood sleep-with-mom, knock-off-your-father wish that Freud termed the oedipal conflict).

Sex, as Freud and Marvin Gaye have posited, may well be for good for us, but, in fact, it's actually difficult to talk about—even in psychotherapy. Research into what patients talk about in psychotherapy (Farber, 2006) has consistently indicated a significant discrepancy between the importance of sex to patients and the extent to which they discuss this topic with their thera-pist. Peter Frampton ("Show Me the Way") sang about his apparent sexual desire for another, "I wonder if I'm dreaming, I feel so unashamed." He was onto something, because most of the time, even in the confidential confines of a therapist's office, speaking about sex feels shameful to lots of people.

Freud, who was always trying to reconcile the tenets of so-called hard science (biology and neurology) with his psychological theories, believed there were two opposing forces in all of us: a life force (eros) that is primarily driven by sexual energy and yearns for excitement, and a death force (thanatos) whose impulses are driven toward equilibrium, calm, and ultimately death. Turns out that hardly anyone still believes in the death instinct part of this theory (except for a few rarely read European intellectuals), but lots of people still agree with Freud's contention that sex is the great motivating force of life. It turns out, too, that lots of rock lyricists concur with this idea. "I have only one burning desire," sang Jimi Hendrix ("Fire"), "let me stand next to your fire." Similarly, Jim Morrison yearned to have someone "light his fire."

But Freud also argued that the sexual drive is contained somewhat by the demands of society. That is, the raw impulse toward unbridled expressions of sexuality (and aggression) is softened somewhat by the laws and moral code of societies. Both sides of this equation have been played out in rock music. The strong, biological drive toward sex is almost always represented in rock songs as the need and willingness for men to have sex with whomever and whenever without any sense of commitment or shame. Godsmack ("Get up Get Out") found a clever way of phrasing this idea: "You were the love of my life for a day." Equally cleverly, The Doors ("Hello I Love You") sang: "Hello, I love you, won't you tell me your name?" Aerosmith ("Shut up and Dance") expressed this thought far more crudely: "Sex is like a gun. You aim, you shoot, you run." Note too how this mixing of sex and aggression also occurs in such common idioms as *hitting on* someone. Finally, Michael Jackson may or may not have realized how ironic it is that he titled his song about sexual feelings, "Dangerous," but his lyrics here are an excellent repre-sentation of how sex can sometimes feel like a powerful, biologically driven force: "Deep in the darkness of passion's insanity, I felt taken by lust's strange inhumanity."

All these lyrics represent what Freud called the id—that part of the psyche that has as its aim the need to fulfill the drive toward either sex or aggression. The other side of the equation, that which insists on traditional societal values regarding the avoidance of sex outside of marriage, is very well reflected in the lyrics of Georgia Satellites' song, "Keep Your Hands to Yourself": "each time we talk I get the same old thing, always 'no huggin no kissin until I get a wedding ring'." Here we get that part of the Freudian psyche called the superego, that part of ourselves made up of moral strictures passed down from our parents and the community that influence our actions and sometimes lead to feelings of shame connected with sex.

It's quite common for the dictates of the id and superego to clash. This is evident in the internal debate between "I want sex now" versus "Is this right?" or "How will the other feel?" Or, from a male point of view: "I want a woman who's totally and completely sexual" versus "I want the purest woman in the world." This latter dialectic has been termed the Madonna-Whore complex, the belief of some men that love and sex don't mix, and that love is reserved for so-called good women, while sex is reserved for so-called bad women. The Eagles ("One of These Nights") understood this conflict well: "I've been searching for the daughter of the devil himself, I've been searching for an angel in white." In this song, at least, the resolution is a good one—we're led to believe that the singer understands the need to find someone who has a combination of both ingredients. However, in real life, many men and women struggle to allow themselves to be fully sexual with their partners, fearing that their partner would lose respect for them or that they would lose self-respect. The lyrics I started this chapter with, "Could it be the devil in me or is this the way that love's supposed to be?" contain the idea of sex as somewhat devilish or shameful, a part of oneself that may take some work to accept.

This leads to another, related set of issues dealt with in rock music, one that is more explicitly focused on women's sexuality. There is an enormously wide range of lyrics that address this topic, ranging from those suggesting that a women's sexual needs are not very different from men's, to those suggesting that women still have greater needs than men to combine sexuality with tenderness and perhaps even permanence. So, on the one hand, there are lyrics that celebrate women's sexuality, including acceptance of the idea that women can be every bit as blatantly sexual as men. "Gonna use my style, gonna use my sidestep…gonna use my imagination" sang Chrissie Hynde of The Pretenders in "Brass in Pocket." Even more explicitly, Blondie ("Call Me") sang: "Cover me with kisses baby, cover me with love. Roll me in designer sheets, because I never get enough." And Tori Amos' lyrics in "Precious Things" are a wonderfully cynical example of a woman's ability to be just as callously disregarding of a man's need for affirmation as men have traditionally been of women: "So you can make me come, doesn't make you Jesus."

On other hand, though, many rock lyrics suggest that women do want something more than just sex for sex's sake, and that, in comparison to men, they take greater pains to distinguish between love and lust. From an evolutionary psychology perspective, this makes sense: men produce trillions of sperm in their lifetime and must compete with other men for opportunities to keep their gene pool going. Women, on the other hand, produce relatively few eggs in their lifetime and, for the most part, bring one fetus to term at a time. Hence, the well-turned phrase: men to seek to reproduce widely, women wisely. Not surprisingly, then, while Aretha Franklin proudly acknowledged that "What you want, baby I got, what you need, you know I got it," she also made it abundantly clear that for this to transpire, she has to have "a little respect." Presumably, this means that there has to be some possibility of a relationship. What makes this somewhat ironic is that this song ("Respect") was actually written and originally sung by a man, Otis Redding.

Reflecting values similar to those of Aretha Franklin, the all-girls group the Shirelles, in a song written for them by Carole King and Gerry Goffin ("Will You Love Me Tomorrow"), delicately posed the important question, "Is this a lasting treasure or just a moment's pleasure?" Again, we see the assumed importance for women to differentiate between love and lust. Moreover, while some songs do suggest that women may be as accepting of casual sex as men are (many of Madonna's lyrics intimate as much), there's also a strong indication in many songs that there has to be a mutual acceptance of these terms; women do not want be seduced under false pretenses. A very poignant perspective on this is offered by Stevie Nicks ("Sometimes It's a Bitch"): "I've laid down with love and I woke up with lies."

What needs to be kept in mind in thinking about these lyrics is that until fairly recently, American society was still under the sway of Victorian notions that proper women had no sexual desire. Kinsey's volume on female sexuality (published in 1953, five years after the male version) was seen not only as immoral but also as undermining family values. Its great supposed sin was in normalizing female sexual desire. Since Kinsey, much has changed, a reflection of the real successes of the Women's Movement that began sometime in the 1960s and a consequence, too, of the introduction of effective oral contraception. The 1976 Hite Report, though shocking many, approved and even recommended female masturbation as a more effective means of orgasm than intercourse, an activity that Cyndi Lauper ("She Bop") later did her best to enthusiastically endorse: "they say I better get a chaperone, because I can't stop messin' with the danger zone." But, she added, she's not going to fret, because "there ain't no law against it yet."

Nevertheless, despite dramatic changes in the acceptance of a woman's right to be sexual and sexually satisfied, there are still significant vestiges of a double standard. Christina Aguilera's lyrics in "Can't Hold Us Down" are probably only slightly exaggerated: "A guy gets all the glory the more he can score, while the girl can do the same and you call her a whore." There still remains this implicit sense that, for the sake of propriety, some women need to hide the full extent of their sexuality and/or not respond fully to men. Dylan alluded slyly to this situation in "Stuck Inside of Mobile with the Memphis Blues Again": "Your debutante just knows what you need, but I know what you want."

The psychological evidence is strong that men do think about sex more than women. In one study (Leitenberg & Henning, 1995), researchers asked people at random times of the day whether sex had crossed their minds during the past five minutes. Among 14- and 15-year-olds, this was true for 57 percent of boys and 42 percent of girls; in the 26- to 55-year age bracket, it was true for 26 percent for men and 14 percent for women; and among 56-to 64-year-olds, 19 percent of men and 12 percent of women. In a study of sexual fantasies, in which nearly 3,500 people were surveyed, Laumann and colleagues (1994) found that 54 percent of men and 19 percent of women said they thought about sex every day or several times a day. As George Michel put it in his right-to-the-point song, "I Want Your Sex," "It's playing on my mind, it's dancing in my soul."

Men and women are attracted to different features in a potential, heterosexual partner. Men are attracted to women whose physical appearance, including a youthful face and form, suggests fertility. By contrast, women are attracted to men whose wealth and power seem to indicate an ability to protect and nurture offspring (Myers, 2002). Similarly, the sexual fantasies of men and women differ. In one study of college students (cited in Doskoch, 1995), 41 percent of the women but only 16 percent of the men said that while fantasizing they focused on the personal or emotional characteristics of their partner. Men, however, were four times as likely to focus on their fantasy partner's physical characteristics. Men's greater interest in bodily form also makes them by far the greater consumer of visual pornography. The Dave Matthews Band acknowledged the allure of voyeurism: "I watch you there through the window and I stare at you. You wear nothing, but you wear it so well" ("Crash into Me").

Another important aspect of sex and sexuality is one's "first time." In most countries, including the United States, losing one's virginity is considered a significant rite of passage. Recent statistics compiled by The Alan Guttmacher Institute (2002) indicated that the average age for first sexual intercourse in the United States is about 17 for boys and 16 for girls, considerably younger than decades ago. (The 1953 Kinsey report indicated that only 5 percent of 16-year-old unmarried women had had sex, a figure that had risen to about 38 percent by 1980). Apparently, more than a few adolescents in this country have concurred with the sentiments of Billy Joel ("Only the Good Die Young"): "they say there's a heaven for those who will wait, some say it's better but I say it ain't."

While there is research to suggest that women in particular tend to regret early loss of virginity (Dickson, Paul, Herbison, & Silver, 1998)—early being defined as before 16—for many women as well as men, a first sexual experience is intensely meaningful and important, often serving as an affirmation of their attractiveness, self-esteem, and emerging sense of adulthood. For most, it is a never-to-be forgotten experience. Do rock lyrics about adolescent sexuality and loss of virginity echo these themes? Absolutely. The words to the Four Seasons song, "December, 1963," certainly suggest as much: "Hypnotizing, mesmerizing me, she was everything I dreamed she'd be. Sweet surrender, what a night." In Bob Seger's wonderful song, "Night Moves," he invokes the memory of a hidden, wooden area and the backseat of his 1960s Chevy to so aptly describe youthful sex as "workin' on mysteries without any clues."

However, my old-time favorite lines about this theme are definitely those of Meat Loaf in "Paradise by the Dashboard Light." This is the record, some readers may remember, where ex-Yankees baseball great Phil Rizzuto lends a hand by narrating, in baseball lingo (first base, second base, etc.), the singer's increasingly aggressive sexual advances. The song is both funny and poignant; it captures so very well the excitement, awkwardness, fear, and intensity of adolescent sex. A sample: "Ain't no doubt about it, we were doubly blessed/ Cause we were barely seventeen and we were barely dressed."

On the other hand, all lyrics about sexual initiation are not etched in such positive tones; Bon Jovi's, "Blood on Blood," for example, contains a rather sordid account of such experiences: "Danny knew this white trash girl, we each threw in a ten/she took us to this cheap motel and turned us into men."

Sex has often been seen as the chief form of recreation for the poor. As the Smiths sang in "I Want the Ones I Can't Have": "A double-bed and a stalwart lover, for sure, these are the riches of the poor." But, of course, this is a rather narrow view. Sex, at its best, is a source of riches for all. A good place, then, to end this chapter is to offer some well-turned lyrics that have extolled the unequalled gratifications of sex, especially its power to evoke both intense individual pleasure and an exquisite sense of mutuality and merger with another. First, words from Fleetwood Mac from "Say You Love Me" (written by Christy McVie) that speak to the way that good loving creates its own min-iature universe: "'Cause when the lovin' starts and the lights go down, there's not another living soul around." And last, poetic words and beautiful imagery from Shawn Colvin ("Set the Prairie on Fire"): "the feeling burns down to one solitary color, the velocity of longing melting into each other."

Chapter 9

DRUG AND ALCOHOL USE

One pill makes you larger, and one pill makes you small.
—Jefferson Airplane, "White Rabbit"

The three words in the English language so often used to stand for fun are *sex, drugs,* and *rock 'n' roll.* The last chapter dealt with sex, and this whole book is essentially an homage to the underappreciated smartness of rock 'n' roll lyrics, and so that leaves the topic of drugs. It's probably fair to say that just as our culture is ambivalent in its attitudes toward alcohol and illicit drug use, so has been rock music. In both cases, there's a great acceptance of alcohol and recreational drugs (especially marijuana); a disparagement (with moralistic overtones) of the use of hard drugs (especially heroin); and all sorts of tangled, inconsistent attitudes toward binge drinking (often, but not always associated with good times and partying) and the use of cocaine, pills, and hallucinogens (often, but not always thought of as on the acceptable edges of excess and experimentation). On the one hand, then, there was and still is a great deal of rock music that rejoices in the disinhibiting effects of drugs and alcohol ("Feed your head," famously sang Jefferson Airplane in "White Rabbit"). On the other hand, there's also a fair amount of this music that reflects an attitude of caution, regret, and even disapproval ("Wasting away again in Margaritaville," sang Jimmy Buffett).

Attitudes, in life and in songs, are also influenced by how damaging one's substance use is to oneself and others. As noted above, drinking alcohol or smoking pot is usually acceptable and sometimes even glorified. Most of us know a friend or two who still enjoys either or both pursuits and seems to suffer no ill effects; indeed, some of these friends likely claim that their lives are greatly enhanced by these activities. But heavy drinking (consistent binges) and drunk driving are talked and sung about in different ways. A recent study by the National Institute of Alcohol Abuse and Alcoholism (*Substance Abuse*, 2006) found that 1,700 college students die each year from alcohol-related incidents, and awareness of such tragic consequences has begun to filter into our popular music. Even into the music of such good-time icons as Jimmy Buffett. There are, indeed, differences between occasionally getting high or intoxicated, having an intermittent substance abuse problem, and being addicted to or dependent ondrugs.

But before checking out those lyrics on both sides of the equation—those that seem to endorse drug and alcohol use, and those that are more cautionary—let's take a quick, historical step backward. Rock music, even before the '60s, has been indelibly associated with drugs and alcohol. Actually, even before the age of rock, jazz musicians were reported to be avant-garde partakers of drugs of all sorts, from marijuana to heroin, with lots of alcohol thrown in the mix. But rock music—primarily because it's now far more high-profile than jazz—is seen by the public as the drug and alcohol center of the music industry, perhaps of the entire entertainment industry. And the history of rock, including that of its most famous concerts and performers, provides little data for disputing the image. Not only is it virtually impossible to attend a concert without seeing large amounts of alcohol consumed in parking lots before the show and large amounts of marijuana consumed during the show, but a good many rock artists seem to be constantly battling drug and/or alcohol problems. Trent Reznor of Nine Inch Nails and Pete Doherty of Babyshambles are two of the current faces of rock-star addiction. Many rock celebrities—including Janis Joplin, Jimi Hendrix, Jim Morrison, Jerry Garcia, Sid Vicious (Sex Pistols), John Bonham (Led Zeppelin), Keith Moon (The Who), Gram Parsons (The Byrds), David Ruffin (The Temptations), and, of course, Elvis Presley—have died from their addictions, and scores more have been unabashedly high on stage.

But even outside of concerts, listening to rock seems very connected to drinking alcohol and smoking dope. Rock music is often seen as party time and as inextricably connected with singing, dancing, and getting high— whether it be in a campus dorm room, a backyard, a rooftop, a beach, or a concert setting. Although music and parties have long gone together, the '60s introduced drugs into this mixture in a big way. The ethos of that era included the belief that getting high was an integral part of growing up and expanding one's consciousness. The Beatles ("With a Little Help from My Friends") were hardly the only ones getting "high with a little help from [their] friends." David Crosby has been widely quoted as saying that "if you can remember the '60s, you weren't there." It's a terrific line, one that looks back fondly at the drug-friendly nature of that period. On the other hand, it's only fair to point out that in a recent *Time* magazine interview (Sachs, 2006), Crosby is quoted as saying that "we were right about everything [in the '60s] except the drugs."

Not surprisingly, then, a good many rock songs deal with drugs and alcohol. Three pages of lists of songs dealing with drugs and alcohol are in *The New Book of Rock Lists* (Marsh & Bernard, 1994). Some songs, particularly those that came out in the 1960s and 1970s, reflect this very relaxed, mostly positive attitude toward recreational drug use. The Beatles lyrics in "A Day in the Life" are a good example: "Found my way upstairs and had a smoke, and somebody spoke and I fell into a dream." In combination with the lush instrumentation that followed, these words convey a sense of mellownesss, an intimation that having a little something to smoke is a very nice way, indeed, of taking a break from life. Smoking marijuana is thus seen as a relatively benign, pleasant form of either self-medication (warding off stress) and/or self-enhancement (enabling one to get in touch with dreamy, creative forms of consciousness). While these may not be the most creative or wise words ever penned by the Beatles, they do have the virtue of having a texture that matches the message. There is something about the phrasing and peacefulness of these words that are consistent with the mild high they imply.

A smattering of other songs that have espoused a very tolerant view of marijuana include the Byrds' "Eight Miles High," Harry Chapin's "Taxi" ("I'm flying so high when I'm stoned"), the Mamas and the Papas' "Creeque Alley" ("McGuinn and McGuire couldn't get much higher, but that's what they are aiming at"), Arlo Guthrie's "Coming into Los Angeles" ("Comin' into Los Angeles, bringing in a couple of keys, don't touch my bags if you please, Mr. Customs Man"), and the Steve Miller Band's "The Joker" ("I'm a joker, I'm a smoker, I'm a midnight toker"). More recently, Counting Crows wrote some words for "Perfect Blue Buildings" that are also worth mentioning: "Gonna get me a little oblivion, baby/try to keep myself away from me (myself and) me." While it's not entirely clear whether the oblivion sought is simply sleep or something stronger (illicit drugs or alcohol), the latter possibility feels right. Moreover, the word *oblivion* here is such a good choice: whereas for some, getting high is a means of accessing a different kind of (supposedly higher) consciousness, for others it's a way of tuning out the hardships of life (a theme of much of Counting Crows' music).

Nirvana ("Alcohol") and Nine Inch Nails ("Happiness in Slavery") also offer narratives that justify getting high. From Nirvana: "My baby taught me how to be…how to fight…how to die." Alcohol is portrayed here as a teacher, offering important lessons on life. No irony is implied. From Nine Inch Nails: "I have found you can find happiness in slavery." If there's wisdom in either of these sets of lyrics, it's in the realization that for some individuals life is overwhelming and often incomprehensible, and that giving oneself over to the demands of drugs offers a seemingly better alternative. Cults offer a similar allure.

Some of Bob Dylan's songs might also fit into the category of drug-friendly— *might* because there's controversy over the meaning of many of his ambiguously worded lines. Dylan's "Mr. Tambourine Man" ("Take me for a trip upon your magic swirlin' ship"), "Rainy Day Women #12 and 35" ("Everybody must get stoned") and "Quinn the Eskimo" ("Everybody's in despair, every girl and boy, but when Quinn the Eskimo gets here everybody's gonna jump for joy") all seem suggestive of the joys of getting high, but each can be read as having a different meaning as well. In "Rainy Day Women," for example, the notion of "stoned" can easily be read as "criticized"—that regardless of what you're doing in life, whether it's "trying' to go home" or "when you're there all alone," you're going to get flack from others. But assuming that "Mr. Tambourine Man" is about drugs—and it's quite easy to read the lines this way—Dylan's song gives us an extraordinary glimpse into the temptation of being high. There's a "magic swirlin' ship," there's a readiness "to go anywhere," there's an inner "parade," and there's even a "dancing spell" to go under. In this song, there's a sense of playfulness, a tension between fear and joyful anticipation, a sense of abandon, an eagerness to learn more about the self as well as the readiness to trust another as a guide, and an Alice-in-Wonderland quality of strangeness, intrigue, and adventure. In this regard, the lyrics from Jefferson Airplane's "White Rabbit" that I began this chapter with—"One pill makes you larger, and one pill makes you small"—are meant to suggest that the experience of "tripping" (using LSD) provides this Alice-in-Wonderland quality.

What is surprising, though, is that the tone of the great majority of rock songs is cautionary in regard to drug and alcohol use—or, somewhat more accurately, cautionary in regard to blatant overuse. That is, most rock songs offer admonitions to refrain or note the consequences for those who've gone too far. Examples include Jimmy Buffet's manifestly comic but ultimately serious acknowledgment of the self-deluding qualities of alcohol abuse in *Margaritaville* ("Some people claim that there's a woman to blame but I know it's my own damned fault") and the Eagles' depiction in "Witchy Woman" of someone being driven "to madness with a silver spoon." Harder drugs have led to even harder-edged lyrics. Examples here include Lou Reed's allusion ("Heroin") to the terrible power of this drug ("Heroin, be the death of me; heroin, it's my wife and it's my life") and Neil Young's awareness in "The Needle and the Damage Done" of the sad inevitability of terminal burnout in heroin users ("every junkie's like a setting sun").

Surprisingly (and ironically, given Jerry Garcia's fate and the usual state of consciousness reached by their fans), even the Grateful Dead penned lyrics ("Casey Jones") that can be seen as warnings against excessive drug use: "Drivin' that train, high on cocaine, Casey Jones you better watch your speed."

It's not hard to see the train as a metaphor for life and the song as a warning for those using drugs, cocaine in particular, to be careful. Stated somewhat differently: it's easy to get in too deep without realizing it, and when you do become aware, it may be too late to avoid a fatal crash. Furthermore, in "Truckin'," they bemoan the fate of someone who has wasted herself on drugs: "livin' on reds, Vitamin C and cocaine, all a friend can say is 'ain't it a shame'." Here, of course, the message is that beyond a certain point even well-meaning friends are often helpless to do very much with a person caught up in drug abuse—like the other members of the Grateful Dead in terms of their efforts to help heroin-addicted Jerry Garcia. This is far from the captivating, life-enhancing image of getting high in "Mr. Tambourine Man"; in fact, it speaks to the opposite, to the real possibility of a wasted life, or at least, a tragic end to one.

How many people in this country face the possibility of a wasted, "wrecked" life? Let's examine some recent statistics. In 2005, 22.2 million persons aged 12 or older in the United States (slightly more than 9 percent of this age group) were classified by the Department of Health and Human Services as having a substance abuse or dependence problem in the past year (*Substance Abuse*, 2006). Dependence is considered to be a more severe problem than abuse because it involves the psychological and physiological effects of tolerance and withdrawal. Addiction (in any form) is usually viewed by the public as a problem involving heroin, cocaine, or alcohol. However, according to the National Center on Addiction and Substance Abuse at Columbia University (CASA, 2005a), more than 15 million Americans abuse controlled prescription drugs, including opioids (for example, Oxycontin or Vicotin), central nervous system depressants (for example, Valium or Xanax), and stimulants (for example, Ritalin). Abuse among 12- to 17-year-olds tripled in the period between 1992 and 2003, while abuse in the adult population nearly doubled. The 15 million people abusing prescription drugs exceed the combined number of people in this country abusing cocaine (nearly 6 million), heroin (300,000), hallucinogens (4 million), and inhalants (2 million). Fifteen million is also about the same number as those individuals using marijuana in this country, by the far the most widely used illicit street drug. As for that rock line most reminiscent of marijuana use, my choice would be an infamous phrase from Brewer and Shipley, "One toke over the line, sweet Jesus, one toke over the line." It's a good line because it suggests that there can be too much, even of a presumed good thing.

As for the damage done: alcohol and drug-abusing parents are three times likelier to abuse their children and four times likelier to neglect them than parents who do not abuse these substances (National Center on Addiction and Substance Abuse, 2005b). John Prine ("Sam Stone") said it very well: "There's a hole in daddy's arm where all the money goes." Children of alcohol and drug abusers are more likely to suffer conduct disorders, depression, anxiety, and academic failure, conditions that increase the probability that they will smoke, drink, and use drugs. Moreover, there were 3.9 million persons aged 12 or older (1.6 percent of the population) who received some kind of treatment for a problem related to the use of alcohol or illicit drugs in 2005.

What causes addiction? Is it a disease, an unfortunate habit, a series of bad choices, a lifestyle, a moral failing, a mental disorder, a natural craving for stimulation gone awry, or all of the above? The answer actually depends on several factors, including one's scientific biases, political leanings, religious stance, and personal familiarity with addictive substances. Almost certainly though, addiction is the result of an inherited predisposition interacting with environmental stressors. Or, stated more basically, addiction is yet another example of something that is a combination of nature and nurture—of biology and life circumstances. Furthermore—and here's the basic problem—getting high (whether through drugs or alcohol) does two things very well. It produces pleasurable, frequently euphoric sensations. "Picture yourself in a boat on a river, with tangerine trees and marmalade skies," sang the Beatles in "Lucy in the Sky with Diamonds." In addition, at least in the short run, it reduces unpleasant sensations, including boredom, sadness, anxiety, and the fear of death. The Ramones ("I Wanna Be Sedated") speak to the boredom: "Nothing to do, nowhere to go, I want to be sedated." The Rolling Stones ("Mother's Little Helper") have sung about alleviating anxiety through pills: "And I'll come running for the shelter of mother's little helper." In a similar vein, the Eagles ("Tequila Sunrise") used a perfectly accurate metaphor to denote the anxiety-reducing effects of drinking: "Take another shot of courage." And Bon Jovi, in "Dry County," astutely noted how alcohol mitigates what may be the greatest source of anxiety of all, the awareness of death: "Some say it's a savior in these hard and desperate times; for me it helps me to forget that we're just born to die."

It's not surprising, then, that most attempts to treat alcoholism and substance abuse fail, or don't even begin. Kanye West's lines ("Addiction") are a strikingly accurate depiction of the problem: "Everything they told me not to is exactly what I would; man I tried to stop man, I tried the best I could." Like most others who try to stop their substance abuse habits, he failed. Relapses after treatment are the norm; it often takes multiple efforts to effectively end a drug or alcohol problem. The most often reported reasons for not receiving substance abuse treatment among persons who acknowledge needing such treatment are (a) not being ready to stop using, (b) cost or insurance barriers, and (c) stigma, including negative opinions from neighbors and community, and negative job consequences (*Substance Abuse*, 2006). Many addicts are also in denial of their need for help, a point very astutely noted by Black Crowes ("She Talks to Angels"): "She never mentions the word addiction in certain company; yes, she'll tell you she's an orphan after you meet her family."

Taken together, though, the lyrics in this chapter suggest a philosophy that many members of society—baby boomers and otherwise—have ultimately adopted in regard to drug and alcohol intake: all things in moderation. But these lyrics suggest something else too—that what brings some degree of peace to some, brings ruin to others. Joni Mitchell captures this general thought rather beautifully in the song, "Amelia": "Where some have found their paradise, others just come to harm."

Chapter 10

MONEY

I don't need no money, fortune or fame.
—The Temptations, "My Girl" (Written by Smokey Robinson)

There are people who need neither money, fortune, nor fame; none, however, will ever make it into the glamour pages of *People* magazine. We are intrigued by those who are rich or ultrasuccessful. Moreover, despite the advice of spiritual leaders to eschew materialistic pursuits, so many of us cannot help but strive to make as much money as possible. We ignore the warnings that it will lead to trouble and regret. We disavow the existential mantra that money is but an illusion. Indeed, in the decades following the idealistic (and somewhat naïve) era of the '60s, making money has once again become a primary objective of both young and old. Tom Wolfe in his best-selling book, *Bonfire of the Vanities,* coined the phrase "masters of the universe" to describe those whose successful pursuit of money (most often in the financial industry) provided them with an extraordinary aura of power, influence, and self-importance. Pink Floyd ("Money") understood this need well: "Money, it's a hit, don't give me that do goody good bullshit."

Some celebrity members of the music industry seem to be highly socially conscious and philanthropic (Bono, of U2 fame, comes to mind), while others seem to be far more interested in collecting bling than giving money to needy others. Not surprisingly, then, lyrics reflect a good deal of ambivalence about the importance and value of money and financial success. "Sometimes," observed Prince ("Condition of the Heart"), "money buys you everything and nothing."

Money is often portrayed as all-important. In the oft-quoted words of the "Money Song" from the Broadway show *Cabaret*, it "makes the world go 'round." In the famous words of the Beatles in "Money (That's What I Want)," "Money don't get everything it's true [but] what it don't get, I can't use." Or, in words that are less famous but at least contain an intriguing simile, "when you get right down to it, no matter who you are, it rules your life like a virgin queen" (The Alan Parson Project, "Money Talks").

Similarly, money is often considered the great motivating force in life. The late Irish playwright George Bernard Shaw contended that the "lack of money is the root of all evil," meaning that people and nations get desperate when they haven't enough to survive and that inequalities among groups lead to wars and other degradations. Conveying much the same sentiment, albeit with opposite-sounding words, Pink Floyd (paraphrasing the apostle Paul as well as the novelist Ayn Rand in *Atlas Shrugged*) suggested that money is "the root of all evil today" ("Money"). Again, the message is that the obsessive pursuit of money is corrupting, that competition for it makes the world a very difficult place, and that even the winners in this battle never feel they have enough. Nevertheless, Pink Floyd's basic point in this song is that it's okay to get as much as you can and that it's hypocritical to imagine that everyone isn't on this same page. Consistent with this message, Pink Floyd sold more than 34 million copies of the album, *The Dark Side of the Moon*, on which the song "Money" appears.

But the pursuit of money often leads to the following dilemma: laboring for the affluence we feel we need leaves little or no time to enjoy the money we make. In "Working Man," the group Rush described this situation with these words: "I get up at seven and I go to work at nine. I got no time for living, yes, I'm working all the time." Of course, there are those working in law offices or the financial industry who are already at work by 7:00 A.M. and not likely to make it home till 8 or 9 P.M.; their financial compensation is considerably higher than the so-called working man, but they too feel locked into a situation that leaves them (and their families) feeling resentful over the lack of leisure time. In their hit song, "Take It to the Limit," the Eagles were quite discerning in writing about such circumstances: "You can spend all your time making money, and then spend all your love making time." That's as good a summary of one of the great problems in modern life as can be found anywhere.

This leads to a consideration of the struggles we often face between competing needs. Abraham Maslow, one of the founders (along with Carl Rogers) of humanistic psychology, proposed the concept of a hierarchy of needs. According to this somewhat old (1943) but still useful theory, love, friendship, and family relationships are basic needs. But here's the rub: there are needs that are even more basic and primary, including those related to physiological prerequisites (like food) and safety/security requirements (like housing, health, and a steady job) that must be attained before an individual can focus on the higher-order needs of love, self-esteem, and self-actualization. As it turns out, Maslow wasn't exactly right: after all, an individual can have friends while still lacking job security or health insurance. But still, he was onto something important. So, while the Beatles were surely right that "money can't buy me love," they overlooked the fact that money can buy me absolutely needed stuff. Money is a very basic need; or, more accurately, money is the usual means to secure very basic needs.

In fact, several studies have found that there is a significant relationship between socio-economic status (an index of income and education) and physical health: the lower one's socioeconomic status, the poorer one's physical health (Adler & Snibbe, 2003). Or, from Maslow's perspective: The less money available to us, the less able we are to achieve our most basic needs. Financial woes lead to physical vulnerability (substandard housing and less access to health care) and, thus, illness. In addition, not having enough money to make ends meet often causes stress and unhealthy coping behaviors, including smoking and drinking. All of which may leave people feeling desperate. The rapper Grandmaster Flash ("The Message") got right to the heart of the matter: "'cuz it's all about money, ain't a damn thing funny/You got to have a con in this land of milk and honey." It is, he suggests, ultimately about survival, and Maslow would agree.

What about those on the other end of the financial continuum? One stereotype alluded to earlier is that the rich are every bit as stressed and overwhelmed as everyone else. But another stereotype is that the rich live healthy and stress-free lives. As the Smiths ("This Charming Man") so charmingly put it: "why pamper life's complexities when the leather runs smooth on the passenger seat?" So which is it? Are the rich really happier? From one perspective, the answer is actually yes. Research has shown that income is related to perceived life satisfaction (Johnson & Krueger, 2006). Money provides a sense of security and a feeling of control over one's life. At least temporarily, money may even chase the blues away. Shopping comes to mind, as does dressing elegantly. Paul Simon played on this theme particularly well in one of his many wonderfully crafted songs, "Diamonds on the Souls of Her Shoes": "She got diamonds on the souls of her shoes/well, that's one way to lose these walking blues."

When a person's income increases, his or her well-being improves, though *only* when the increase is slow and steady. A person must feel that he or she had some hand in controlling the change in his or her financial status; otherwise, even change in a positive direction is perceived as precarious. When an individual wins the lottery, for example, the results are quite mixed: for some, life satisfaction improves, for others, it worsens. Sudden rises in income are actually linked with heightened risk for divorce (Diener & Seligman, 2004). The explanation for the paradox of unhappy consequences of sudden fortune may be seen in The Cars' song "It's All I Can Do": "Once in a moment, it all comes to you. As soon as you get it, you want something new."

Thus, excessive pursuit of money, or sudden riches, may easily result in skewed priorities. "All I want is everything. Am I asking too much?" ("All I Want Is Everything"). Well, yes, Def Leppard, you are. But greed is a central theme when it comes to money. As Steve Winwood's first band, Traffic, noted in "State of Grace": we all tend to get lost in things we don't need, because "we all lose direction in a world of greed." Once we start acquiring goods and possessions, it may be very hard to stop the habit. We tend to admire those who somehow manage to keep their priorities straight even when they have a great deal of disposable income.

Neil Young captures the seductive and manipulative qualities of material wealth in his song "Days That Used to Be": "Possessions and concessions are not often what they seem; they drag you down and load you down in disguise of security." Or, as the rap group Notorious B.I.G. says in "Mo Money Mo Problems," "The more money we come across, the more problems we see." Why might this be the case? One possibility is that when we focus on such extrinsic symbols of success as money and possessions, we become less focused on more humanistic values, including the potential for personal growth. Gordon Lightfoot ("Sit down Young Stranger") framed this quite beautifully: "Will you gather daydreams or will you gather wealth? How can you find your fortune when you cannot find yourself?" Indeed, the importance of the goal of financial success is negatively associated with happiness, self-actualization, and self-esteem (Diener & Seligman, 2004). The more important the pursuit of money is to you, the less you tend to feel happy or existentially satisfied. This finding may seem contradictory to what I reported a few paragraphs ago, but it's not really. While having the means to make ends meet is generally associated with well-being, placing a high value on money or caring too much about making a great deal of money decreases overall life satisfaction. Ben Harper, a contemporary singer-songwriter, had it right when he advised in "Diamonds on the Inside" that you "make sure the fortune that you seek is the fortune that you need."

Another psychological issue related to money is the perception of relative wealth. That is, we tend to judge our fortune not against that of the whole world—which would make everyone reading this extremely well off—but rather in comparison to the income and assets of our family members, friends, and neighbors. Sad but true: gains in income are more likely to increase subjective well-being when the gain is relative to other people. If everyone gets a raise, for example, the increase in income does little for our individual happiness (Diener & Seligman, 2004). We tend to want more than others. Our sense of what we have is affected by our perception of what those around us have. What the group Boston said in their song "Peace of Mind" is admirable but rare: "I don't care if I get behind/People living in competition, all I want is to have my peace of mind."

The "power of gold" (the title of a song by Dan Fogelberg) is something psychologists have been very keen on studying in recent years. Researchers have found that when people are given subliminal cues to think about money, they are less likely to want to help or be helped by others (Stevens, Cushman, & Hauser, 2004). Although it's sometimes a stretch to generalize results from a laboratory study to so-called real life, these results do suggest that people who think more about money act more independently and less communally than those who think about it less. In addition, research indicates that people often lie to their partners about their spending habits (Henry & Miller, 2004). In fact, as I alluded to earlier on the chapter on love lost, financial matters are among the most commonly cited marital problem in many research studies. Again, money comes with problems.

Is all of this just bad news about human nature? Are we inherently greedy creatures, looking out primarily for ourselves, and insatiable in our desire for riches? Not exactly. But not terribly far from the mark either. Freud thought that we have all been socialized—that is, learned to be kind to one another—only under very heavy societal pressures. It's the *Lord of the Flies* view of the world: without the constraints of civilization and its rules, we'd all be savages, acting only to satisfy our own needs. Thus, while aspects of selfishness are probably part of our biological inheritance, most of us, at least most of the time, have learned to play nicely. That is, we've learned to share, use some of our money for the pursuit of the common good, focus on less materialistic needs, and even curtail our impulses to pursue wealth at all cost.

But we still need to be reminded of these perils, and rock lyrics have done their share in this regard. In "Simple Man," the rock band Lynyrd Skynyrd advises, "forget your lust for the rich man's gold, all that you need is in your soul." Similarly, other groups have suggested that the important things in life have nothing to do with money and everything to do with love. The Beatles conveyed this message in both "Money Can't Buy Me Love" and "All You Need Is Love," as did the Temptations in "My Girl" ("I got all the riches, baby, that one man can claim"). The idea is, you "can't buy what [you] want because it's free" (Pearl Jam, "Corduroy"). That is, what you *really*, existentially want.

It's also worth returning to a point I made briefly at the beginning of this chapter: some of the wealthiest musicians in the world are also some of the most generous. U2's Bono is known for his humanitarian gestures through-out the developing world. He has established an organization that has raised millions of dollars to ease the extraordinary financial and health burdens in much of Africa. Jewel Kilcher ("Jewel") also developed a nonprofit organiza-tion, *Higher Ground for Humanity,* with the intent of enhancing access to clean water in developing countries. The majority of the funding for this charity comes from Jewel herself. Good publicity for these individuals? Sure, but it would be hard to argue that this is their primary motivation. Even if our philanthropic acts are self-preserving at heart, they still serve other good purposes. Finally, we should all probably take the advice of the rock group (Supertramp) who tells us to "give a little bit," if only to (selfishly) keep our values in perspective. The members of this group seem to have honored their own advice in real life: in order to preserve the integrity of their music, they purportedly turned down a $5 million offer from Greyhound to use their song "Take the Long Way Home" in bus commercials!

Part IV

ON COPING WITH LIFE

The four chapters within this part use rock lyrics to illustrate a variety of ways that we cope with the inevitable difficulties of life. The initial chapter of this section (Chapter 11) is actually about why our attempts to change who we are, and how we act, are often doomed to fail. The theme in this chapter, especially reflected in the lyrics of Paul Simon and the Eagles, is that we get locked into patterns early in life that are extremely resistant to change. Their words, and those of some others, including Ani DiFranco, are very consistent with what has been written in the psychology literature about the near-permanence of early childhood mental models.

The second chapter of this part (Chapter 12) invokes rock lyrics to illustrate the large variety of defense mechanisms we use to make reality more palatable. Drawing heavily on the Who's "Tommy," as well as lyrics by Smokey Robinson, Dylan, and Pearl Jam, this chapter traces the controversy in psychology between those who believe repressing painful emotions is inevitably problematic, and those who suggest that repression is a perfectly acceptable way of defending against thoughts and feelings that are just too overwhelming.

Chapter 13 is about secrets and self-disclosure. Here I've tried to integrate some very wise lyrics by the likes of Bruce Springsteen, David Bowie, Billy Joel, and Pink Floyd with recent research on what, and why, individuals will and will not disclose to others. The great lyricists here understand the extraordinary power of shame to inhibit our usual need to be known, comforted, and understood by others.

The final chapter in this section (Chapter 14) focuses on coping with life through religion and spirituality. The power of believing in God, or another kind of higher power, is something that many songwriters have addressed in thoughtful ways. Most, like Sarah McLachlan, Stevie Wonder, Eric Clapton, and Van Morrison, have found great comfort in their beliefs; others, however, including Elton John and the late singer-songwriter Laura Nyro, have been critical and even cynical of the power of organized religion and the uses (including justifications for wars) to which God has been put. Given the importance of this topic to most people, it should not be surprising that the lyrics in this chapter seem very close to the heart of these songwriters.

seemingly puzzling phenomena of individuals continuing to perform the same (often maladaptive) behaviors or seeking the same sorts of (inappropriate) love-objects even in the face of constant frustration or failure. Freud's explanation for this was a bit arcane, having to do with the continued symbolic expression of inner conflicts that never quite get resolved because the actual behaviors mask the true aggressive or sexual need. But, of course, repetitive behaviors make sense on a simpler psychological level—these actions undoubtedly paid off early in life. They either resulted in a reduction of stress or an increase in the intensity or frequency of some reward, such as affection. Now, however, even when these same behaviors have no payoff, we tend to repeat them.

In fact, we tend to ignore information in the environment that might change our feelings or attitudes. *Cognitive dissonance*, a term used in social psychology, is the technical way to describe our penchant for attending to (indeed, seeking out) information we agree with and for avoiding other input. Paul Simon—perhaps we should give him an honorary psychology degree?—is apparently well aware of this: "a man hears what he wants to hear and disregards the rest," he sang in "The Boxer." Nothing prevents change so effectively as the failure to allow ourselves to listen to opinions, feedback, or advice that challenges our sense of the world. We do this (listen primarily or exclusively to confirmatory evidence; avoid contrary evidence) even in terms of relatively small things, like buying CDs or appliances or cars. It's much easier and more affirming to hear that others agree with the wisdom of our choices. Indeed, good salespeople are invariably wise to this tendency. But we cling even more tenaciously to our views and opinions when listening to alternative opinions or advice that would require us to give up or dramatically alter dreams, hopes, values, beliefs, comforts, or self-images. The boxer, in Simon's song, listened to half-baked promises that he knew were "all lies and jest," but the potential for glory was so great that he suspended serious consideration of other, more rational views. So often, we fail to listen to others whose words imply that we need to change, that we are not perfect, that we could do far better. It just hurts too much to admit these things. And even if we do admit that we need to change, visions of how hard this would be to accomplish—or how terribly gratified others might be when hearing of our efforts—often prevent us from taking any steps at all.

So, change is hard and we resist it. We become defensive in the face of even well-meaning and sensitive feedback from friends and significant others, and we stay far more attuned to the idiosyncrasies and flaws in others than we do to these same issues in ourselves. If we are even aware of our flaws at all, we tend to acknowledge them to ourselves and others rather than doing anything much about them. We are surprised, disappointed, and even infuriated that our partners don't always take our side; we are wounded by their criticisms. In therapy, we still secretly hold onto the wish that our therapist will one day come to agree with our sense that everyone else is wrong and misguided and that we are, indeed, innocent, right, entirely lovable, and free from blame. Shawn Colvin's poignant words ("Polaroids") resonate with this deep wish we all have to simply be affirmed and not have to change a thing: "Please no more therapy, mother take care of me."

I would like to end this chapter, though, on a somewhat more positive note. A note that acknowledges that psychologists, as well as some smart rock lyricists, believe that change—at least in small but powerful amounts—is possible. As the Eagles have wisely noted (in "Already Gone"), "So often times it happens that we live our lives in chains and we never even know we have the key." This is a brilliant lyric, containing elements of Sartre and Camus, of Freud, of social psychologists studying the nature of learned helplessness, and of contemporary psychotherapists who strive to convince their clients that they can and must take responsibility for changing that which has seemed unchangeable. Believing that we have the key—that we have the power within us to effect change—is a substantial first step in this direction. The Beatles understood this too ("Within You, Without You"): "Try to realize it's all within yourself—no one else can make you change." Meaning, of course, that loving friends and sensitive therapists will inevitably fail in their attempts to help if a person resists being helped, but that he or she who truly wants to change can often find the way. In "Carry On," Crosby, Stills, Nash, and Young also articulated the constant possibilities for renewal: "A new day, a new way, and new eyes to see the dawn." Similarly, Led Zeppelin, in "Stairway to Heaven" reflected on the fact that change is always a possibility: "in the long run there's still time to change the road you're on." Who knew there were at least some reasonably smart lyrics in the aftermath of the most famous, overplayed opening notes in rock history?

Finally, these astute, beautifully rendered lyrics by the Beatles in "Blackbird": "Blackbird singin' in the dead of night, take these broken wings and learn to fly; all your life, you were only waiting for this moment to arise." Here we are reminded that change is often sought most by those who have been most hurt in life. And we are reminded too that despite the hurt, despite intimations of the futility of trying to change, we can and must find moments of strength to begin living life differently.

Chapter 12

PSYCHOLOGICAL DEFENSES

Every form of refuge has its price.

—The Eagles, "Lyin' Eyes"

No one likes being accused of being defensive. It implies that we are being childish and stubborn, refusing to acknowledge what everyone else knows to be the case. "You're so defensive" is a frequent taunt used in couples' fights, a charge that the offending partner is maddeningly unwilling to admit his or her responsibility for a problem or own up to long-standing annoying behaviors. When we're defensive we're willing to do almost anything to deflect our frustration. For example, we may deny that there's any problem at all, blame others for our own flaws, or take our frustrations out on inanimate objects (or, worse, on innocent people or pets). Or, we may rationalize that something awful is really for the best, withdraw from the world and retreat to a safe place, regress to remarkably childish states (for example, have a fit or temper tantrum), or even dissociate (space out). We might also use big words to avoid feelings, use feelings to avoid thoughts, or become physically sick or hyperenergized to avoid emotionally distressing thoughts or feelings.

Although many of these psychological defense mechanisms sound a bit perverse and even a bit pathetic, the truth is that we're all defensive sometimes. In fact, we all need to be defensive at times because we're all vulnerable to feeling overwhelmed and shamed. Each of us has different triggers, different defensive tendencies, and different thresholds for what we can bear. But without our defenses we would feel besieged by the power of all those things and all those people that threaten our physical and emotional well being. Some things are just too hard to hear, process, or react to in an appropriate, realistic, or mature way. As Billy Joel sang ("And So It Goes"), "this is why my eyes are closed, it's just as well for all I've seen." So the question is not whether defenses are necessary or not—they simply are—but rather, "what, if anything, is the price we pay for this part of our lives?" Before answering this question, though, let's delve a bit more deeply into the nature of defense mechanisms, and let's start with a Dylan lyric to illustrate further how and why they get used.

While defenses are likely to have their biological roots in physical fear, in modern life our defenses are usually brought into play when we feel threatened psychologically, a dynamic that Dylan understood well. In "My Back Pages," Dylan's guard was evoked when "threats too noble to neglect deceived me into thinking I had something to protect." What Dylan understood so well here is that it's the *perception* of threat that counts—our sense that someone has been too demeaning or hurtful, or that some circumstance is too emotionally intense for us to fully take in. These situations, or rather the feelings that they provoke, overwhelm us, threaten our sense of self, and create an intense need to protect ourselves from further hurt. That others may be telling us "you're overreacting" or "you're too sensitive" doesn't mean much (or enough) at the moment. We may even know that we should just let this remark or behavior go, but we can't, or at least don't. Right then, something must be done to alleviate or minimize our frustration or anger, or displace it onto someone or something else. Dylan also grasped that it's shame, or relatedly, the need to preserve an easily bruised sense of pride, that typically sets our defenses into motion. Our self-esteem is often more fragile than we realize; our tolerance for shame often has a low threshold.

Anna Freud—Sigmund's daughter, and a famous therapist in her own right—wrote the first book (1936) on common psychological defenses. She noted that our preferred defenses have usually been adopted in childhood and tend to be remarkably enduring. We keeping using them because they work; that is, at least temporarily, they alleviate painful aspects of our existence. And, yes, a surprising number of rock songs describe, often quite accurately, some of the most common defense mechanisms that Ms. Freud (she never attained a formal professional degree) noted all those years ago. For example, Carole King's song, "Up on the Roof," contains a perfect example of withdrawal: "When…people are just too much for me to face/I climb way up to the top of the stairs where all my cares just drift right into space." John Cougar Mellencamp ("Hard Times for an Honest Man") sang about displacement in these lyrics: "His frustration running very high/he takes it out on the ones he loves because it's safe." Eric Clapton clearly understood projection (seeing in others what we can't face up to in ourselves): "Before you accuse me, take a look at yourself," he sang. Smoky Robinson got the idea of reaction formation (turning an unwanted feeling into its opposite) exactly right in his great song "Tracks of My Tears": "My smile is my make-up I wear since my breakup with you." The Beatles also sang about this phenomenon in "A Day in the Life": "And though the news was rather sad, well, I just had to laugh."

As I noted earlier, defenses are necessary, but some are far less adaptive than others. The healthier defenses don't distort reality as much, nor do they harm oneself or others as much. When the world gets you down or feels too much, there's a big difference between climbing "way up to the top of the stairs" (a bit of reasonable withdrawal) and taking frustrations out on loved ones "because it's safer" (displacement).

A particularly problematic defense is that of "acting out"—behaving in inappropriate, often hurtful ways instead of talking about why or how we're hurting. In therapy, unhappy patients act out by coming late to sessions, failing to pay their bills, or even engaging in self-destructive behavior. In marriage, unhappy spouses act out by having affairs. On a larger canvas, disenfranchised people act out by refusing to adhere to conventional social rules. A good example of this form of acting out can be heard in a smart, biting lyric in Rage Against the Machine's song "Calm Like a Bomb": "A riot be the rhyme of the unheard." This lyric speaks to the idea that people who feel they haven't been well heard may vent their frustration—act out—by not adhering to typical norms of behavior. On the other hand, some individuals who experience awful frustrations and hurts can channel these feelings into creative or artistic projects. An example of this very healthy defensive mechanism of sublimation can be found in Don McLean's poignant song "Vincent (Starry Starry Night)." Here, Vincent Van Gogh is pictured as sublimating his demons onto his canvas: "weathered faces lined in pain are soothed beneath the artist's loving hand/And now I understand." Of course, given the fate of his ear (chopped off) and his life (ended by suicide), Van Gogh's use of sublimation can hardly be considered a rousing success. What one might say is that, like many defense mechanisms, it worked reasonably well for a short while.

Sigmund Freud thought that repression was the most basic of all defense mechanisms, the means by which we keep painful thoughts and feelings out of conscious awareness. Pink Floyd, though usually not mentioned in the same paragraph as Freud, nevertheless got the concept exactly right in "The Hero's Return": "a memory that is too painful to withstand the light of day." In keeping these memories in the dark, we prevent ourselves from taking control of our lives. In Freudian theory, children who witness or who are forced to participate in inappropriate sexual or aggressive activities are especially likely to repress memories of these events. Examples include a child's observing his or her parents' sexual activity, viewing violent acts of others, or (worst of all) being the victim of sexual or physical abuse. In the Who's rock-opera *Tommy*, we're led to believe that a boy who has seen his father kill his mother's lover becomes deaf, blind, and mute as a result. In "What About the Boy," Tommy's father sings: "You didn't hear it, you didn't see it!/You won't say nothin' to no one, ever in your life." Indeed, the boy is not haunted by these memories; he has success-fully repressed them, and he has no conscious awareness that these actions ever occurred. Although *Tommy* is a great album (one of the first so-called concept albums), the Who is not going to be given honorary psychology degrees: this scenario lacks any scientific credibility. Children (or adults) who witness or experience personal violence may develop symptoms of posttraumatic stress disorder (including flashbacks, distressing dreams, and numb feelings) but do not become disabled in the manner of Tommy. Nevertheless, the story is a powerful, if exaggerated, illustration of the basic process of repression. If you can't deal well with what you see, push it down, forget it ever existed.

While Freud suggested that repression was an inevitable feature of life, he also believed that it had unfortunate consequences. He thought repression, as well as other psychological defenses, consumed psychic energy that could be used in far more vital, life-enhancing ways. Moreover, he thought that repres-sion would always come back to haunt us—that we could not repress traumatic events forever, and that sooner or later, these memories would reemerge in intrusive thoughts, in troubling dreams, or in the guise of various somatic ailments (for example, headaches, stomachaches, back pain). "He who forgets will be destined to remember" is what Freud meant, but these actual words were not said by him but rather sung by Pearl Jam ("Nothingman"). These ingenious lyrics speak to the assumption of most mental health workers that while repression protects us from pain, its use comes with an inevitable cost. Or, in the astute words of the Eagles that I began this chapter with: "every form of refuge has its price."

This seems intuitively right—that every form of refuge or defense comes with a cost. But is it? There's now lively debate in the psychological world as to whether repression is as unfortunate a practice as Freud and others have contended. Some contemporary researchers, including a colleague of mine at Teachers College (Dr. George Bonanno), have argued that for many people repression is actually a quite appropriate and adaptive strategy—one of sev-eral pathways toward successful coping (Bonanno, Papa, O'Neill, Westphal, & Coifman, 2004). According to this perspective, psychologists shouldn't be cautioning people against using repression as a defense because some people do just fine by keeping awful memories far away from consciousness. These individuals (called repressors) seemingly don't need to replay old traumatic memories in order to work through them. They don't need to discuss them in therapy or in posttraumatic debriefing sessions. For many, repressing painful memories is a highly successful and low-risk strategy. Of course, there are also those of us who are so-called sensitizers, who seem to need to obsessively replay and endlessly analyze those things that bother us.

So is there a significant cost to repression? Some smart and persuasive lyrics have been written supporting one side or the other in this debate. For example, Melissa Manchester sang of the lure of pushing painful affect away: "Don't cry out loud, keep it inside, learn how to hide your feelings." Even more powerfully, Carly Simon ("That's the Way I've Always Heard It Should Be") wrote of despairing couples who, in order to keep going, "close the wound [and] hide the scar." These lyrics suggest that repression is a necessary part of life, one we must adopt when the pain is just too much to bear. Similarly, Ms. Simon sang the words, "I haven't got time for the pain," in the song with this title. A last example: Jackson Browne, in one of his early hits ("Doctor My Eyes"), questioned the wisdom of allowing pain to be experienced fully: "Doctor, my eyes—tell me what is wrong/Was I unwise to leave them open for so long?"

On the other hand, a number of rock artists have disagreed with such sentiments, believing (along with Freud) that keeping feelings down and memories out of awareness exacts a heavy price. This side of the issue suggests that you can distance yourself from feelings, but there are consequences. Keeping things out—or in the words of Pink Floyd, being "comfortably numb"—is the high price we pay for emotional safety. The world is no longer all there. We can push things out of awareness, but we often become a bit more detached as a result. Springsteen said this exceedingly well in "Human Touch": "You can't shut off the risk and the pain/Without losin' the love that remains."

And thus, the Eagles' great line, surely among the smartest metaphors in rock history: "some dance to remember, some to forget." They're probably right. Apparently there's no great virtue or benefit in choosing either strategy. Some of us are better off expressing our feelings ("I'm not one of those who can easily hide," sang Elton John in "Your Song"); some of us benefit from repressing painful feelings. In fact, what might be most adaptive of all is the ability to be cognitively flexible—sometimes to express feelings, sometimes to repress them. What's certain is that defenses—including repression—help make life more bearable.

Chapter 13

SECRETS AND SELF-DISCLOSURE

Everybody's got a secret, sonny / Something that they just can't face.
—Bruce Springsteen, "Darkness on the Edge of Town"

"The Boss" (Springsteen) is surely right. All of us do have secrets we can't face. It may not even be something that most others in the world would regard as awful or embarrassing. It may not even be something that is our fault. And yet we simply cannot or will not talk about it. We may even try not to think about it. But it is there, sometimes close to the surface, pressing for disclosure, and sometimes in the far recesses of our consciousness, barely remembered. We may consciously decide we want to finally share this thought with a good friend or maybe a therapist. Or, if we believe the secret is really awful, we may take it with us to our grave. As David Bowie said so well in the song, "Janine": "You'd like to know me well, but I've got things inside my head that even I can't face."

In fact, Springsteen and Bowie have both unintentionally alluded to one of the reasons that people go into therapy: to talk about the kinds of things that seemingly can't be faced but yet continue in some way to make life difficult. From Freud onward, there's been an assumption among psychotherapists that talking about problems helps. Research has also shown that keeping a secret can have a rebound effect—the more one tries to hide a thought or feeling, the more one becomes obsessed with it (Wegner & Lane, 1995). Nevertheless, even in the safe, confidential confines of a therapist's office, it may take a while before clients share their secrets with their therapists. A great deal of trust and an effective therapeutic alliance must first be established. Thus, many patients will give their therapists the so-called B material for a while, sharing semi-important, semi-intimate material before they feel comfortable and safe enough to divulge their innermost thoughts and feelings. Still, some patients may never feel comfortable enough to disclose their most private, intimate thoughts. This tends to be true as well outside of therapy, a pattern that, once again, Springsteen seems to understand. One can say all the right words to a lover, Springsteen notes in "Secret Garden," and yet: "She'll let you deep inside, but there's a secret garden she hides." Some of us are high self-concealers, consistently less comfortable than others with sharing the deepest parts of ourselves.

What kinds of thoughts or feelings are hardest to acknowledge and share with others? The answer is probably what you'd expect: sex, traumatic events, and feelings of inadequacy or failure (Farber, 2006). Despite the ease with which the characters on *Sex and the City* constantly and unabashedly discuss their sexual exploits, most individuals do not readily divulge this kind of information with others. Dylan in his song "Dirge," offers a clever line to illustrate this point: "The naked truth is still taboo." The research that I and others have done on disclosure in therapy indicates that it's especially difficult for people to talk about their sexual fantasies, interest in pornography, and masturbation. This is the very private stuff of life. It was way back in 1958 that the Everly Brothers ("All I Have to Do Is Dream") sang these seemingly innocent lines: "when I want you and all your charms…all I have to do is dream." In real life, they'd probably have trouble sharing the specific content of those dreams or fantasies with their friends or even their therapist. Gordon Lightfoot ("Sundown") wrote explicitly about the impossibility of disclosing certain sexual experiences: "I can see her lying back in her satin dress, in a room where you do what you don't confess." Among others, Cyndi Lauper ("She-Bop") and Britney Spears ("Touch of My Hand": "I love myself, it's not a sin, I can't control what's happenin'") have written songs about masturbation, and both have been severely criticized for doing so; open discussion of this topic violates cultural assumptions about what can or should be talked about publicly.

It's also hard to talk about traumatic events, especially acts of sexual or physical abuse that one has either experienced or perpetrated. It is unfortunate but true that those who have been abused are often acutely ashamed of what happened to them. Not infrequently, they blame themselves for these horrendous acts. This is especially common when the abuser is a family member. In such cases, the victim of the abuse may struggle terribly to resist believing what they've so often been told: "it's your fault," "you're asking for it," or, "if you weren't so bad, I wouldn't have to do this to you." But whether they blame themselves or those who have hurt them, survivors of abuse struggle to talk about what happened. Almost all treatment of abuse assumes that survivors must learn to talk about what happened to them, despite their justifiable reluctance to do so. It's impossible to know from the lyrics what exactly The Dave Matthews Band wants to forget in "So Much to Say." Some speculate that it may be a girlfriend's unwanted pregnancy, a band member's gay identity, or some kind of abuse. "Keep it locked up inside," they sing, "don't talk about it, talk about the weather." Regardless of what they're specifically referring to, they've identified well the psychological impulse to avoid talking about traumatic experiences. Doing so runs the risk of feeling retraumatized, of reexperiencing the awful feelings. It's far easier to talk about the weather instead, a notion that is reminiscent of a wonderful line from John Mayer ("Sucker"): "sometimes I wish that I was the weather, you'd bring me up in conversation forever."

We dislike feeling inadequate and so avoid disclosing such feelings. We may apologize to another, but there is a significant difference between owning up to a mistake and acknowledging that there's a part of one's personality that keeps leading to making these mistakes. The first task is relatively easy; the second, quite difficult. Even personally revealing blogs, memoirs, and songs tend to gloss over acknowledgments of failure and self-doubt. For the most part, our egos are fragile (see Chapter 12 on "Psychological Defenses"), and we avoid dwelling on those things that make us look less capable to others. One of the great musical exceptions to this general rule is the late Kurt Cobain's admission (in Nirvana's "Smells Like Teen Spirit") that "I'm worse at what I do best and for this gift I am blessed." A plausible interpretation of these clever lines is that he felt inadequate to the task of being a major rock star, and yet also felt that he should be grateful for the fame and adulation that it brought him.

Shame is the common denominator here, the chief reason that certain topics are kept secret or only minimally disclosed. Lucinda Williams, a superb contemporary lyricist, sang the following words in "Metal Firecracker": "All I ask, don't tell anybody the secrets." Clearly, there are parts of herself that she revealed to her now ex-lover that are not ever to be shared with anyone else in the world. They are potentially shameful. No one else is to know what happened between them or who she is in her darkest, most secret places. These lines also speak to the fact that we discriminate as to whom we're willing to share our most private selves. What we're willing to tell our significant other is different than what we're willing to disclose to our parents or best friend. As is so often the case, Dylan found a way to express this psychological truth in two smart, compact musical lines: "Oh, ev'ry thought that's strung a knot in my mind, I might go insane if it couldn't be sprung/But it's not to stand naked under unknowin' eyes, it's for myself and my friends my stories are sung" ("Restless Farewell").

In general, then, we strive to balance the wish to be known by others (especially intimate others) and the need to safeguard our most shameful thoughts and feelings. Another way of saying this: we try to find an appropriate tension between wanting to feel understood and accepted and wanting to keep private those parts of ourselves that we don't like and fear that others won't like or accept either. To a great extent, we do this through what's called impression management: sharing only the best parts of ourselves with others (Goffman, 1956). Billy Joel put this perfectly well in "Always a Woman": "She only reveals what she wants you to see." The question, then, that we all wrestle with is, what parts of our private world will we share with the outer world? Or, when do the demands of intimacy and authenticity trump the need for disclosing only that which will aggrandize us?

In fact, this is a rather complicated question, one that I've devoted much of my recent academic life studying. In my previous book, *Self-Disclosure in Psychotherapy* (2006), I suggested that there were so many questions that typically go through our heads as we make a decision as to whether to disclose a private thought or secret to another: Is this an appropriate thing to share? Is it worth the risk (of shame, guilt, regret)? Is it worth the reward (of feeling proud, authentic, or more intimate)? Do I expect something back, perhaps advice, or reassurance, or an equal amount of sharing? Can I trust this person with my secret? What will he or she think of me if I disclose this part of myself? What will I think of myself? Sarah McLachlan, whose lyrics consistently reflect a high degree of psychologically mindedness, has pondered some of these questions in her song, "Black": "If I cried me a river of all my confessions, would I drown in my shallow regret?"

As Sarah McLachlan has suggested, it is hard to know in advance whether confessions will feel courageous, foolish, or self-defeating. However, some recent research has begun to trace typical patterns of emotions that accompany moderate to intimate disclosures (Farber, Berano, & Capobianco, 2006). Immediately before sharing a secret or intimate thought, we tend to feel apprehensive, wanting to unburden ourselves but also fearing our own shame and the possible negative reactions or judgments of the person to whom we're disclosing. During disclosures, we tend to feel vulnerable or exposed. Immediately after disclosing we continue to feel somewhat vulnerable but, even more so, tend to feel relieved, authentic, and proud. In short, there seem to be far more positive emotions following hard disclosures than negative ones— and very little regret. Moreover, difficult disclosures tend to make subsequent disclosures somewhat easier.

Sidney Jourard, a psychologist who pioneered the study of self-disclosure in the late 1960s, believed that individuals needed to find the courage to share deeply held thoughts and secrets. According to Jourard (1971), "No man can come to know himself except as an outcome of disclosing himself to another person." In revealing ourselves to another, we necessarily learn a great deal about ourselves. We become more fully aware of our thoughts and feelings; in addition, others' responses to our disclosures provide information about how we are perceived in the world. The '60s era spawned a great variety of activities meant to facilitate interpersonal disclosure, including t-groups, encounter groups, peer counseling, and the now very quaint-sounding rap sessions. And while most of these events seem like ancient history now, we are once again in a self-confessional age. This time around it is media and technology that are promoting confession: TV talk shows, tabloid newspaper columns, radio call-in shows, and online diaries and chat rooms all reflect a tell-all mentality. However, despite, or perhaps as a result of the media blitz, many individuals still resist disclosing themselves to others. In their postsurfing years, when they started writing songs with more serious messages, the Beach Boys ("In My Room") found a poignant way to describe the loneliness of not being able to disclose to another: "there's a world where I can go and tell my secrets to, in my room." The image is similar to that offered by Simon and Garfunkel in "I Am a Rock," wherein they describe a self-imposed fortress that "none may penetrate."

Keeping secrets has been associated with physical and emotional distress. By contrast, disclosure has been shown to have multiple positive consequences (Farber, 2006). It facilitates intimacy, a sense of emotional closeness. It provides opportunities to be validated and appreciated. It leads, as I noted above, to greater self-awareness and a more fully developed sense of identity. It allows one to feel more authentic and honest. Lastly, and perhaps most importantly, disclosing intimate parts of oneself, including secrets, has been shown to relieve the burden of unexpressed pain. Disclosing, to use an old psychoanalytic word, is *cathartic*.

James Pennebaker (1990) has published a series of studies demonstrating rather conclusively that writing about secrets has tangible health benefits. Students who have been directed to write about personally meaningful secrets routinely make far less use of campus health centers than peers who have been told only to write about any topic whatsoever. Apparently, writing about a secret helps individuals make new sense of situations or thoughts that have often been impossible to master; it also reduces rumination and worry, freeing up mental space for more positive thoughts and experiences. Another Sarah McLachlan line (from "Building a Mystery") will illustrate what disclosure is meant to overcome: "you're working, building a mystery, holding on and holding it in."

Self-disclosure offers a few other relational benefits. When we disclose it makes others feel special or privileged. We've shared an important part of ourselves that presumably hasn't been shared with a multitude of others. Moreover, it leads to a far greater willingness on the part of our listeners to disclose to us. Research has repeatedly shown that disclosure begets disclosure, a phenomenon labeled the reciprocity principle. Billy Joel seemingly understood this phenomenon well. In "The Stranger," he notes that we shouldn't be surprised at not being allowed to see the secret side of a beloved if we don't grant the same privilege to him or her. He phrased this, though, far more elegantly than I just did: "Why were you so surprised that you never saw the stranger/Did you ever let your lover see the stranger in yourself?"

Whereas disclosure has been shown to have a number of significant benefits, there are also risks and downsides. One risk is that the person to whom we disclose may not listen very attentively or caringly to our words, may criticize the content of what we've shared, or even reject us outright. Pink Floyd ("Final Cut") sang about this very concern: "if I show you my dark side, will you still hold me tonight?" Any hint of rejection can be hurtful given the fact that disclosure is often a courageous and intimate gesture. We also may regret the disclosure because it makes us feel too vulnerable, as if we've given away too much of ourselves. We may feel shaky afterward and resolve never to share so much again. Joni Mitchell's advice in "Both Sides Now" was "Don't give yourself away." Finally, we sometimes risk burdening others with our secrets and intimate disclosures. What we tell others may be hurtful to them. Lovers do not have to know, even if they say they do, the intimate details of all previous relationships. Knowing when, where, what, and how to disclose to others, that is, knowing how to be tactful, is a great asset to any relationship. As I've noted elsewhere (Farber, 2006) "total and complete honesty is not only impossible in a relationship, it is usually not even desirable" (p. 16). The best rock lyric illustrating this point? My vote would be for Carly Simon's words in "We Have No Secrets": "Sometimes I wish, often I wish, I never knew some of those secrets of yours."

Research also shows that most individuals want their inner lives and/or secrets to be pursued a bit (Farber, Berano, & Capobianco, 2004). Joni Mitchell's words in "Song to a Seagull" seem to reflect a keen understanding of this need: "Humans are hungry for worlds they can't share." While these words could mean that we yearn to have private space for ourselves, my sense is that they're about our desperate need to be found, even as our silence and secrecy would suggest otherwise. Patients in psychotherapy often wish their therapists would be more active in questioning them and getting them to talk about difficult topics. Outside therapy, in what patients often call real life, many harbor the fantasy—or have actually had the experience—of opening up to that special, gentle, extraordinarily empathic but persistent friend or lover. James Taylor's words in "Something in the Way She Moves" reflects his experience of being understood this way: "She has the power to go where no one else can find me." We need to feel so very trusting in order to open ourselves up; many of us need to hear words like these offered by The Pretenders in "I'll Stand by You": "Nothing you confess could make me love you less." These words of Neil Young ("Down by the River") might also make us feel reassured that our disclosures would be lovingly accepted: "Be on my side, I'll be on your side, there is no reason for you to hide."

All of this is hard stuff to accept and act on. Our impulse is to dissemble, to lie, to put only our best foot forward. As Dylan suggested in one of the great rock songs of all time, "Like a Rolling Stone," only those who've removed themselves from the everyday rhythms of humanity "have no secrets to conceal." An ideal world might be one where it would be relatively simple to be always trusting and open and totally self-disclosing. Alanis Morisette ("Utopia") certain seems to concur: "accept and admit and divulge and open and reach out and speak up, this is utopia."

Chapter 14

RELIGION AND SPIRITUALITY

In the arms of the angel, may you find some comfort there.
                                        —Sarah McLachlan, "Angel"

Rock is rich with songs concerning faith. Whereas country music consistently affirms the notion and power of a higher being, songs in the rock tradition have been far more ambivalent. Some rock songs uphold a belief in a higher power and consider faith to be a healing force. The words of the Beatles in "Let It Be" are a good example of this view: "When I find myself in times of trouble, Mother Mary comes to me, speaking words of wisdom, let it be." Other songs, however, adopt a more cynical stance, suggesting that belief in God is a myth that is too often used as a substitute for reason. James Taylor's words in "Up from Your Life" come to mind here: "So much for your moment of prayer; God's not at home, there is no there, there." Then there are song-writers like Billy Joel ("The River of Dreams") who just aren't sure and waver in their belief: "In the middle of the night, I go walking in my sleep/From the mountains of faith to the river so deep." Sometimes, he suggests, the river (life's journey) is just too deep or wide (impossible to cope with) to accept the plausibility of a helpful, higher power. Finally, there are those like Sarah McLachlin ("Angel") who don't take a position on whether religious belief is an illusion, but who nonetheless hope that those who need it can find comfort in the "arms of the angel." Multiple Internet sites have reported that she wrote this song following the drug overdose of a musician friend.

According to *Time* magazine ("America by the Numbers," October, 2006), 66 percent of Americans "have no doubts that God exists." An additional 14 percent believe in a higher power or cosmic force, and 11 percent affirm a belief in God, but with some doubts. Only 5 percent among those surveyed indicated that they did not believe in anything beyond the bounds of the physical world. In fact, the concept of God (or gods) has been endorsed by all human societies over all of record history. Many social scientists believe that such belief protects us against the intolerable idea of our own mortality. As Norman Greenbaum sang in "Spirit in the Sky"—probably the most frequently requested and catchiest religiously oriented groove ever played on mainstream radio—"Gotta have a friend in Jesus, so you know that when you die, he's gonna recommend you to the spirit in the sky." More eastern-oriented religions hold to the idea of eternal life through reincarnation; the idea of karma suggests that we continue to reincarnate until we develop compassion toward all sentient beings. As the Indigo Girls sang in their spiritually-oriented song "Galileo," "how long till my soul gets it right?"

Importantly, too, religion provides a moral structure (including rules of behavior) necessary for the survival of a community. Religion is an effective social organizer. But religion is also the means by which many of us cope with circumstances that push us beyond our usual capacities. Religion and spirituality offer meaningful ways of dealing with personal adversity, man-made and environmental disasters, and troubling existential questions. Religious or spiritual coping may involve praying, meditating, reading scripture, attending religious services, pondering the mysteries of existence, or, as Neil Young put it, "looking for faith on the forest floor" ("You're My Girl"). Some scientists, like molecular biologist Dean Hamer, contend that the ubiquity of religious belief points to the probability of a specific spirituality gene or genes. According to Hamer's 2004 book, *The God Gene: How Faith Is Hardwired into Our Genes,* we are programmed to believe because it helps to ensure survival.

Before proceeding further, it's important to distinguish between organized religion and spirituality. Unfortunately, the lack of consistent definitions of these concepts, along with the intermingling of them, makes it impossible to provide a universally accepted distinction. Thus, the following definitions describe my use of these terms in this chapter, but there are many others used. Religion is an organized system of beliefs, practices, and rituals of a community. It is designed to increase a sense of closeness to the transcendent (whether that be God, another kind of higher power, or ultimate truth/reality). It tends to be authoritarian in terms of prescribed behaviors and responsibilities and is often concerned with doctrines that attempt to separate good from evil.

Spirituality, on the other hand, involves a more personal quest for meaning and purpose. While concerned with a relationship to the divine, a spiritual path may or may not lead to religious beliefs and rituals. The spiritual person is committed to trying to understand the natural order of the universe and living in harmony with it. Stevie Wonder ("Race Babbling") provides a good example of what would usually be considered a spiritual idea: "God's induction, life's construction...can't you see that life's connected?" Another good example is from the Beatles' "Within You, Without You": "And the time will come when you see we're all one, and life flows on within you and without you." It was George Harrison who wrote this song for the *Sgt. Pepper* album, and he did so after the Beatles came under the influence of a prominent proponent of transcendental meditation, Maharishi Mahesh Yogi, sometime in 1966. The song, with a background of sitar music by Ravi Shankar, is based on ideas of one branch of Hindu philosophy—essentially, that we are here to experience the bliss of oneness with God.

What is psychology's stance on faith? From a historical perspective, psychology's attitude toward religion and spirituality has undergone several significant shifts. The mental health benefits of religion were initially acknowledged and even supported by the field. In fact, the first form of psychiatric care in the United States—beginning in the late-eighteenth century and lasting throughout most of the nineteenth—was known as so-called moral treatment, in which religion played a significant role. Early American psychiatric hospitals routinely hired clergy to live on the grounds, both holding religious services and providing spiritual counsel. Several of psychology's early luminaries also acknowledged the mental health benefits of religion. Foremost among this group was William James, whose *Principles of Psychology* (1890) represented the state-of-the-art text in psychology at the time (and is still in print) and whose *The Varieties of Religious Experiences* (1902) is still considered the classic work on the intersection of religion and psychology. James, who served as the president of the American Psychological Association, was deeply interested in religious phenomena and believed that understanding an individual's religious experience and values was essential to psychological treatment. He believed that those afflicted with so-called sick souls (that is, those who tended toward depression or pessimism) would benefit greatly from mystical or spiritually meaningful experiences. He criticized the scientific establishment for not taking seriously the unseen aspects of life.

Despite James' beliefs, the relationship between religion and psychology shifted dramatically over the next century. In particular, Sigmund Freud had an enormous influence on psychology's attitude toward religion. In Freud's first paper on the topic, *Obsessive Acts and Religious Practices* (1907), he described religion as an "obsessional neurosis" and compared the act of prayer to the obsessive-compulsive actions of the neurotic. Largely as a result of Freud's disparaging views, psychologists began to interpret religiosity as a primitive need and considered its practice as inimical to emotional maturity. Religion, according to this perspective, was an illusion, a defense against mankind's frailty, mortality, and inability to control the forces of nature. This view has its modern-day corollary in Billy Joel's cynical words in "Innocent Man": "Some people hope for a miracle cure, some people just accept the world as it is."

Psychology's negative attitude towards religion endured well into the 1990s. In fact, until 1994, the *Diagnostic and Statistical Manual of Mental Disorders* (the clinician's diagnostic bible!) commonly used religious examples to illustrate serious cases of mental illness. This skepticism more than likely impacted the personal views of many practicing psychologists. Surveys in the 1980s and 1990s found that approximately 65 period of psychologists did not believe in God, compared to only 4 percent of nonbelievers in the general population (Princeton Religious Research Center, 1996). However, in more recent years, several developments have combined to suggest that the field is experiencing a resurgence of interest and acceptance. These include the establishment of professional journals devoted to research on religious and spiritual topics, the birth of a division of the American Psychological Association dedicated to the psychological study of religion, and the renewed awareness that an understanding of an individual's religious and spiritual beliefs may be necessary for effective diagnosis and treatment. Some of these trends can be traced back to William James, some to Carl Jung (the most avowedly spiritual among Freud's colleagues), some to Carl Rogers and Abraham Maslow (pioneers of humanistic psychology), and some to cultural changes in the 1960s that encouraged spiritual exploration and development. Another perspective on this is that spirituality, mysticism, and religion have never entirely disappeared from the purview of psychology, but that the field has once again become ripe for serious consideration of these issues. Indeed, many of these ideas coalesced within a Positive Psychology movement that, in the last decade, has reemphasized age-old notions of growth, meaning, happiness, and transcendence. The title and theme of Stevie Wonder's song "Higher Ground" ("Gonna keep on trying till I reach my highest ground") approximate well the ideas contained in Positive Psychology.

Whereas those in the mental health professions and the music business have been somewhat ambivalent about the value of religion, far less uncertainty has existed among the public. Consistent with the fact that the vast majority of people in this country believe in God, a study published in the *New England Journal of Medicine* (Schuster et al., 2001) reported that 90 percent of Americans coped with the stress of 9/11 by "turning to religion." Unable to make sense of this horrific situation, and unable to mitigate overwhelming feelings, many looked to God or other forms of faith for answers. In other words, being able to comprehend tragedy—to make it meaningful—is at the heart of successful coping; and for most people, religion performs this role quite well. But religious and spiritual coping are not restricted to handling crises; many people turn to God or other forms of spiritual beliefs to deal with more common problems of living, including depression, substance abuse, and existential concerns.

Because religion can be a source of hope and meaning, it is not surprising that studies have consistently found that religious belief in individuals is a protective factor in regard to depression: such belief is associated with fewer depressive symptoms in individuals and faster recovery from depression over time. Like the Beatles ("Let It Be"), Bruce Springsteen ("Mary's Place") has sung about battling depression with the help of faith: "My heart's dark, but it's rising. I'm pulling all the faith I can see." Jewel makes a similar point with "Hands," in words that seem almost biblical: "I won't be idle with despair, I will gather myself around my faith, for light does the darkness most fear." Even Dylan, the eternal iconoclast, affirmed the power of faith to overcome despair. In fact, he spent most of the eighties rejoicing about it with songs like "Saved": "Nobody to rescue me, Nobody would dare, I was going down for the last time, But by His mercy I've been spared." During this time, Dylan released two spiritually oriented albums, both of which were testaments to his newfound Christian faith (since renounced for several other faiths, including Judaism). Legend has it that he saw a vision of Christ after a fan threw a silver cross on stage. He then began an intense study of Christianity that greatly influenced his songwriting for the next several years.

Death of a loved one, particularly when it involves a child, is a major stressor that often results in depression. Undoubtedly, one of the greatest tragedies in life is losing a child. Probably the most well-known song regarding this issue is Eric Clapton's "Tears in Heaven." In 1991, Clapton's four-and-a-half-year-old son Connor died when he fell from a 53rd-story window in a New York City apartment. This death had a deep impact on Clapton. For nine months he concentrated on coming to terms with his loss rather than on performing, and when he returned to the stage, his music had changed, becoming softer and more reflective, and yet also more powerful. In "Tears in Heaven," Clapton seems to find some inner peace in believing that his child has found a safe place in a heavenly afterlife. In the song, he expresses a deep desire to be reunited with his son, but also acknowledges that despite his terrible loss, he has to continue living and loving here on earth: "I'll find my way, through night and day, 'cause I know I just can't stay, here in heaven."

Johnny Cash suffered from depression and drug addiction for much of his life, yet his faith in God was just as hard-fought as his vices. Cash expresses this long-standing battle in "I Came to Believe": "In childlike faith I gave in and gave him a try, and I came to believe in a power much higher than I." In a 1984 interview with Scott Ross of *The 700 Club* (a talk show on the Christian Broadcasting Network), Cash was asked where he would be today without faith in God. He replied, "I'd be dead a long time ago. I have a terminal disease called chemical dependency…And with all the alcoholic/drug treatment centers in the world, if they don't have that spiritual element that returns you to a one-on-one communication with God, then they're not worth the land they're built on." In at least one respect, Cash's views have been confirmed by research: most research studies on this topic have found significantly less substance abuse among the more religious. For example, in 2001 the National Center on Addiction and Substance Abuse (CASA) at Columbia University released the findings of their two-year investigation entitled, "So Help Me God: Substance Abuse, Religion and Spirituality." The results showed that adults and teens who reported that religion was very important in their lives were far less likely than others to smoke, drink, or use illegal drugs. Additionally, results indicated that individuals who received professional treatment and attended spiritually based support groups such as Alcoholics Anonymous were far more likely to remain sober than if they received therapy alone.

Then there's the other side, the position of those, including songwriters, who are skeptical of faith or the healing power of religion. Especially during those times when faith and prayer seemingly have no effect on enduring pain, it is not uncommon for people to feel punished or abandoned by God, angry at God, or uncertain about God's love or capacity to make a difference. Like many who've suffered from wars, genocide, torture, child abuse, floods, or earthquakes, Elton John and his lyricist, Bernie Taupin, question how a loving, all-powerful God can allow for so much human suffering ("If There Is a God in Heaven"): "If he can't hear the children, then he must see the war/ But it seems to me, that he leads his lambs to the slaughter house, and not the promised land." Some theologians attempt to answer the implied question here (Why?) by acknowledging that God's ways are unknowable, some by assuming that wide-scale disasters are punishment for man's sins, and others by believing that mercy and goodness abide in an afterlife. Some individuals, including songwriters, also seem resigned to the limitations of faith. The Beatles, in one of their most memorable and moving songs, "Eleanor Rigby," ponder the inevitability of loneliness and the impotence of religion to overcome this state: "Father Mackenzie, wiping the dirt from his hands as he walks from the grave, no one was saved."

In addition, some challenge or renounce faith completely when they begin to view organized religion as more a source of political and social influence than of spiritual meaning. One of the most sophisticated and sensitive songwriters of all time (who died far too young), Laura Nyro, spoke to this disturbing realization in "Stoney End": "I was born from love and my poor mother worked the mines. I was raised on the good book Jesus till I read between the lines." Joni Mitchell, another deeply introspective songwriter, made a similar point in "The Priest": "Then he took his contradictions out, and he splashed them on my brow/So which words was I then to doubt, when choosing what to vow?" She's hardly the first artist to rail against the apparent hypocrisy of some religious figures, but here she's given a folk-rock voice to sentiments that many have felt. Elton John and Bernie Taupin addressed the issue of misplaced religious priorities in "God Never Came There." In this song, their anger is apparently directed at organized religion's obsession with what many have sarcastically called the edifice complex: "We starve and you demand we pray to the faces etched in stone/Auction up your ancient wealth, so we can build ourselves a home." In "Tiny Dancer"—and has there ever been a better use of a rock song in a movie than this one in *Almost Famous?*—this duo directed their wrath at the efforts of those so-called religious true believers who recruit others for their cause: "Jesus freaks, out in the street, handing tickets out for God." By contrast, Jackson Browne ("Looking East") reserved his cynicism for sanctimonious and shallow celebrities who pursue faith and spiritual meaning half-heartedly at best. It is on the West Coast, he says, "where the search for truth is conducted with a wink and a nod, and where power and position are equated with the grace of God."

Even more angrily, some rock stars have expressed the opinion that belief in God is misused as a means to rationalize the morality of unjust wars. This position is clearly voiced by the Eagles in "The Last Resort": "We satisfy our endless needs, and justify our bloody deeds, in the name of Destiny, and in the name of God." This is a point also made by Dylan in his powerful antiwar song, "With God on Our Side": "You never ask questions when God's on your side." Other rocks stars have pointedly suggested that organized religion has become a voice of repression, attempting to overly socialize individuals and curb their sexuality. Billy Joel captures much of this in "Only the Good Die Young." His words here reflect his sense that there's a great price to pay for religious devotion and that abstaining from secular pleasures is unfortunate and regrettable. The most prominent scientific voice raised in opposition to the influence of religion in all spheres of personal and political life is now that of evolutionary biologist Richard Dawkins. In his 2006 book, *The God Delusion,* he argues vehemently for the view that religious belief is an illusion that has led, and continues to lead, to oppression of women and children, bigotry, the obstruction of scientific progress, terrorism, and wars.

Despite these criticisms, it's important to remember that the flaws or excesses of organized religion are not their only defining features. Many individuals have found their salvation in the words of the Bible; their community churches, mosques, or synagogues; or in the rituals, songs, or traditions of their religion. Moreover, organized religion is not the only means to a spiritually meaningful life. As noted earlier, some find religious meaning, including a profound sense of security and well being, in the formation of a personal relationship with what might be called the sacred or the divine. Van Morrison beautifully captures a sense of merging with the sacred in "Into the Mystic": "Smell the sea and feel the sky, let your soul and spirit fly into the mystic."

This merging, sometimes referred to as a mystical experience, is often described as a kind of energy or unconditional love that envelops the soul; many believe that this love is the essence that connects every living thing in the universe. For example, Depeche Mode in "Personal Jesus" extorted us all to "reach out and touch faith." But it's the Beatles that have probably addressed this theme more than any other prominent rock band in the history of music. In "Across the Universe," they brilliantly capture this notion: "Limitless undying love which shines around me like a million suns." They also present it as a kind of energy, assumedly experienced through meditation, in "Within You without You." Finally, in words that have probably been quoted as much as any in the history of rock 'n' roll, they suggest that this love is governed by karma in "The End": "And in the end, the love you take is equal to the love you make."

While many seek transcendence through explicitly spiritual pursuits (for example, meditation) or loving relationships, others seek it in nature, others in music, and still others in the appreciation of life's myriad events. Anyone who has witnessed the birth of a child or experienced the power and beauty of crashing waves knows that the sacred can be felt in the eternal rhythms of human existence. John Denver's gentle words from "Rocky Mountain High" are one good example of this type of transcendence: "Now he walks in quiet solitude the forest and the streams, seeking grace in every step he takes." Another example is Van Morrison's entreaty to his lover in "Come Here My Love": "Become enraptured by the sights and sounds in intrigue of nature and beauty."

"God," sang John Lennon in a song with this title, "is a concept by which we measure our pain." A provocative notion, to be sure. Do we need to create a god to rely on, to believe in, to assess our value and significance in life? There can be no proof positive in matters of faith. As many have said in different ways: for those who believe, no proof is necessary; for those who don't believe, no evidence of God or godliness will ever suffice. For some, then, living without the concept of God is a courageous act. The lyrics of Robert Hunter of the Grateful Dead in "Box of Rain" are a good illustration of this line of thinking— one can think of the title as a metaphor for that which is intangible, but perhaps sacred, in the world: "It's just a box of rain, I don't know who put it there; believe it if you need it, or leave it if you dare." On the other side of the spiritual ledger, think of the inspirational words of country singer Lee Ann Womack's song "I Hope You Dance": "Promise me that you'll give faith a fighting chance."

Part V

ON AGING AND GROWTH

The last section of this book is broadly divided between two chapters that focus on the psychological process of growing up and two chapters that address the personal growth that occurs as we become more socially, politically, and existentially aware.

In Chapter 15 ("Growing Up"), the lyrics I've chosen offer various interpretations of childhood innocence and various ways of understanding the nature of adolescence. Don Henley and Joni Mitchell, among other notable songwriters, have written emotionally evocative and psychologically astute phrases that depict the terribly confusing period between the end of childhood and the beginning of adolescence. Songs by Alice Cooper, John Mayer, and Rod Stewart, for example, have accurately conveyed the difficulties and pride of teenagers and their parents, as adolescents grow toward adulthood. The second chapter here (Chapter 16) focuses on the path from adulthood through old age. Like lyrics that address the transition from adolescence to adulthood, the words in this chapter acknowledge that the aging process is replete with feelings of great pride, but also experiences and thoughts that are tinged with anguish and regret. In particular, our mortality is so very hard for most of us to accept, an idea that Jackson Browne, Harry Chapin, and Pink Floyd have all addressed in their music.

Chapter 17, on the search for social justice, explores several themes, including racial, economic, and environmental concerns. Dylan, of course, comes immediately to mind as a champion of the underserved, and his lyrics are in the forefront of this chapter. But many other artists, including Bob Marley,

Marvin Gaye, Bruce Hornsby, and Creedence Clearwater Revival, have also expressed impassioned sentiments on various injustices and horrors, especially that of war. The common denominator among these diverse voices is that to be fully human is to be caring about others and the planet we all inhabit.

Chapter 18, the last chapter in the book, focuses on existential concerns. The primary question addressed is, "How do we live meaningful lives?" Pearl Jam, Dylan (again), the Rolling Stones, the Beatles, and Leonard Cohen have all contributed wise reflections on issues of authenticity, awareness, and personal responsibility. Their words are worth hearing and remembering.

Chapter 15

GROWING UP

Didn't have a care in the world with mommy and daddy standing by, but this is the end of the innocence.
>   —Don Henley, "The End of the Innocence" (written by Don Henley &
>   Bruce Hornsby)

The innocence: what exactly was Don Henley referring to when he evoked this concept? It feels like he's referencing that time of life when the seemingly idyllic, blissful state of childhood begins to erode forever. More specifically, his words suggest how the idea of mommy and daddy always standing by—an image borrowed from Gershwin's sublime "Summertime"—no longer feels realistic or sustainable when the world begins to feels complex and confusing. Childhood innocence may be impossible to define precisely, but many musicians have attempted to provide a sense of it in their songs over the years. Joni Mitchell sang of "cartwheels" and "painted ponies" ("Circle Game"); and Kansas of a "sweet child of innocence, living in the present tense" ("Child of Innocence"). This notion of living in the present tense was also one that Joni Mitchell evoked in "Chelsea Morning," alluding to the power of love to make time disappear. At their purest, both childhood and love are states of glorious innocence.

Thus, this innocence of youth that many of us recall is typified by an undemanding sense of time—of years lingering like decades, of an endlessness unaffected by any sense of urgency. It's also typified by a simple set of needs and priorities, a feeling that this period of life is relatively uncomplicated. Play and food and sleep are the effortless essentials, the building blocks of life. It's not a rock song, but the words from "Try to Remember," from that longest-running off-Broadway show ever, *The Fantasticks,* bring to mind the timelessness and easiness of childhood at its imagined best: "Try to remember the kind of September, when life was slow and oh so mellow."

But as most of these songs quickly reveal, there is another side to such childhood purity. Don Henley, describing the end of the innocence, explains that "happily ever after fails and we've been poisoned by these fairy tales." This, he instructs us, is especially true in families in which children witness parental acrimony or divorce. For children in these situations, images of happy, carefree childhoods are the stuff of myths. Kansas' message in "Child of Innocence" is starker still, as the singer explains to the sweet, innocent child that "father time will take his toll, rack your body and steal your soul."

Even more poignantly, Joni Mitchell reminds us of how quickly it all changes: "cartwheels turn to car wheels through the town." And, in lines that I still find haunting despite hearing them hundreds of times, she tell us that well-wishing adults will say to kids who are eager to grow up, "take your time, it won't be long now, till you drag your feet to slow the circles down" ("Circle Game"). But kids immersed in the giddiness of young adulthood can't listen. They're too caught up in their need to feel grown-up to heed these well-intentioned words. They may be hurt by life; indeed, they may have to be: "Without a hurt, the heart is hollow" ("Try to Remember"). It is one of those tragic elements of life that for the most part, we cannot protect our children from experiencing firsthand those hurts and disappointments that we ourselves encountered.

There's another famous song whose theme is the transition from childhood to adolescence/adulthood—"Puff (The Magic Dragon)." In the words of this seemingly innocent Peter, Paul, and Mary hit that we probably all sang a thousand times as kids and never thought much about, "dragons live forever, but not so little boys." Somewhat sadly, if inevitably, "painted wings and giant strings make way for other toys." This is arguably the most popular image in rock history for the end of the innocence. (Although the lyricists, Peter Yarrow and Leonard Lipson, adamantly deny any intentional double-meanings—puff? drag-on?—the song has been banned in Singapore along with other supposedly drug-explicit tunes, such as the Beatles' "Lucy in the Sky with Diamonds.")

Had we taken this song a bit more seriously, or not gotten caught up in the allegedly hidden drug references, we might have reflected more on the bittersweet message in it. Springsteen's "Glory Days" actually evokes much the same sentiment, though his words, embedded in a far more up-tempo rhythm, are more about the transition from adolescence to adulthood: "glory days, well they'll pass you by; glory days, in the wink of a young girl's eye" ("Glory Days"). John Cougar Mellencamp, in a nostalgic song about two kids who grow up together in Middle America ("Jack and Diane") also weighs in on this theme of lost innocence and lost grandeur. Like Springsteen, but invoking a more somber tone, his message is that "life goes on, long after the thrill of living is gone." In short, this terribly complex transition from childhood to adulthood—one that brings pain and pride to growing up children and their confused parents—has served as inspiration for many thoughtful rock lyrics, with their juxtaposed metaphors of lightheartedness and regret, sweetness and pain, and hope and loss.

One of George Bernard Shaw's grand assertions was that "youth is wasted on the young." Some would surely agree, claiming that the privileges and characteristics of youth—freedom, health, exuberance, and idealism, for example—can only be appreciated and used wisely by those who have had a lifetime's worth of experience in the world. Others would surely oppose his proposition, either because they think of their childhood years as particularly well spent (and therefore not wasted), or, conversely, because they cannot see anything enviable about youth at all—what about it is there to waste? Of course, Shaw's axiom is unprovable, if provocative. Nevertheless, it does feel like one of those great ironies of life that we spend much of our youth wanting to be older and much of our old age wishing we were young. Contrast the lines of Antony and the Johnsons in "For Today I Am a Boy"—"One day I'll grow up, I'll feel the power in me"—with the words of Dolly Parton in "Coat of Many Colors": "Back through the years I go wonderin' once again, back to the seasons of my youth." Erik Erikson, a psychologist to whom I referred on the chapter on "Identity" (and to whom I shall further refer in the next chapter (on "Aging and Mortality"), explained that each age of life has its own challenges and rewards. But it can be very difficult for all of us to accept this premise. Our essential narcissism compels us to want all the advantages of each age and none of the problems.

Of all the factors that determine whether childhood will be happy or not, a child's relationships with his or her parents is most important. Virtually all psychologists believe that parents must provide a so-called holding environment for their child (Winnicott, 1958); that is, they must physically and emotionally hold the child so that he or she develops a sense of trust in the world. It is this burgeoning sense of trust that allows children to develop a healthy, stable identity as well as effective, satisfying relationships with others. The late psychoanalyst D. W. Winnicott, who coined the term *holding environment*, also wrote (1958) about the "good-enough mother" as someone who adapts to the changing needs of her developing child. Winnicott, one of the giants in the history of child psychology, preached unceasingly about the need for parents to nurture and respect the individuality of each of their children. Alanis Morissette, in "Perfect," provides a perfect example of what Winnicott thought parents should not be doing. In singing about those who use their children to satisfy their own narcissistic needs, her sarcasm and anger are unmistakable: "Be a good boy, push a little farther now. That wasn't fast enough to make us happy. We'll love you just the way you are, if you're perfect." This singer knows, perhaps firsthand, that this is the perfect recipe for children to grow up to be miserable and chronically self-doubting. These lyrics approximate all too well the definition of emotional abuse.

But our relationship with parents isn't the only variable that affects us during childhood. Judith Rich Harris made headlines in the late 1990s with her book, *The Nurture Assumption.* Her contention was that peer relationships are a greater influence on a child's development and values than parents. Whereas most psychologists consider her views overstated, it isn't hard for any of us to remember how critical peer acceptance is to our self-esteem. Research has shown that children who are rejected by their peers tend to exhibit a number of problematic behaviors, including social withdrawal, aggression, depression, and poor academic performance (McDougall, Hymel, Vaillancourt, & Mercer, 2001). In her touching "At Seventeen," Janis Ian describes this age through the experience of a girl who feels far less beautiful than some of her peers and, thus, unworthy of love or acceptance: "I learned the truth at seventeen that love was meant for beauty queens…it isn't all it seems, at seventeen." Unfortunately, research confirms Janis Ian's painful memories: those who are less attractive do experience higher rates of peer rejection (Coie & Dodge, 1982).

One route to peer acceptance during late childhood and adolescence is to buy and wear the so-called right things, usually understood as what everyone else (or at least the seemingly coolest group) is buying and wearing. Jack Johnson describes this peer pressure and the demands of conformity in his insightful song "Rodeo Clowns": "She barely understands her dreams of belly button rings and other kinds of things. Symbolic of change, but the thing that is strange, is that…now she's just a part of the herd." Here we see how our search for identity is often merged with our desperate longing to fit in. We want to be unique while still being accepted as one of the crowd. What makes this so daunting is that the demands and changes of puberty exacerbate the near-universal tendency toward doubt, insecurity, and shame. The cognitive changes that come with puberty—the ability to think abstractly, to think about thinking, to imagine what others are thinking about us—give rise to a great increase in self-consciousness and introspection. Adolescents are forever wondering how others are perceiving them and forever changing their perceptions of themselves and others. And, thus, mood fluctuations, frustration, and impatience.

All this seems to be happening earlier than ever. David Elkind, a psychologist at Tufts University, has written extensively about how adolescence seems to begin at increasingly lower ages in the United States. His thesis is that not only has the age of menarche (first menstruation) decreased considerably over the past 100 years as the result of better nutrition, but we have allowed and even encouraged children to dress, talk, play, compete, and act as adults at ages when they should be treated as kids. His sense (2001) is that while we were primarily concerned about spoiled children in the 1950s and 1960s, we should now be more concerned with the hurried child—those who grow up too fast, too soon. Suzanne Vega, in "The Queen and the Soldier," gave voice to the idea of a too-hurried adolescence in these touching lyrics: "You won't understand, and you may as well not try, but her face was a child's and he thought she would cry." These lyrics seemingly refer to a young girl's first feelings of love. What may be even harder to handle, for both parents and their adolescent children, are adultlike sexual feelings. Melissa Etheridge, in "Silent Legacy," sang of the pain that often accompanies the dawning of sexual feelings: "The natural progression is the coming of your age, but they cover it with shame and turn it into rage." She's assumedly speaking here about the how the world doesn't want to acknowledge such feelings, much less allow them expression.

Adolescence is also the time of life that demands that we separate from our parents. Psychologists have thought that the turmoil experienced by this developmental imperative has much in common with what originally occurred in childhood. In both periods of life, there is a push-pull: a need to feel independent and a simultaneous fear of being separate and alone in the world. In John Mayer's song "Stop This Train" he vacillates anxiously between not wanting to grow up—"don't want to see my parents go…so scared of getting older"—and accepting the fact that "we'll never stop this train."

According to Anna Freud (1958), one of the first psychologists to write extensively about this time of life, adolescents typically despise the first half of this equation, that of feeling a need for their parents. In fact, her sense was that teens often deal with their unwanted feelings of connectedness by transforming them into their opposite: love becomes hate, admiration turns into derision, and closeness turns into rebellion. Chuck Berry, one of the earliest pioneers of rock 'n' roll, got it right in his well-titled 1959 tune, "Almost Grown": "Don't bother me, leave me alone. Anyway, I'm almost grown." Or, better still, in what I'd argue is the single best phrase the Beatles' ever wrote, "she's leaving home after living alone for so many years."

Yielding to the values or dictates of parents or adult society is often rejected out of hand. Schools often become a target of adolescent resentment and frustration. Has anyone articulated these feelings better than Paul Simon in "Kodachrome?": "When I think back on all the crap I learned in high school, it's a wonder I can think at all." Well, actually, maybe Pink Floyd did by getting dozens of English children to chant angrily alongside them in "Another Brick in The Wall, Part 2," "we don't need no education, we don't need no thought control." Alice Cooper in "School's Out" also captured quite well this well-known vein of adolescent "screw you" by invoking an image of a school's being "blown to pieces" and by writing the terrific, pun-filled line, "we got no class and we got no principals and we got no innocence."

Adolescence is, indeed, a confusing time of life. To continue the focus on Alice Cooper—this time in "I'm Eighteen"—"I've got a baby's brain and an old man's heart, took eighteen years to get this far." They got the confusion right but may have gotten confused themselves in coming up with these phrases: these lyrics would have been more accurate had they written of adolescence in terms of an old man's (still well-functioning) brain and a baby's heart. Adolescents are quite capable of thinking well and more than capable of acting tenderly toward others. But most teens do want it to get easier—and for most, it does. The agonizing contradictions of adolescence become a bit more muted. As Springsteen put it in "Blood Brothers," "what once seemed black and white turns to so many shades of grey." Still, even as we grow to adulthood, most of us hold on to some very precious pieces of childhood and adolescence. It may be with a brother or sister or oldest, best friend, but a great part of life is when we get to trot out old memories, feelings, reminiscences, and great knowing smiles. "Ain't we all a little juvenile?" Rod Stewart sang in "Ain't Love a Bitch." And don't we all love it.

I'll conclude this chapter by focusing on parents' reactions to their children growing up. After all, I suspect that many reading this are not only remembering their own teenage years but also have more recent memories of their own children moving away. Rod Stewart's version of an original Bob Dylan song ("Forever Young") is one that I suspect brings tears to many parents whose sons and daughters have left home: "And when you finally fly away, I'll be hoping that I served you well. For all the wisdom of a lifetime, no one can ever tell." On a similarly tearful but positive note, I'll close the chapter with one last set of lyrics from the Indigo Girls. Their song, "Someone to Come Home," reminds us that of the three critical tasks of parenthood—dedication, education, and abdication—it's the last that's often the most difficult: "Take my advice," they sing to a grown-up child, "go ahead and live your own life; everybody's waiting for someone to come home."

Chapter 16

AGING AND MORTALITY

Don't let the past remind us of what we are not now.
                    —Crosby, Stills, and Nash, "Suite: Judy Blue Eyes"

Despite the Peter Pan–like resistance of so many of us, we all grow up. For many years (and especially on birthdays), the aging process is a source of familiar quips and gag gifts. Yet, at some point, the truth of getting old is likely to sink in. This is ever more evident since most of us are living longer than those in previous generations. In 1915, only 4.5 percent of the population was 65 and older, but in 2006 that figure had increased to 12.3 percent. In fact, the number of older adults in the United States is expanding such that by the year 2030, it is expected that 20 percent of Americans will be over the age of 65 (Hoover Institute, 2006). Despite the fact that we look younger and feel younger at older ages, for many baby boomers, growing older is an experience that's hard to make sense of—it doesn't seem quite real: "Who knows where the time goes?" sang Judy Collins (covering a song by that title written in 1967 by Sandy Denny).

Perhaps, more than a particular chronological time, psychological aging begins when we realize that time is going by too quickly, that the past is stretched far behind us, and that it contains far more years than does our future. Perhaps it comes with an acute awareness of our own mortality. Pink Floyd, in their well-named song, "Time," evoked an image of running after the sun as it sinks below the horizon: "The sun is the same in a relative way/you're older, shorter of breath, and one day closer to death." This line holds in it the irony of aging: so much remains the same in the external world and yet how we experience it continually changes. A new perspective brings with it new emotions, new realities. Being "one day closer to death" can grant us the most beautiful view of a sunset and the poignancy of life's colors, or it can summon the fear and darkness of life's inevitable end.

Aging, then, is an experience that elicits a wide range of emotions, though in general we tend to fight the reality of it: we dye our hair, exercise obsessively, apply endless cosmetics of dubious worth, submit to plastic surgery, watch our diets, and dress as if we were far younger than we actually are. Of course, it's one thing to grow older and another thing to be truly old. Getting older may involve dealing with creeping insecurities and the so-called sandwich pressures of taking care of children as well as aging parents, but it also typically means gaining wisdom, self-assurance, and respect. On the other hand, being old, though often full of small pleasures, inevitably brings losses—of people, physical vitality, independence, career, and hope for change in the future. More frighteningly still, it means nearing the end of life. As my 85-year-old mother says (almost every day), "It ain't easy growing old." It also isn't easy to imagine the experience. As we deny thinking about death, we also tend to avoid thinking about old age and old people. We ask so few questions of older people and get so few lessons about what it's like to grow old. Still, there have been some songwriters who've tried to envision their lives decades later. When they were in their 20s, Simon and Garfunkel ("Old Friends") wondered what it would be like to be "old friends [who] sit on the park bench like bookends." They imagined it would be "terribly strange to be seventy." And the pace of the music that accompanies these lyrics also suggests to us a terrible somberness, a slowing down of mind and spirit. Springsteen ("Glory Days") imagines that as "time slips away" we're left only with "boring stories of glory days."

So, was the singer Meatloaf right in his provocative declaration ("Everything Louder Than Everything Else") that "a wasted youth is better by far than a wise and productive old age"? From his perspective, there's no contest: the vitality of youth, even when it goes astray, is so full of possibility and passion, so ripe to be enjoyed even to excess, that it simply must be seen as the best time of life. But as these lyrics also suggest, there is another side—one that might not argue that old age is better but rather that old age allows, indeed requires, a very different set of satisfactions. Erik Erikson, as noted in the previous chapter on "Growing Up," observed that each stage of life contains its own psychosocial challenges and rewards. Middle age, he contended, challenges us to be generative—for example, by raising children or by contributing to the welfare of future generations through teaching or community service. Old age, he thought, was one in which the challenge was to combat despair and achieve what he called ego integrity. By this, Erikson meant the ability to accept the course of one's life and the choices made. This acceptance leads to wisdom, including a true generosity of spirit that may not be possible earlier in one's life.

But though aging might lead to certain satisfactions not available earlier in life, does growing older lead to a greater sense of happiness? Or does it lead to despair and disdain for life, including one's own? Research has struggled to answer these questions conclusively. Some studies show that depression and anxiety decrease as we age, in part because we have more practice regulating our emotions (Charles, Reynolds, & Gatz, 2001). However, other studies suggest the opposite, indicating that age-sensitive measures actually reveal higher levels of anxiety and depression in aging populations (Fuentes & Cox, 1997). But there is a middle position here that makes intuitive sense. This line of thinking holds that we experience a fair amount of anxiety and depression through our young adult years as we struggle with relationship and career challenges, a decline in these negative feelings during the midadult years as we become more settled, and an increase in depression and anxiety later in life as health concerns and losses begin to mount (Teachman, 2006). Thus, while wisdom and generosity may be part of the later stages of life, we may still need to battle hard not to succumb to despair and feelings of uselessness. Edwin McCain ("Sorry to a Friend") expresses this sentiment beautifully, if ruefully: "Like a stone in a stream, life smoothes all our edges/'Til we barely make a ripple any more."

Despite the fact that we are living longer, we still must deal with the knowledge of the inevitability of death. To truly realize that "in the end there is one dance you'll do alone" (Jackson Browne, "For a Dancer") is one of the most existential and frightening insights a person can have. How do we cope with the magnitude of facing this unknown? Psychologists, writers, and musicians alike have suggested that one of the most meaningful ways of dealing with our mortality is by using this knowledge to live fully in the moment. In their hit single, "Dream On," Aerosmith expressed this sentiment well: "Sing with me, just for the day, maybe tomorrow the good lord take you away." Interestingly, too, in contrast to the slow, somber tones of Simon and Garfunkel's "Old Friends," Aerosmith employed an upbeat tempo to punctuate their belief in combating mortality with joy and passion. Bonnie Raitt expressed similar thoughts in "Nick of Time": "With so much more at stake, life gets mighty precious when there's less of it to waste." We need to live well for as long as we can.

This belief, however, can be so very hard to play out. The realities of old age can overwhelm all but the most resilient of spirits. Harry Chapin ("Anthem") tells us that of all things, "the old man couldn't tell him how to make the long years sing." Equally poignantly, John Prine ("Hello in There") observed that, while old trees grow stronger, "Old people just grow lonesome/Waiting for someone to say, 'Hello in there, hello'." It's painful to reflect on this image, but surely we've all known those for whom these words reflect a terrible and depressing truth.

Others become more important to us as we age. Psychological research has shown that social support is one of the most important predictors of happiness and adjustment in old age. One study found older married persons to be less distressed than their single counterparts (Hagedoorn et al., 2006). However, it seems that single people who invest in social relationships may reap similar benefits (Arber, 2004), suggesting that it is socialization itself—the process of interacting with others—that is beneficial. Even though we ultimately die alone, we don't want to be alone when we die. David Kuhl, a palliative care physician who wrote *What Dying People Want* (2002), called the importance of socialization in old age the need to "be touched and be in touch," emphasizing that older people facing death still need to feel *alive* and they do this primarily through interactions with others. Even though we may be old and our time on this earth shortened, we need to feel that we are important to others and that we will be cared for. The Beatles recognized this when they queried: "Will you still need me, will you still feed me, when I'm sixty-four?" ("When I'm Sixty-Four"). The song has the feel of a somewhat silly ditty, but its sentiments are quite real.

Another way we deal with our own mortality, and the process of aging in general, is through remembering. We are all familiar with the stereotype of a grandparent who tells the same story time and time again, the when-I-was-your-age tale. These stories are not just meant to entertain or educate; they are reminders of what we were and how vital we once felt. Although I started this chapter with these imploring words from Crosby, Stills, and Nash—"Don't let the past remind us of what we are not now"—the admonition contained in this phrase needs to be deconstructed a bit. Sometimes the past is a cruel reminder, and sometimes it is more life-affirming than it is painful. In this lovely song ("Suite: Judy Blue Eyes"), a lover desperately wants to avoid memories of a passion that is no longer possible. It is clear, though, that there will be new passions and new excitement; the singer is still young. In old age, however, while past glories may be painful to remember, they are also affirmations that our lives have been meaningful and satisfying. "Son, can you play a memory, I'm not really sure how it goes, but it's sad and it's sweet." And most readers can probably fill in the rest of the line from Billy Joel's great ballad, "Piano Man."

Another way of saying this is that nostalgia seems to have two competing sides. One side pushes toward sweetening the past, the other clings to old regrets. The first is a way of persuading ourselves that our life has been well lived; the second is about berating ourselves that it could have or should have been better. In fact, some become preoccupied with their failures, the bad decisions they made, or their lack of good luck. As for the first side of nostalgia: the older we grow, the easier it seemed back then. In fact, research has shown that remembering actually becomes increasingly enjoyable with age; older people show the most pleasure in recalling their past (Piolini et al., 2006). We tend to forget, or at least minimize, the pains, mistakes, and heartaches of earlier years. Paradoxically, we seem to rely more and more on our sense of the past, even as our ability to remember wanes. Perhaps, as our mortality becomes more pressing an issue and advancing age not quite so funny anymore, we need to re-create an especially memorable and meaningful image of our younger years. I find these old lines from Simon and Garfunkel ("Bookends Theme") a lovely example of this process: "Time it was, and what a time it was/It was…A time of innocence, a time of confidences."

John Mellencamp (in a song cowritten with George Green) explicitly reflected on this re-creation process: "When I was a young boy, said, put away those young boy ways. Now that I'm getting older, so much older, I love all those young boy days" ("Hurts So Good"). There is value in our ability to reconstruct our pasts. We all need to feel important; we all want to feel we've lived a good life. So we look back fondly to the intimacies we've experienced, the pleasures we've felt, the neighborhoods we've lived in, the friendships we've created, the lives we've influenced, the successes we've earned. In fact, memories may be the most precious image we have of ourselves: "We don't even have pictures, just memories to hold, that grow sweeter each season as we slowly grow old" (Toad the Wet Sprocket, "Walk on the Ocean"). In this way, we let our memories sustain us as we age, giving us a sense of purpose, value, and identity.

But memories and regrets can haunt us as well. Paul Simon calls a "good day" one that "ain't got no rain" but "a bad day is when I lie in bed and think of things that might have been" ("Slip Slidin' Away"). If only's and what if's are ways of saying "As good as it was, I had the potential to be truly great, to have an extraordinary life." Yes, reminiscent of that memorable Marlon Brando line in *On the Waterfront*, "I coulda been a contender." As we grow older and the opportunity to do all we had hoped for in our lives fades, regrets become stronger. Sometimes, though, even young people are aware of just how short life is. When he was in his 20s, the late folksinger Phil Ochs (once hailed as the "next Dylan"), noted poignantly that when he's gone he won't be able to feel the "flowing of time" or the "pleasures of love" or do his share to heal the world, and so, he sang, "I guess I'll have to do it while I'm here" ("When I'm Gone").

Anecdotal evidence suggests that older people most regret not having spent more time with their families. Research, though, actually reveals that, at least in England, the greatest single regret of retired individuals—both men and women—is that they hadn't had more sex (Liddle, 2006). Really. Fully 70 percent of those surveyed. The second most common regret? Not having traveled more. Apparently, hardly anyone regrets not making more money, acquiring more possessions, or working more hours. But, as John Lennon astutely observed in "Beautiful Boy (Darling Boy)," "life is what happens when you are busy making other plans." As we grow older we dwell on the things we missed.

Growing up, having lived through many experiences, enables us to do what Stevie Nicks of Fleetwood Mac ruefully wonders whether she can do in "Landslide"—to "sail through the changing ocean tides" and "handle the seasons of [our] live[s]." In dealing with many "changing ocean tides," we come to know who we are and we become more rooted in this identity. Personality traits do become more stable over time, especially after the age of 50 (Roberts & DelVecchio, 2000). "Landslide" is another one of those songs that's hard to listen to without crying if one has children; in it, Stevie Nicks seems to suggest a growing understanding of who she is as distinct from her family and a sad awareness that it's time for her to become more independent. Listening carefully, we become aware that the main theme of the song is her relationship with her father, who, when the song was written, was scheduled for an operation at the Mayo Clinic the following day. The point is that, as our parents age, we implicitly recognize our own aging. And as we "get older too," we come into our own. This is a phenomenon not only noted by Stevie Nicks but also by researchers: it's been shown that individuals achieve a closer match between their actual self-perceptions and their ideal self as they grow older (Ryff, 1991). While this finding might be explained by a lowering of self-ideals, it's more likely that, as we age, we come to recognize and accept who we are.

This acceptance may be taken one step further as we approach the limits of our own mortality. David Kuhl, in his work with people at the end of their lives, recognized the importance of self-realization and "speaking the truth." This truth speaking—and seeking—may have to do with forgiveness, with sharing long-held secrets, with expressing gratitude, with understanding the past, and with saying good-bye. Graham Nash understood this so very well in one of the lines made famous by Crosby, Stills, and Nash ("Teach Your Children"). To cite just the last part of the phrase that's directed to children of aging parents: "And so please help them with your youth. They seek the truth before they can die."

So much of life—from our fantasies to our children to the art we create—reflects the wish to be more than mortal. *The Denial of Death* (Ernest Becker) is one of the great books of the twentieth century, a comprehensive look at the ways our need to deny death play out in every sphere of our lives. Some, though not many, songs have recognized this tendency as well. One powerful example is in Simon and Garfunkel's "Flowers Never Bend with the Rainfall": "And so I continue to continue to pretend that life will never end and flowers never bend with the rainfall." But a great many more rock songs have opted for the opposite, reminding us, as the group Kansas did, that "all we are is dust in the wind" or, as the Youngbloods did in a song first recorded by Chet Powers in 1963 ("Let's Get Together"), that "we are but a moment's sunlight, fading on the grass."

And so, how do we make sense of all these ideas about aging? How do we reconcile the warnings about not living too much in the past, the advice about the need to make sense of the past, the belief that it all goes by so quickly, the suggestion that we need to be aware of our mortality in order to live fully? Perhaps rock 'n' roll's best advice about how best to cope with aging resides in the compromise notion that while we need to look back in order to give our lives meaning, we also cannot stop looking toward. As Billy Joel ("Keeping the Faith") has wisely noted, "You can linger too long in your dreams...the good ol' days weren't always good and tomorrow ain't as bad as it seems."

Chapter 17

THE SEARCH FOR SOCIAL JUSTICE

No need for greed or hunger, a brotherhood of man / Imagine all the people sharing all the world.

—John Lennon, "Imagine"

The lyrics noted in previous chapters speak primarily to people's desire to improve their lives in whatever way they can—be it by finding love or friendship, conquering depression, making money, surviving a loss, or adopting a spiritually meaningful path. But even as we strive toward inner calm and happiness, we may also work toward making the world around us a healthier, safer, more equitable place. At our ethical best, we feel a sense of responsibility for our fellow citizens as well as for the planet we inhabit. Bob Dylan's famous line from "Subterranean Homesick Blues"—"you don't need a weatherman to know which way the wind blows"—mocked those who didn't realize how quickly and significantly the world was changing. It can still be thought of as a call for all of us to be aware of, and part of, the winds of change.

Rock 'n' roll exploded as a social phenomenon in the 1960s and 1970s, so it makes sense that so many rock lyrics reflect the social upheaval of those times. Moreover, much of the music of that time owed a great deal to the influence of folk artists such as Woody Guthrie (Dylan's hero) and Pete Seeger, individuals whose careers and lives were devoted to protesting social injustice. Woody Guthrie (father of Arlo, of "Alice's Restaurant" fame) was a lifelong socialist and fierce advocate of working-class people. He wrote his most enduring song, "This Land Is Your Land," in 1940; in part, it was meant as an alternative to the near-perfect vision of American offered by Irving Berlin's "God Bless America." In Woody Guthrie's words, "this land is made for you and me." No one, he thought, should be excluded from our country's abundant riches. Peter, Paul, and Mary popularized this song in their *Moving* album of 1963. A stanza in the original song that now rarely gets heard or sung (and was not in the Peter, Paul, and Mary version) includes these words:

> In the squares of the city, in the shadow of the steeple
> near the relief office, I saw my people
> And some are grumbling, and some are wonderin'
> If this land's still made for you and me.

It's not hard to see how this sentiment, this hope for true equality in the midst of manifest inequities, might inspire something like Dylan's masterpiece "Blowin' in the Wind." This latter song contains some of the most powerful and moving metaphors in rock history, including the haunting opening line that become the rallying point for racial justice: "How many roads must a man walk down before they call him a man?"

"If I Had a Hammer" was written in 1949 by Lee Hays and Pete Seeger (original members of the influential and politically controversial folk-singing group, the Weavers); this song was also popularized in the early 1960s by Peter, Paul and Mary (a group, by the way, that like the Monkees after them, were put together by a promoter with an eye toward creating a best-selling musical troupe). The most powerful lyrics are in the last verse: "it's the hammer of justice, it's the bell of freedom, it's the song about love between my brothers and my sisters, all over this land." Justice, freedom, and brotherhood remain to this day the three prominent themes in socially-conscious songs.

It's probably not much of a stretch to believe that all three of these songs ("This Land Is Your Land," "Blowin' in the Wind," and "If I Had a Hammer")—along with another Pete Seeger song, the antiwar ballad, "Where Have All the Flowers Gone"—were sung at every campfire at every summer camp for an entire decade. The image of mostly white, middle-class kids singing or listening to protest songs at summer camps or college campuses is easy to deride. But there was an earnestness to it all that's not so easily dismissible. Moreover, these songs—even the mellower Peter, Paul and Mary versions—provided the backdrop and at times the inspiration for wide-scale social activism. They sensitized an entire generation or two of America's youth to a wide range of pressing social issues. These recordings, along with subsequent harder-edged, nonacoustic rock songs influenced by them, helped young people find their voices and allowed them to express their dissatisfaction with the poverty, war, racism, violence, and environmental devastation that were (and still are) part of society.

Let's see what wisdom rock lyrics can offer about each one of these social injustices, beginning with the most basic, poverty, or more specifically, having enough food to eat. Springsteen, who usually has great insight into class issues, wrote the following words for "Badlands": "Poor man wanna be rich, rich man wanna be king, and a king ain't satisfied till he rules everything." There's some truth to these lines—people do struggle to accept that what they have is enough. Narcissism and greed are parts of most people's character. But what's missing in Springsteen's words is the awareness that really poor people just want to have enough to eat, and many in the world, including the poor in this country, do not. Another set of lyrics, this from Steely Dan ("Kings"), offers a keen insight into the way in which narcissistic needs for glory and power can have devastating effects on people's lives, including their ability to have enough food to eat: "While he plundered far and wide, all his starving children cried. And though we sung his fame, we all went hungry just the same."

Rock artists who have grown up in the inner city, most of whom are African American or Latino, have written compellingly, and angrily, about hunger. Listen to the strong words of Stevie Wonder in "Village Ghetto Land": "Families buying dog food now, starvation roams the streets. Babies die before they're born, infected by the grief." And the words of the rap star Nas ("I Want to Talk to You") bitterly convey the idea that those of who haven't been there can never fully understand the desperation of hunger and poverty: "Mr. Governor, imagine if it was your kids that starved, imagine your kids gotta sling crack to survive." Finally, there's Bob Marley's trenchant observation in his song "Them Belly Full" that a "a hungry mob is an angry mob." These powerful lyrics could serve as an object lesson to politicians. Moreover, the words of all these artists could probably be used as an introduction to the difference between liberal and conservative political sentiments.

Those who do have enough to eat may avoid facing the harsh truth about poverty because it's easier to look the other way. In Dylan's great words from "Blowin' in the Wind," it's too easy for a man to "pretend that he just doesn't see." Denial, as I noted in an earlier chapter ("Psychological Defenses"), can be a quite effective means to tune out parts of life that are just too unpleasant or overwhelming. Sting, a singer known for his humanitarian activism, reflects on this course of action in the following line: "By pretending they're a different world from me, I shelve my responsibility" (The Police, "One World"). Sting is talking about America's indifference toward third world troubles, but in this era of globalization, it's becoming harder to feign ignorance about the pain of people who are geographically distant. With the instant access of television and Internet news, we can hardly pretend not to see the suffering in far away countries. The perfect contrast to Sting's observation is U2's acknowledgment in "Sunday Bloody Sunday": "I can't believe the news today, I can't close my eyes and make it go away."

When we do open our eyes to the problems around us, it may make us feel guilty for not doing enough. The popular '80s band REO Speedwagon did a good job of describing a sense of collective guilt with the line, "Golden country your face is so red, with all your money your poor can be fed" ("Golden Country"). Similarly, The Steve Miller Band in "Fly Like an Eagle" implores us to do better: "Feed the babies who don't have enough to eat, shoe the children with no shoes on their feet, house the people living in the street. Oh, oh, there's a solution."

Within the context of a raunchy and often misogynistic rap song ("You Can't Win"), L'il Kim found a funny but clever metaphor to describe the state of the "have nots" in society: "Life's a wheel of fortune and y'all can't buy a vowel. " Far more seriously, in what was probably the first concept album by an African-American artist, "What's Going On," Marvin Gaye sang out about the unfairness in society and the need to change the reality around him. He opened the title song with the simple but poignant lines, "Mother, mother, there's too many of you crying. Brother, brother, there's too many of you dying." Gaye sang in the voice of an American soldier who has returned home from Vietnam to find his own country plagued by poverty, racism, political corruption, and drug abuse. Creedence Clearwater Revival's "Fortunate Son" is written in the voice of a soldier lamenting the unfairness of a draft system that rewards wealth with exemption from military service while rewarding poverty with the obligation of fighting and the potential honor of dying. Although the tune is upbeat, the lyrics of the song are actually a harsh social commentary: "Some people are born made to wave the flag, oh, they're red, white, and blue; and when the band plays hail to the chief, oh, they point the cannon at you."

War is among the oldest of all organized human activities, engaged in by people everywhere, in every era. There are many theories of why humans wage war, ranging from those that emphasize inborn aggression or narcissism to those that focus on tribal/ethnic/religious differences or the inevitability of geopolitical conflicts over scarce resources. One constant is that those affected by war suffer terribly. Another is that there have always been those who have tried mightily to find ways to end war. John Lennon sang it most famously: "All we are saying is give peace a chance." Another set of moving, pacifist lyrics comes from a song that was popular in the 1960s, "Last Night I Had the Strangest Dream" (written by Ed McCurdy, sung by, among others, Pete Seeger, and Simon and Garfunkel): "Last night I had the strangest dream, I never dreamed before, I dreamed the world had all agreed to put an end to war." A less gentle song offering a similar antiwar message is that of Edwin Starr; his song (actually more of a rhythmic chant), "War," reached number one on the Billboard charts in 1970: "War, what is it good for? Absolutely nothing." Perhaps, though, the angriest and most poignant antiwar lyrics are those of Dylan in "Masters of War" in which he accuses the government of having "thrown the worst fear that can ever be hurled, fear to bring children into the world."

To state the obvious: a significant, chronic social problem in this country and many others in the world is that of racism. Arguably, the most moving and powerful song ever written about racial injustice was sung by Billie Holiday ("Strange Fruit") in 1939: "Southern trees bear a strange fruit/blood on the leaves and blood at the root." Although it's often assumed that this song was written by Holiday, it was originally penned as a poem by a union activist from the Bronx, New York, who wrote it (and the music) after viewing a brutal picture of a southern lynching. An interesting historical note: the songwriter used the name Lewis Allan, but his real name was Abe Meeropol, the person who later adopted the two sons of the convicted spies, Ethel and Julius Rosenberg.

Unfortunately Bob Seger was right in asserting that "It went on yesterday and it's going on tonight, somewhere there's somebody ain't treatin' somebody right" ("Fire down Below"). Neil Young wrote "Southern Man" in 1970; in it, he offers a biting assessment of the racial and socioeconomic divides he witnessed in the South: "I saw cotton and I saw black. Tall white mansions and little shacks." Young wondered (accusingly), "Southern man, when will you pay them back?" As followers of rock 'n' roll know, an angry response to this song was delivered by Lynyrd Skinner in "Sweet Home Alabama": "Well, I heard old Neil put her [Alabama] down; well I hope Neil Young will remember, a southern man don't need him around." Personal disagreements aside, there can be little doubt that much remains to be done to solve our racial problems and that these problems are hardly unique to the South.

Again, though, it's instructive to hear the voices of African-American artists themselves on the current state of racial relations and justice. More than 35 years after Young wrote "Southern Man," the late rapper TuPac Shakur, known for his biting commentary on the hardships of inner city life, described the way he saw his relationship with this country and its leaders: "Pledge allegiance to the flag that neglects us. Honor a man that who refuses to respect us" ("Words of Wisdom"). The words of Stevie Wonder in "Higher Ground" are also concise and incisive: "Powers keep on lyin', while your people keep on dyin'." The late reggae musician Bob Marley sang so knowingly in his song "War" about the relationship of racism to violence: "Until the philosophy which holds one race superior, and another inferior, is finally and permanently discredited and abandoned, everywhere is war."

It would take far more than a few lines within a single chapter of a single book to explain the psychology of racism, but one persuasive theory is contained in the line of the Creed song, "One": "why hold down one to raise another?" The unfortunate answer to this profound question is that putting others down because of their race, ethnicity, gender, or religion serves a terrible, if psychologically understandable function: it tends to make those individuals or groups carrying out the oppression feel better about themselves. It's another manifestation of the unsolvable problem of narcissism: typically, every individual and every group wants to feel better than others. How fragile we all are, how suspect our self-esteem, that we put others down to feel better ourselves. But we do. We exclude, ridicule, and dehumanize others. Virtually every society has treated one group within its community as other, and less than. And because every society has economic and social problems of one sort or another, the group treated as "other" becomes the focus and presumed cause of all society's ills (Sampson, 1983). This allows the dominant group to avoid the pain of self-scrutiny and continue to position themselves as superior. As Jackson Browne astutely noted ("It Is One"), there is always someone to "speak in terms of what divides us to justify the violence they do."

Finally, a number of rock songs have focused on environmental issues. Though rock 'n' roll is probably not the first place one would look to find environmental advocacy tips, some strong lyrics do address the fears felt by people living in a changing landscape. One of the first rock bands to follow up on Rachel Carson's 1962 best-selling book on environmental destruction and pollution (*Silent Spring*) was the Doors ("When the Music's Over"): "What have they done to the earth, what have they done to our fair sister? Ravaged and plundered and ripped her and bit her." Joni Mitchell's lyrics in "Big Yellow Taxi" are less overtly angry but far more cynical: "They paved paradise and put up a parking lot." Over 30 years later, the Counting Crows' (2002) cover version made the song a hit once again. It's a good, catchy song, but I'd also like to believe that its popularity stems in part from its message about overdevelopment and the consequences of greed. Tom Petty offered similar imagery in "Free Fallin'": "There's a freeway running through the yard." Even The Beach Boys, not usually known for the depth of their lyrics, showed their concern for the earth ("Don't Go Near the Water"): "Oceans, rivers, lakes, and streams, have all been touched by man. The poison floating out to sea, now threatens life on land." I suspect that as we become inevitably more concerned about global warming and the quality of our air and water, more rock songs will focus on these topics.

Many of the songs discussed in this chapter can be seen as attempts at political wake-up calls: a plea to those who do care to do something, and soon. Unfortunately, it is easy to pessimistic about social change. Take, for example, Bruce Hornsby's lines in "The Way It Is," a song about the difficulty in changing racial attitudes: "That's just the way it is, some things will never change." While this is a thoughtful phrase, I think the most psychologically astute line is what follows as an explanation: "because the law don't change another's mind." This specific point is somewhat debatable—there have been demonstrable changes in racial attitudes as a by-product of civil rights legislation—but Hornsby has nevertheless honed in on a crucial psychological fact. It may take a very long time, indeed, for legislation to lead to legal changes that might ultimately result in true attitude change among significant numbers of people.

Moreover, as I noted earlier in the chapter on "The Difficulty of Change," individuals do tend to be resistant to doing or seeing things differently. In Simon and Garfunkel's first hit record ("Sounds of Silence"), they sung about nobody daring to "disturb the sound of silence" and implied that most of us are oblivious to "the words of the prophets [that] are written on the subway walls and tenement halls." Their poetic lines, then, reflect the phenomenon of ignoring the proverbial elephant in the room—in this case, social injustice. A similar, more recent line is Bon Jovi's "no one hears our silent screams in this land of broken dreams" ("When She Comes"). But it's not only people who resist change; organizations and governments do so as well. Hence, Dylan's lines from "The Times They Are A-Changin'" imploring those in authority to use their influence in the service of change: "Come Senators, Congressman, please heed the call, don't stand in the doorway, don't block up the hall."

Those who grew up in the 60s almost surely remember Buffalo Springfield's plea for heightened social consciousness and activism in the charged atmosphere of this era: "Stop, children, what's that sound? Everybody look what's going down" ("For What It's Worth"). The youth culture and deep social awareness of these times fostered a generation that realized that by pooling their energy and voices they could create an entity loud enough to be heard in the highest of places. Creedence Clearwater Revival ("Effigy") understood well the political power of a united front: "Last night I saw the fire spreading to the palace door, silent majority weren't keeping quiet anymore."

Some songs have pleaded for a collective, universal response to social injustices. The message in these songs is consistent with the words of Dr. Harry Stack Sullivan (the "father of American psychiatry"): "We are all more human than otherwise" (1947). Despite our differences, we share so much in common and should be there for each other. Thus, Bob Marley's plea in "One Love": "Let's get together and feel alright." And thus, the sentiment in the Hollies' moving song, "He Ain't Heavy, He's My Brother": "His welfare is my concern. No burden is he to bear, we'll get there." Another famous call for peace and global unity comes from the lyrics of the Youngbloods in "Get Together," "Come on people now, smile on your brother. Everybody get together, try to love one another, right now." Of course, the last words on any utopian sense of shared community must be those of John Lennon with which I opened this chapter: "Imagine all the people living life in peace."

"Into this house we're born, into this world we're thrown" sang the Doors in "Riders on the Storm." True enough—much of life rests on fate and circumstances that we have little control over—but many songs have urged us to do what we can, and as soon as we can, about this flawed world into which we're born. If not for ourselves, these songs suggest, we should work toward improving the world for the sake of the next generation. As Neil Young put it in "Let's Roll," we should "not let our children grow up fearful in their youth." The quest for peace and social justice is an ongoing one because, despite the persistent attempts of good people in every society, there are always competing needs and claims, just as there are different visions of what constitutes fairness or progress. John Fogerty must have understood this when he wrote (presumably about war and its weaponry), "Good men through the ages, trying to find the sun and I wonder, still I wonder, who'll stop the rain?" (Creedence Clearwater Revival, "Who'll Stop the Rain"). A hopeful answer comes from David Bowie ("Heroes"). It is each of us who can help because "we can be heroes, just for one day."

Chapter 18

THE SEARCH FOR A MEANINGFUL LIFE

There is a road, no simple highway, between the dawn and the dark of night, and if you go no one may follow, that path is for your steps alone.

—The Grateful Dead, "Ripple"

Throughout history, people have searched for meaning in their lives. This search has focused variously on the planets and stars, God, the soul, nature, family, community, and the self. Philosophies, religions, and cultures have been built around each of these belief systems. Books, plays, art, and, yes, rock songs have had interesting things to say about our need to make sense of who we are and why we're here. Tom Paxton, one of the many influential folk singers of the 1960s, described this questioning of our place and destiny with a deceptively simple phrase in a song with this same title: "I can't help but wonder where I'm bound." Other songs have focused on the need to take responsibility for the shape of our lives and to be aware of the choices that constantly present themselves to us. Mary Chapin Carpenter, as she usually does in her songs, found just the right words: "We got two lives. One we're given, and the other one we make" ("The Hard Way").

Research has shown that people strive to find meaning in life, attempting to impose structure or logic where none seems to exist (McAdams, 2006). It's as if we cannot tolerate meaninglessness or uncertainty. In part, this is the basis for the infamous Rorschach inkblot test used in psychology: confronted with ambiguous figures and drawings, we fill in the blanks with our sense of what these pictures might or should be. The allure of art is also based on attempting to fathom meaning in paintings or other works that allow multiple interpretations. We ask, "What does it mean?" And we try to find answers—in art and otherwise. In this regard, here's a good line from the Grateful Dead ("Scarlet Begonias"): "Once in a while you get shown the light in the strangest of places, if you look at it right."

Sometimes, though, life presents us with information or circumstances that we struggle unsuccessfully to comprehend; for example, our efforts to make sense of traumatic events (terrorist attacks, natural disasters, childhood abuse) often exceed our capacities. This is one of the ways that psychotherapy can be helpful—with the assistance of a therapist, people are sometimes able to find meaning, or what is now called narrative coherence, in memories, feelings, thoughts, or dreams that once felt confusing and overwhelming (Angus & McLeod, 2003). But whether we choose to enlist the services of a therapist or not, or whether we've suffered from trauma or not, many of us have given considerable thought to the idea of a personally meaningful life. Some of us are generally introspective or thoughtful, perhaps made more so by the fears that seem to permeate modern existence. Queen ("Under Pressure") expressed this kind of anxiety so very well in their phrase, "the terror of knowing what this world is about."

Existentialism is about the search for meaning in life. Among the most noted psychotherapists to focus on this theme is Viktor Frankl, whose 1946 book, *Man's Search for Meaning*, was based on his experience of finding meaning (through helping others) in the midst of a concentration camp. One of Frankl's central points is that we must take personal responsibility for the choices we make. While we may put in situations beyond our control, we can still find meaning in what we choose to do think, feel, and do. Another focus of existentialism is on authenticity—getting in touch with those parts of ourselves that feel most genuine and central to our sense of self. Yet another aspect of a contemporary search for meaning revolves around the idea of living in the moment, in the "here and now." Carl Rogers (1961) talked about moving our awareness from the "there and then" to the "here and now." All these tasks have in common the dual notions of freedom and courage: freedom to make life what you want it to be and the courage to make choices—and stay present—in the face of anxiety. At each moment, a person is free to choose what he or she will do and be. Alanis Morissette ("Innocence") understood well the extraordinary difficulty of this path: "For my ocean is big and my boat is small; find the courage."

Choice, then, is critical to the notion of a meaningful life, and many rock artists have been very aware of this. Pearl Jam, for one, expressed this idea as if they'd been studying philosophy for years ("I Am Mine"): "I know I was born and I know that I'll die, the in-between is mine." The rock group Yes found an appropriate metaphor for this concept in "It Can Happen": "We are architects in life." However, the most famous, and probably most poetically-phrased statement in rock history on the importance of living a life of constant choice and conscious transformation is (not surprisingly) that of Bob Dylan's in "It's Alright, Ma (I'm Only Bleeding)": "He not being born, is busy dying." On some level, Dylan was aware of the existential notion that the failure to continue growing is tantamount to dying. His words are also reminiscent of Socrates' oft-quoted maxim that the unexamined life is not worth living.

Consistent, too, with the ideas in the preceding paragraph, the Rolling Stones have consistently emphasized the importance of exploring possibilities, pursuing dreams, and assuming an active role in life. "You can't always get what you want…but if you try sometimes, you just might find, you get what you need" they sang in "You Can't Always Get What You Want." The song seems to be about connection and relationships, and, like most Rolling Stone tunes, also has a veneer of sexual intrigue; nevertheless, there is the implication here that one needs to keep trying in life and not just accept fate or an occasional defeat. Their words in "Ruby Tuesday" are more explicitly philosophical (and frightening): "Cash your dreams before they slip away; dying all the time, lose your dream and you will lose your mind."

Writing, apparently, from an existential perspective, Rush ("Freewill") offered this astute observation: "If you choose not to decide, you still have made a choice." Why would one avoid making personally meaningful choices? Because, as I've noted, anxiety is one of the perils on the way toward making a life comprised of choices and freedom. The existential philosopher Jean Paul Sartre contended that people try to conceal themselves from an awareness of their unlimited freedom. It can overwhelm or even paralyze us. Freedom—or the awareness of choice—may bring us in conflict with social, theological, and parental dictates of what we're supposed to be doing and how we're supposed to be feeling. It may make us aware of how many choices there are in life, how often we must assume responsibility, and how frequently circumstances thwart our attempts to live consciously and meaningfully. The Indigo Girls' wise lyrics in "Watershed" reflect these difficulties while urging us to stay the course: "You'll never fly as the crow flies, get used to a country mile. When you're learning to face the path at your pace, every choice is worth your while." Harry Chapin in "Circle" personalized this advice: "No straight lines make up my life, and all my roads have bends; there's no clear-cut beginning, and so far no dead-ends."

Bob Marley also understood the importance of examining one's life and making changes when necessary ("Exodus"): "Open your eyes and look within, are you satisfied with the life you're living?" He also believed that one should not postpone the search for a personally meaningful life. Although the Rasta religion he was committed to believes in everlasting life, he wrote these words for his great song "Get up Stand Up": "If you know what your life is worth, you will look for yours on earth." Perhaps he knew on some level that his own life would be short; he died at age 36 of a melanoma he refused to have treated. As John Mayer ("Love Soon") wrote, "The minute hand moves faster than you think it does."

Taking life seriously is not easy. More than one philosopher and songwriter have commented on the absurdity of believing that life is anything but random, and that attempts to render it meaningful are doomed to failure. There's Woody Allen's retort in *Hannah and Her Sisters* to being asked about how to make sense of a world that could permit Nazis: "How the hell do I know why there were Nazis! I don't even know how the can opener works." There's Steve Forbet's very clever words in "About a Dream": "Dogs chase cars and men chase dreams, and the dog is the more practical it seems." And there are these Dylan words made famous by Jimi Hendrix's cover of "All along the Watchtower": "There are many here among us who think that life is but a joke." The question to be asked is whether this philosophy is a defense against making hard choices and taking responsibility for one's life.

Stevie Wonder, like many, has apparently struggled with questions of meaning and the purpose of life. Out of this struggle have come some beautifully turned, and philosophically earnest, words. I'm partial to these in particular from "The Secret Life of Plants": "I can't conceive the nucleus of all beings inside a tiny seed, and what we think as insignificant provides the purest air that we breath." Tennyson, in his poem *(Flower in the Crannied Wall)*, suggests that if we could understand anything in its entirely, like the working of a little flower, we might unlock the key to the universe. Both of these artistic efforts implicitly assume that the search for meaning is a noble and wondrous undertaking, a critical part of being fully human.

Awareness, though, is a far more arduous task than most assume. Staying in the moment means that we can't hide. Leonard Cohen, who recently completed a five-year stay at a monastery, encouraged this practice in his song "Anthem": "Don't dwell on what has passed away or what is yet to be." The ancient practice of Zen Buddhism has emphasized the importance of staying in the moment; it also recognizes that most people need years of practice, often with the help of masters, to accomplish this. We daydream, wander off, reminisce, replay, and anticipate. What we struggle to do is keep our awareness in the moment. Mindfulness training, derived in part from Zen meditative practices, teaches individuals to do just that: to be aware, in the moment, of what they are feeling, thinking, and experiencing. This practice is increasingly being used in this country to help individuals (including children) cope with stress, anxiety, and rapid affective fluctuations. Early reports are quite encouraging; it seems to work (Hayes, Follette, & Linehan, 2004). It is also used by an increasing number of individuals in nonclinical populations to feel more centered and alive. Awareness has a paradoxical quality: as soon as we talk about being aware, we're no longer there. Instead, we're commenting on an experience that has just passed. Thus, our awareness of being aware is what some have called an almost or epi-phenomenon. Another paradox: though learning to be aware is often a solitary pursuit (achieved, for example, through meditation), it's an effective means to feel more fully engaged in the world.

People who search for meaning or yearn for growth—whether in religious texts, philosophy books, therapists' offices, transcendent experiences, or in moment-to-moment awareness—almost invariably experience some doubt along their journey. (A very enjoyable book on this topic is *Ambivalent Zen* by Lawrence Shainberg, 1996.) Not surprisingly, some seek gurus or heroes to guide them; they may even imbue such individuals with superhuman qualities, and far too often, these individuals bask in the idealization and worship. In "Mrs. Robinson," Simon and Garfunkel showed their great understanding of the need for heroes, especially in times of personal or cultural demoralization: "Where have you gone, Joe DiMaggio? A nation turns its lonely eyes to you." While every age has its heroes (including rock stars), most of those who've written about the search for meaning have emphasized the need for us to look inside ourselves for our own path.

Although some religious traditions discourage doubt, many of those seeking truth and meaning seem to regard it as an integral part of the path. That is, they allow doubt—or at least a tolerance for ambiguity and uncertainty—to filter into their consideration of what life is about. My sense is that this is what Dylan meant in these lines that allow for multiple interpretations: "I was so much older then, I'm younger than that now" ("My Back Pages"). I imagine that Dylan is referring to the kind of growth that occurs when we let go of old, often rigid assumptions, and become more accepting of new ways of looking at ourselves and the world. Billy Joel, who consistently turns out sharply observed lines about the human condition, found another way of affirming the value of doubt and skepticism: "Shades of grey, wherever I go, the more I find out, the less that I know." Later in this song ("Shades of Grey"), he suggests that the only people he fears are the arrogant among us who have no doubts.

Thus, the search for meaning can be difficult because it involves giving up previously unexamined notions of what is personally important. As I've noted throughout this book, we all tend to resist these kinds of transformations; it's easier to hold onto long-held beliefs and permit no doubts. Sometimes we need to experience a bit of an epiphany, a sudden realization that old patterns and beliefs are not the only ways of perceiving the world. John Lennon seemingly referred to a moment like this in "Watching the Wheels": "No longer riding on the merry-go-round, I just had to let it go." Similarly, Natalie Merchant's words in "Carnival" suggest how reflexive patterns of understanding the world can blunt growth and awareness: "Have I been blind, have I been lost inside my self and my own mind/Hypnotized, mesmerized, by what my eyes have seen?" Her notion here is that old patterns anesthetize us to new possibilities.

Herman Hesse's *Siddhartha* is one of the great, timeless novels about the search for a meaningful life. After years of wandering, Siddhartha ultimately finds inner peace as a ferryman, watching the endless rhythms of the river. It is in observing and accepting the constant changes in the river's patterns that Siddhartha understands the meaning of life. Although it might be considered sacrilegious to imagine a rock lyric equivalent to a classic book, I'll nevertheless put forward these beautiful words by Carole King ("Tapestry"): "My life has been a tapestry of rich and royal hue, an everlasting vision of the ever-changing view." It is a tapestry, she adds, that is "impossible to hold." Life is indeed complex, and our search for what is important or meaningful may encompass many chapters and span many years. Robert Hunter of the Grateful Dead also brilliantly describes this existential path in "Ripple": "There is a road, no simple highway, between the dawn and the dark of night/And if you go no one may follow, that path is for your steps alone." Hunter implies that we are faced with unlimited choices throughout our lifetime, and that we are sometimes utterly alone on our journey.

Still, we may have more strength for the task of finding personal meaning in our lives than we realize. We may be more capable of courage than we realize. "Oz never did give nothing to the Tin Man, that he didn't…already have" noted the folk-rock group America in "Tin Man." We need to try. The words to Neil Young's song "My My, Hey Hey (Out of the Blue)" resonate with this need to give our all to the pursuit of a meaningful life: "it's better to burn out than to fade away." In colloquial terms, he's imploring us to "go for it," to pursue our dreams (even if that leads to frustration or failure) rather than live a life of untested possibilities.

I'll conclude this chapter with quotes from two very different musical traditions. In "Strawberry Fields Forever," the Beatles pointed out that "living is easy with eyes closed, misunderstanding all you see." The solution to this problem, the path to a personally meaningful life, is articulated very well indeed by Lauryn Hill, a contemporary hip-hop artist ("The Miseducation of Lauryn Hill"): "Deep in my heart the answer it was in me, I made up my mind to define my own destiny."

CONCLUSION: LIFE LESSONS AND ROCK LYRICS

We busted out of class, had to get away from those fools; we learned more from a three minute record than we ever learned in school.
—Bruce Springsteen, "No Surrender"

In recent years, books have seemingly lost their unique place in our culture: they are no longer the sole or even predominant means by which knowledge is acquired, and they are no longer the preferred topic of conversation at lunch, parties, or work (Bosman, 2007). Music, though, remains as strong a presence in social life as ever. Music in the car; music on the eight-speaker home entertainment center; music at concerts and weekend parties; music in the background at the office and in the kids' rooms as they're doing homework; and, most ubiquitously, music on iPods played not only for one's own pleasure but downloaded and shared with multiple friends. It's not hard to find people who don't enjoy reading, or the theater, or even television. It is hard to find people of any age who don't enjoy music and who don't enjoy talking about it.

We rely on the emotional power of music. It is a power that can heighten pleasurable feelings or even evoke them when they're not much there. It can also dampen distressing feelings and even calm us during turbulent moments. "Music soothes the savage breast" (often misquoted as "beast") wrote the now obscure eighteenth-century English playwright William Congreve. Music also has the power to incite passion; note the use of music to rouse a crowd at a sporting event or political rally, to raise spirits at a party, to heighten a sense of spirituality at religious events, or to intensify romantic and sexual feelings.

"I believe in the faith that grows, and the four right chords can make me cry" sang Third Eye Blind ("Semi-Charmed Life").

In "American Pie"—probably the most widely interpreted song in rock 'n' roll history—Don McLean asks, "Do you believe in rock 'n' roll, and can music soothe your mortal soul?" He's probably referring to the transformational power of rock music, its ability to change not only a mood but the very essence of listeners' lives: to get us to feel what we've never quite felt before, even to get us to see things we haven't realized before. For him, rock music was as inspirational and meaningful as any religious, spiritual, or cultural movement. This song is a brilliantly composed paean to the magic of rock 'n' roll with some-what disguised references to rock's early pioneers, its reigning king at the time (Elvis), and the folk-rock jester (Bob Dylan) who was about to make his mark on the music scene. But, no, the music didn't die that day the plane went down, even though some inspirational musicians (including Buddy Holly and Richie Havens) did. The music has gone on, and still evokes intense feelings. Roberta Flack sang about this very process so exquisitely and personally: "Strumming my pain with his fingers, singing my life with his words, killing me softly with his song." The wonderful twist here is that, as the story goes, she composed these words while listening to Don McLean in concert.

The assumption, though, underlying this book is that just as music itself is capable of generating intense emotional feelings, wise words accompanying these notes are capable of generating considerable intellectual understand-ing or insight. Listening to both the words and music makes excellent use of both the right (more intuitive, creative) and left (more analytic) parts of our brains. That may be why it is easier to remember the words with the musical accompaniment. That may also be why lyrics seem enhanced by music. The phrasing, the rhythm, and the passion with which songs are sung all add immeasurably to the pleasure of the words. There is a wonderful interaction when smart words are embedded in engaging melodies.

But, even when they stand by themselves, the lyrics of some rocks songs are quite powerful and meaningful. What, then, of Springsteen's words that I began this chapter with? ("We learned more from a three minute record than we ever learned in school.") On the one hand, while affirming the wisdom and value of rock lyrics, these words can be seen as overstated. It's too easy a pleasure to denigrate education in this country, and too consistent with that part of rock 'n' roll that is reflexively rebellious and antiestablishment. Surely, not all schooling is useless, and not all lyrics are instructive. On the other hand, this line of criticism is probably too literal: Springsteen's primary message here is probably that rock lyrics can sometimes be at least as effective as formal schooling in teaching something important about life, and that they're often far more "experience-near" than what is taught in school. These sentiments are easy to agree with. The better lyricists within the rock tradition tell stories about life and use creative phrases and imagery to do so. Like novelists, poets, and other artists, their best efforts teach us something about ourselves, or offer a new way of seeing old, familiar phenomena. In addition, like other artists, rock lyricists often succeed best when they leave space for multiple interpretations. Finally, like other artists, great songwriters offer the virtue of a more palatable way of learning than through the often-tedious pages of textbooks.

Across these hundreds of lyrics is there a consistent message? Yes, there probably is an overall old-time liberal sentiment lurking among these words, one that emphasizes "love between my brothers and my sisters" ("If I Had a Hammer"), the need to work for social justice, and the belief that, despite the inevitable hardness of life, things can and will get better on both a personal and communal level if we keep trying. Paul Simon rendered this last thought quite beautifully in "Train in the Distance": "the thought that life could be better is woven indelibly into our hearts, and into our brains." Similarly, Lou Reed ("The Day John Kennedy Died") sang the following words: "I dreamed that I was young and smart, and it was not a waste. I dreamed that there was a point of life, and to the human race." Of course, these themes reflect the choices I've made regarding which lyrics and songs to include in this book. Whereas most prominent rock stars have been politically progressive (if not downright radical) and have espoused such positions in their music, it surely would have been possible for another person writing this book to have compiled lyrics with a far more conservative or even nihilistic flavor. Attending to the songs of country music and punk, respectively, would easily have brought about these results. It would also have been relatively easy for someone to write a book about rock lyrics that would conclude that most are not worthy of any serious consideration regardless of the political sensibilities of the songwriter.

I chose lyrics that I believed had something wise to say about the human condition. Assumedly without benefit of psychology degrees, the songwriters behind these words seemed to have a profound understanding of many of the most important issues facing individuals as they grow up, form relationships, struggle with life, attempt to cope, and ultimately grow old. Moreover, it was not difficult to find many songs and words that respect the intelligence of listeners and deserve attention. I also know that there are many exceptionally good lyrics than I have not included in this volume, especially in those forms of rock music that I have only cursorily attended to, including country-rock, punk, and rap. Despite Bob Seger's sense in "Old Time Rock and Roll" that "today's music ain't got the same soul [as] old time rock and roll," there is lots of music now being made and played that contemporary listeners consider soulful and wise. I suspect they're right, but that it may take a while for the rest of us to give this music its proper respect. There's a good quote on this theme in Zadie Smith's (2005) wonderful book, *On Beauty:* "Levi loved rap music; its beauty, ingenuity and humanity were neither obscure nor unlikely to him, and he could argue a case for its equal greatness against of the artistic products of the human species" (p. 181–182).

There's also the whole phenomenon of "indie" music, of singers or groups who are independent of major labels or unsigned by any label whatsoever. Some are performing within traditional rock genres (classical rock, folk rock, punk), while others are more alternative and hard to define. (An excellent Web site for independent music is http://www.amiestreet.com.) The point, though, is that whereas there is limited distribution of this music, there are still many wise and creative lyrics lurking there, waiting for a few more appreciative listeners. I'll offer but two small examples among the thousands of indie songs on the web or in clubs. The group Notes from the Road ("Stop My Time") had this to say about the wonderfully disruptive power of early love: "I script the conversation and forget all the words." That's very good stuff—there's a great awareness here of both the wish to present ourselves at our prepackaged best and the near impossibility of maintaining a pose when we feel so enamored of another. In a related vein, Elana Arian's song "This Time" features psychologically smart and beautifully crafted lyrics on love: "You said, 'baby you're the only one for me' and you know how I can't stand regret; and I know that you and I could be forever, I guess I'm just not ready for forever yet." These words are somewhat reminiscent of what Linda Ronstadt sang about long ago in "Different Drum" ("I'm not saying you ain't pretty, all I'm saying is I'm not ready for any person, place, or thing"), but Arian's lyrics are simply smarter; they're far more reflective of the interpersonal context of most difficult, personal decisions.

I don't think we listen to rock songs in order to learn about life. We're all far more likely to listen in order "to forget about life for a while," in the wise words of Billy Joel's "Piano Man." I know, too, that there's far more wisdom, "pound for pound," in the works of great writers or great psychologists. I suspect, in the end, I'm arguing for the "words" part of rock 'n' roll to be listened to with more attention and taken more seriously. In many ways, they are our most accessible art form, enjoying a far greater reach to a far wider audience than most other forms of art. Although our primary intent may not be to learn from rock music, we may do so anyway if we're a bit more aware of the wisdom lurking there. Sometimes it takes a bit of work—using an iPod doesn't guarantee listening carefully, and many songs contain words and phrases that are difficult to discern. But there's always the Internet to help out, and sometimes CDs even come with lyrics (and I wish they all did). As I hope I've demonstrated, there's hardly a worthy topic that rock songs haven't addressed, and sometimes quite wisely. Despite the stereotype, rock music is not just about love. As Blues Traveler ("The Hook") reminds us, "I sing to thee of love, sure, but also rage and hate and pain and fear."

As it stands, rock lyrics are most often quoted in high school and college yearbooks. In this sense, they're like poetry. The difference, though, is that most of us continue to listen to rock well past our high school or college days. If we listen hard—if we replay the words, think about whether they're true, consider their meaning–we may learn far more than we thought from this mode of expression. Truth and knowledge come in many forms. It's only appropriate, though, that I end with a final set of lyrics, this courtesy of Billy Joel ("Say Goodbye to Hollywood"): "Life is a series of hellos and goodbyes, I'm afraid it's time for goodbye again."

THE 50 BEST ROCK LYRICS

Choosing the best lyrics of all time is fun, challenging, and enormously subjective. Contemporary thought in the social sciences holds that all our choices, opinions, and thoughts are inevitably influenced by our gender, race, age, socioeconomic status, religion, and place in the social order. In plain English, then, my choices are biased by who I am. Thus, this list reflects only my views—and those of a few music-loving research assistants—and probably overrepresents songs from the mid-1960s to the mid-1980s. The other problem in compiling a list of this sort is that one's choices are limited by copyright laws. Some great lyrics are longer than the one to two lines allowable, and so can't be reprinted without mountains of legal permissions. Nevertheless, there are some terrific, smart words here—some of which I've already used earlier in this book, others that I haven't because their message didn't quite fit into one of the book's thematic chapters. I've also included very brief phrases indicating why I consider these lyrics particularly wise.

Although I made an attempt to rank-order the lyrics listed here by so-called degree of wisdom, ultimately I just couldn't make these discriminations; from my point of view, all of these phrases represent an extraordinary degree of psychological wisdom. In alphabetical order (of the singers or groups represented here), my best 50:

1. "And in the end the love you take is equal to the love you make"
   The Beatles, "The End"
   It's too often not true, but what an exquisite thought.

2. "Blackbird singin' in the dead of night, take these broken wings and learn to fly/All your life, you were only waiting for this moment to arise"

   The Beatles, "Blackbird"

   There are times when we must risk changing our sense of what we cannot be.

3. "She's leaving home after living alone for so many years"

   The Beatles, "She's Leaving Home"

   Has the distance between parents and children ever been captured so accurately and concisely?

4. "There are places I'll remember all my life, though have some changed/Some forever, not for better, some have gone and some remain"

   The Beatles, "In My Life"

   In great part, we are what we remember.

5. "I'd rather stay here with the madmen than perish with the sadmen roaming free"

   David Bowie, "All the Madmen"

   Better to err on the side of passion.

6. "I thought I was a child until you turned and smiled"

   Jackson Brown, "I Thought I Was a Child"

   Adolescents can become adults in just that moment, and life is never the same again.

7. "It's the smell and the taste and the fear and the thrill/It's everything I understand, and all the things I never will"

   Mary Chapin Carpenter, "Where Time Stands Still"

   The universe can make us feel insignificant, and yet love can heal.

8. "We can leave tonight or live and die this way"

   Traci Chapman, "Fast Car"

   A whole life can turn on a moment's decision.

9. "Like a bird on the wire, like a drunk in a midnight choir, I have tried in my way to be free"

   Leonard Cohen, "Bird on a Wire"

   Freedom is so elusive and so personal a quest.

10. "It's the damage that we do and never know/It's the words that we don't say that scare me so"

    Elvis Costello, "Accidents Will Happen"

    It's so easy to stay hidden and forget how it hurts others.

11. "Fear is the lock, and laughter the key to your heart"

    Crosby, Stills, and Nash, "Suite: Judy Blue Eyes"

    Finding ways to reach others is so central to all our lives.

12. "You've decided to love me for eternity/I'm still deciding who I want to be today"
    Ani DiFranco, "Light of Some Kind"
    Finding a cohesive self may be the job of a lifetime.

13. "Ah, but I was so much older then, I'm younger than that now"
    Bob Dylan, "My Back Pages"
    Sometimes it takes growing up to loosen up.

14. "I once loved a woman, a child I'm told/I gave her my heart but she wanted my soul"
    Bob Dylan, "Don't Think Twice, It's Alright"
    Love can overwhelm, and no one's ever said it better.

15. "How many roads must a man walk down before they call him a man?"

    Bob Dylan, "Blowin' in the Wind"
    The need to put down others to elevate ourselves is a terrible part of the human condition.

16. "Come mothers and fathers throughout the land/And don't criticize what you can't understand"
    Bob Dylan, "The Times They Are A-Changin'"
    Yielding to the next generation is always painful and rarely noted.

17. "Go to him now, he calls you, you can't refuse/When you got nothing, you got nothing to lose"
    Bob Dylan, "Like a Rolling Stone"
    Pride is so difficult to acknowledge and so often gets in the way.

18. "Just remember this my girl when you look up in the sky/You can see the stars and still not see the light"
    The Eagles, "Already Gone"
    We're all sometimes so blind to what is so obvious to others.

19. "How they dance in the courtyard, sweet summer sweat/Some dance to remember, some dance to forget"
    The Eagles, "Hotel California"
    The last line speaks more wisely about psychological defenses than most books.

20. "It seems to me some fine things have been laid upon your table,/But you always want the ones that you can't get"
    The Eagles, "Desperado"
    We all know people like this, including at times ourselves.

21. "Mother, mother, there's too many of you crying/Brother, brother, there's too many of you dying"
    Marvin Gaye, "What's Going On"
    The mournful sounds of injustice must be heard.

22. "There is a road, no simple highway, between the dawn and the dark of night/ And if you go no one may follow, that path is for your steps alone"

    The Grateful Dead, "Ripple"

    Finding our own way takes great courage.

23. "Darkness has a call that's insatiable and lightness has a call that's hard to hear"

    The Indigo Girls, "Closer to Fine"

    Finding hope in a difficult world can be excruciatingly hard.

24. "And my bitter pill to swallow is the silence that I keep/That poisons me I can't swim free the river is too deep"

    The Indigo Girls, "Ghost"

    We all fear being seen—and the consequences are great.

25. "I'd rather laugh with the sinners than cry with the saints,/The sinners are much more fun"

    Billy Joel, "Only the Good Die Young"

    As Freud knew, we become socialized only reluctantly, and rarely entirely.

26. "She only reveals what she wants you to see,/She hides like a child but she's always a woman to me"

    Billy Joel, "She's Always a Woman"

    The power of seduction is in its evasiveness.

27. "Do you still feel the pain of the scars that won't heal,/Your eyes have died but you see more than I"

    Elton John and Bernie Taupin, "Daniel"

    Seeing so clearly is such a mixed blessing, another price of abuse.

28. "My life has been a tapestry of rich and royal hue/An everlasting vision of the ever-changing view"

    Carole King, "Tapestry"

    A stirring celebration of life's complexities and surprises.

29. "Freedom's just another word for nothing left to lose"

    Kris Kristofferson, "Me and Bobby McGee"

    We sometimes forget the price of what we think we want.

30. "Imagine all the people, living life in peace"

    John Lennon, "Imagine"

    Hard to imagine, and yet, is there a more important problem?

31. "Until the philosophy which holds one race superior, and another inferior, is finally and permanently discredited and abandoned, everywhere is war"

    Bob Marley, "War"

    It may just be this basic.

32. "If you know what your life is worth, you will look for yours on earth"

    Bob Marley, "Get up Stand Up"

    Here and now is where we need to live our lives.

33. "Have I been blind, have I been lost inside myself and my own mind,/Hypno-tized, mesmerized, by what my eyes have seen?"

    Natalie Merchant, "Carnival"

    It's so hard to acknowledge our preconceptions, much less overcome them.

34. "We can't return we can only look, behind from where we came/And go round and round and round in the circle game"

    Joni Mitchell, "Circle Game"

    Growing older is impossible to understand, but looking back sometimes helps.

35. "Well, something's lost but something's gained in living every day"

    Joni Mitchell, "Both Sides Now"

    And the task, indeed, is to recognize both sides.

36. "Oh, won't you stay, we'll put on the day/And we'll wear it till the night comes"

    Joni Mitchell, "Chelsea Morning"

    If we could only feel this alive forever.

37. "She holds the hand that holds her down"

    Pearl Jam, "Daughter"

    It's agony to leave a parent, even when he or she is abusive.

38. "The child is grown, the dream is gone/I have become comfortably numb"

    Pink Floyd, "The Wall"

    Too often the default position in middle-age life.

39. "Maybe you'd go away and never call/And a taste of honey's worse than none at all"

    Smokey Robinson, "I Second That Emotion"

    Debatable, but certainly we've all felt this pain and regret.

40. "Dying all the time, lose your dream and you will lose your mind"

    The Rolling Stones, "Ruby Tuesday"

    Without hope and dreams, life is often unbearable.

41. "She has danced into the danger zone, when the dancer becomes the dance"

    Michael Sembello, "Maniac" (from the movie *Flashdance*)

    Some life for those transcendent moments of merger of the self and the world.

42. "And the course of a lifetime runs over and over again"

    Paul Simon, "Mother and Child Reunion"

Early patterns are so very hard to change, even when we desperately want to change them.

43. "Hiding in my room, safe within my womb, I touch no one and no one touches me"

     Paul Simon (Simon and Garfunkel), "I Am a Rock"

     Hiding is so very understandable and so very costly.

44. "Where have you gone, Joe DiMaggio? A nation turns its lonely eyes to you"

     Paul Simon (Simon & Garfunkel), "Mrs. Robinson"

     People need heroes and every culture needs icons.

45. "And so I continue to continue to pretend that life will never end and flowers never bend with the rainfall"

     Paul Simon (Simon & Garfunkel), "Flowers Never Bend with the Rainfall"

     We defend so mightily against the idea of our own mortality.

46. "People talking without speaking, people hearing without listening, / People writing songs that voices never share"

     Paul Simon (Simon and Garfunkel), "The Sounds of Silence"

     How do we get to really hear each other?

47. "The door is open, but the ride ain't free"

     Bruce Springsteen, "Thunder Road"

     What choice doesn't bring risk?

48. "From the moment I could talk I was ordered to listen"

     Cat Stevens, "Father and Son"

     Some parents just don't understand the way to love and never will

49. "Once upon a time I was falling in love, but now I'm only falling apart / There's nothing I can do, a total eclipse of the heart"

     Bonnie Tyler (written by Jim Steinman), "Total Eclipse of the Heart"

     So good a metaphor for one of life's most terrible pains.

50. "We're one, but we're not the same / We get to carry each other"

     U2, "One"

     We may deny it, but even lovers have separate selves.

REFERENCES

INTRODUCTION

Bangs, L. (1971, Fall-Winter). James Taylor marked for death. *Bomp Magazine*, 1–8.

Buchanan, S. (1994). *Rock 'n roll: The famous lyrics.* New York: HarperCollins.

Christgau, R. (1992). The Rolling Stones. In A. DeCurtis and J. Henke (Eds.), *The Rolling Stone illustrated history of rock and roll* (3rd ed.) (pp. 238–251). New York: Random House.

Deligiannakis, T., & Green, L. (2006, December 27). Adults can't tune out their fave teen songs. *New York Post*, 6.

Goldstein, R. (1969). *The poetry of rock.* New York: Bantam.

Gutterman, J. (2005). *Runaway American dream: Listening to Bruce Springsteen.* Cambridge, MA: Da Capo Press.

Hansen, B. (1992). Doo-wop. In A. DeCurtis and J. Henke (Eds.), *The Rolling Stone illustrated history of rock and roll* (3rd edition) (pp. 92–101). New York: Random House.

Harris, J. F. (1993). *Philosophy at 33 1/3: Themes of classic rock music.* Peru, IL: Open Court Publishing.

Holden, S. (1994, October 20). Dylan's children, without the sanctimony. *New York Times*, Section 2, pp. 1, 4.

Hornby, N. (2003). *Songbook.* New York: Riverhead Books.

Klosterman, C. (2004). *Sex, drugs, and Cocoa Puffs.* New York: Scribner.

Leitenberg, H., & Henning, K. (1995). Sexual fantasy. *Psychological Bulletin, 117*, 469–496.

Leland, J. (July 8, 2001). It's only rhyming quatrains, but I like it. *New York Times Magazine*, p. 36–39.

Light, A. (1992). Bob Dylan. In A. DeCurtis and J. Henke (Eds.), *The Rolling Stone illustrated history of rock and roll* (3rd edition) (pp. 299–308). New York: Random House.

Marsh, D., & Bernard, J. (1994). *The new book of rock lists.* New York: Simon & Schuster.

Michaelis, D. (2002, August). Sgt. Pepper's words. *The American Scholar*, 130–135.

Pareles, J. (1997, September 28). A wiser voice blowin' in the autumn wind. *New York Times*, Section 2, p. 1, 4.

Ricks, C. (2004). *Dylan's vision of sin*. New York: HarperCollins.

CHAPTER ONE

Burt, R. S. (1986). Strangers, friends, and happiness. GSS Technical Report No. 72. *Chicago National Opinion Research Center*, University of Chicago.

Kohut, H. (1971). *The analysis of the self: A systematic approach to the psychoanalytic treatment of narcissistic personality disorders*. New York: International Universities Press.

Schofield, W. (1964). *The purchase of friendship*. Englewood Cliffs, NJ: Prentice-Hall.

Twain, M. (1897/2003). *Following the equator*. Rockville, MD: Wildside Press. (Original publication date, 1897.)

Wright, P. H. (1978). Toward a theory of friendship based on a conception of self. *Human Communication Research, 4*, 196–207.

CHAPTER TWO

Freud, A. (1958). Adolescence. *The Psychoanalytic Study of the Child, 13*, 255–278.

Geller, J. D., & Farber, B. A. (1993). Factors influencing the process of internalization in psychotherapy. *Psychotherapy Research, 3*, 166–180.

Keith, M., & Schafer, R. B. (1980). Role strain in two-job families. *Family Relations, 29*, 483–488.

Laurenceau, J.-P., Feldman Barrett, L., & Pietromonaco, P. R. (1998). Intimacy as an interpersonal process. *Journal of Personality and Social Psychology, 74*, 1238–1251.

Sternberg, R. J. (1988). *The Triangle of love: Intimacy, passion, commitment*. New York: Basic Books.

CHAPTER THREE

Americans for Divorce Reform. What are the most common causes of divorce? Retrieved October, 2006, from http:www.divorcereform.org/cau.html.

Brinig, M., & Allen, D. W. (2000). These boots are made for walking: Why most divorce filers are women. *American Law and Economics Review, 2*, 126–129.

DiCaro, V. (2005). NFI releases report on national marriage survey. *Fatherhood Today, 10*, 4–5.

Gottman, J. (2001). *The relationship cure*. New York: Crown Publishers.

Harris, L. (1987). *Inside America*. New York: Vintage.

Hazan, C., & Shaver, P. (1994). Attachment as an organizational framework for research on close relationships. *Psychological Inquiry, 5*, 1–22.

Hurley, D. (2005, April 19). Divorce rate: It's not as high as you think. *New York Times*, F7.

Pattison, M. (2001, May 5). Time, sex, money biggest obstacles for young married couples. Retrieved October, 26, 2006 from http://lists101.his.com/pipermail/smartmarriages/2001-May/000616.html.

CHAPTER FOUR

Bowlby, J. (1969). *Attachment.* New York: Basic Books.

Chodorow, N. (1978). *The reproduction of mothering: Psychoanalysis and the sociology of gender.* Berkeley, CA: University of California Press.

Gilligan, C. (1982). *In a different voice: Psychological theory and women's development.* Cambridge, MA: Harvard University Press.

Kuriansky, J. (2004). *The complete idiot's guide to a healthy relationship* (2nd ed.). New York: Alpha Books.

CHAPTER FIVE

American Psychiatric Association. (2000). *Diagnostic and Statistical manual of mental disorders* (Text Revision.). Washington, DC: Author.

Beck, A. T., Rush, A. J., Shaw, B. F., & Emery, G. (1987). *Cognitive therapy of depression.* New York: Guilford.

Farber, B. A. (1983). Psychotherapists' perceptions of stressful patient behavior. *Professional Psychology, 14,* 597–605.

Feder, B. (2006, September 10). Battles lines in treating depression. *New York Times,* Section 3, p. 1.

Frank, J. D. (1974). *Persuasion and healing: A comparative study of psychotherapy* (rev. ed.). New York: Shocken Books.

Kessler, R. C., Chiu, W. T., Demler, O., & Walters, E. E. (2005). Prevalence, severity, and comorbidity of twelve-month DSM-IV disorders in the National Comorbidity Survey Replication (NCS-R). *Archives of General Psychiatry, 62,* 617–627.

Nemeroff, C. et al. (2005). Differential responses to psychotherapy versus pharmacotherapy in patients with chronic forms of major depression and childhood trauma. *Focus, 3,* 131–135.

Peterson, C., Maier, S .F., & Seligman, M. E. P. (1995). *Learned helplessness: A theory for the age of personal control.* New York: Oxford University Press.

Taylor, S. E., & Brown, J. (1988). Illusion and well-being: A social psychological perspective on mental health. *Psychological Bulletin, 103,* 193–210.

CHAPTER SIX

Erikson, E. (1968). *Identity: Youth and crisis.* New York: Norton.

Lasch, C. (1979). *Culture of narcissism.* New York: Norton.

Marcia, J. E. (1966). Development and validation of ego identity status. *Journal of Personality and Social Psychology, 3,* 551–558.

Mitchell, S. (1993). *Hope and dread in psychoanalysis.* New York: Basic.

CHAPTER SEVEN

American Psychiatric Association (2000). *Diagnostic and statistic manual of mental disorders* (Text Revision). Washington, DC: Author.

Kaysen, S. (1994). Girl, interrupted. New York: Vintage.

Pine, F. (1986). On the development of the "borderline-child-to-be." *American Journal of Orthopsychiatry, 56,* 450–457.

CHAPTER EIGHT

The Alan Guttmacher Institute (2002). *In their own right.* New York: Author.

Dickson, N., Paul, C., Herbison, P., & Silva, P. (1998). First sexual intercourse: age, coercion, and later regrets reported by a birth cohort. Retrieved on September 22, 2006 from http://www.bmj.com/archive/7124/7124pr.htm.

Doskoch, P. (1995, September-October). The safest sex—sexual fantasies. *Psychology Today. 28,* no. 5, 46–50.

Farber, B. A. (2006). *Self-disclosure in psychotherapy.* New York: Guilford.

Freud, S. (1959). *Collected papers. Vols. 1-V.* New York: Basic Books.

Gore, T. (1987). *Raising PG-kids in an X-rated society.* Nashville, TN: Abington Press.

Hite, S. (1976). *The Hite report: A national study of female sexuality.* New York: MacMillan.

Kinsey, A. C., Pomeroy, W. B., Martin, C. E., & Gebhard, P. H. *Sexual behavior in the human female.* Philadelphia, PA: W. B. Saunders.

Laumann, E. O., Gagnon, J. H., Michael, R. T., & Michaels, S. (1994). *Social organization of sexuality: Sexual practices in the United States.* Chicago: University of Chicago Press.

Leitenberg, H., & Henning, K. (1995). Sexual fantasy. *Psychological Bulletin, 117,* 469–496.

Myers, D. (2002). *Social Psychology* (7th ed.). New York: McGraw-Hill.

CHAPTER NINE

The National Center on Addiction and Substance Abuse at Columbia University (2005a, July). More than 15 million Americans abuse opioids, depressants, stimulants; teen abuse triples in 10 years. *CASA Reports.* New York.

The National Center on Addiction and Substance Abuse at Columbia University (2005b, March). Family matters: Substance abuse and the American family. *CASA Reports.* New York.

Sachs, A. (2006, November). Rock survivor. *Time,* p. F. 10.

Substance Abuse and Mental Health Services Administration. (2006). *Results from the 2005 national survey on drug use and health: National findings.* Rockville, MD: Office of Applied Studies, NSDUH Series H-30, DHHS Publication No. SMA 06–4194.

CHAPTER TEN

Adler, N. E., & Snibbe, A. C. (2003). The role of psychosocial processes in explaining the gradient between socioeconomic status and health. *Current Directions in Psychological Science, 12,* 119–123.

Diener, E., & Seligman, M. (2004). Beyond money: Toward an economy of well-being. *Psychological Science in the Public Interest, 5,* 1–31.

Henry R. G., Miller, R. B. (2004). Marital problems occurring in midlife: Implications for couples therapists. *The American Journal of Family Therapy, 32,* 405–17.

Johnson, W., & Krueger, R. F. (2006). How money buys happiness: Genetic and environmental processes linking finances and life satisfaction. *Journal of Personality and Social Psychology, 90,* 680–691.

Maslow, A. H. (1943). A theory of human motivation. *Psychological Review, 50,* 370–396.

Stevens, J. R., Cushman, F. A., & Hauser, M. D. (2004). Evolving the psychological mechanisms for cooperation. *Annual Review of Ecology, Evolution and Systematics, 36,* 499–518.

CHAPTER ELEVEN

Bowlby, J. (1969). *Attachment.* New York: Basic Books.

Bowlby, J. (1988). Developmental psychiatry comes of age. *The American Journal of Psychiatry, 145,* 1–10.

Kabat-Zinn, J. (1994). *Wherever you go, there you are.* New York: Hyperion.

CHAPTER TWELVE

Bonanno, G. A., Papa, A., O'Neill, K., Westphal, M., & Coifman, K. (2004). The importance of being flexible: The ability to both enhance and suppress emotional expression predicts long-term adjustment. *Psychological Science, 15,* 482–487.

Freud, A. (1936/1971). *Ego and the mechanisms of defense: The writings of Anna Freud, Vol. 2.* New York: International Universities Press. (Originally published, 1936.)

Goffman, E. (1956). *The Presentation of self in everyday life.* New York: Doubleday.

CHAPTER THIRTEEN

Farber, B. A. (2006). *Self-disclosure in psychotherapy.* New York: Guilford.

Farber, B. A., Berano, K. C., & Capobianco, J. A. (2004). Clients' perceptions of the process and consequences of self-disclosure in psychotherapy. *Journal of Counseling Psychology, 51,* 340–346.

Farber, B. A., Berano, K. C., & Capobianco, J. A. (2006). A temporal model of patient disclosure in psychotherapy. *Psychotherapy Research, 16,* 463–469.

Jourard, S. (1971). *The transparent self* (rev. ed.). New York: D. Van Nostrand.

Pennebaker, J. W. (1990). *Opening up: The healing powers of confiding in others.* New York: Guilford.

Wegner, D. M., & Lane, J. D. (1995). From secrecy to psychopathology. In J. W. Pennebaker (Ed.), *Emotion, disclosure and health* (pp. 25–46). Washington, DC: American Psychological Association.

CHAPTER FOURTEEN

America by the numbers: What we believe. (2006, October 30). *Time, 168,* p. 50.

Dawkins, R. (2006), *The God delusion.* New York: Houghton-Mifflin.

Freud, S. (1907) Obsessive acts and religious practices. In J. Strachey (Trans. and Ed.), *Complete psychological works of Sigmund Freud* (standard ed.). London: Hogarth Press (published in 1962).

Hamer, D. (2004). *The God gene: How faith is hardwired into our genes.* New York: Doubleday.

James, W. (1890). *Principles of psychology.* New York: Macmillan and Co.

James, W. (1902/1997). *The varieties of religious experience.* New York: Touchstone. (Original publication, 1902.)

The National Center on Addiction and Substance Abuse (CASA) at Columbia University (2001, November). *So help me God: Substance abuse, religion and spirituality.* New York.

Princeton Religion Research Center. (1996). *Religion in America: Will the vitality of the Church be the surprise of the 21st century?* Princeton, NJ: The Gallup Poll, 22.

Schuster, M. A., Stein, B. D., Jaycox, L. H., Collins, R. L., Marshall, G. N., Elliott, M. N., Zhou, A. J., Kanouse, D. E., Morrison, J. L., & Berry, S. H. (2001). A national survey of stress reactions after the September 11, 2001, terrorist attacks. *New England Journal of Medicine, 345,* 1507–12.

Ross, S. (1984). An interview with the man in black. Interview posted to http://www.cbn.com/700club/scottross/interviews/Johnny_Cash.aspx.

CHAPTER FIFTEEN

Coie, J. D., & Dodge, K. A. (1983). Continuities and changes in children's social status: A five-year longitudinal study. *Merrill-Palmer Quarterly, 29,* 261–282.

Elkind, D. (2001). *The hurried child: Growing up too fast, too soon* (3rd ed.). New York: Perseus Publishing.

Harris, J. R. (1998). *The nurture assumption.* New York: The Free Press.

McDougall, P., Hymel, S., Vaillancourt, T., & Mercer, L. (2001). The consequences of childhood peer rejection. In M. Leary (Ed.), *Interpersonal rejection.* London: Oxford University Press.

Winnicott, D. W. (1958). *Collected papers: Through paediatrics to psycho-analysis.* London: Tavistock Publications.

CHAPTER SIXTEEN

Arber, S. (2004). Gender, marital status, and ageing: Linking material, health, and social resources. *Journal of Aging Studies, 18,* 91–108.

Becker, E. (1973). *The denial of death.* New York: Free Press.

Charles, S. T., & Reynolds, C. A., & Gatz, M. (2001). Age-related differences and change in positive and negative affect over 23 years. *Journal of Personality and Social Psychology, 80,* 136–151.

Fuentes, K. & Cox, B. J. (1997). Prevalence of anxiety disorders in elderly adults: A critical analysis. *Journal of Behavioral Therapy and Experimental Psychiatry, 28(4),* 267–279.

Hagedoorn, M., Van Yperen, N. W., Coyne, J. C., van Jaarsveld, C. H., Ranchor, A. V., Von Sonderen, E., Sanderman, R. (2006). Does marriage protect older people from distress? The role of equity and recency of bereavement. *Psychology and Aging, 21,* 611–620.

Hoover Institute. (2006, October 24) Facts on policy: U.S. population milestones. Retrieved on January 16, 2007 from http://www.hoover.org/research/factsonpolicy/facts/4444946.html.

Kuhl, D. (2002). *What dying people want: Practical wisdom for the end of life.* New York: Perseus Books.

Liddle, R. (2006, October 22). Regrets they've had a few—mainly over not having more sex. *The Sunday Times.* Retrieved on December 1, 2006 from http://www.timesonline.co.uk/article/0, 24393–2415596,00.html.

Piolino, P., Desgranges, B., Clarys, D., Guillery-Girard, B., Taconnat, L., Isingrini, M., & Eustache, F. (2006). Autobiographical memory, autonoetic consciousness, and self-perspective in aging. *Psychology and Aging, 21,* 510–525.

Roberts, B. W. & DelVecchio, W. F. (2000). The rank-order consistency of personality traits from childhood to old age: A quantitative review of longitudinal studies. *Psychological Bulletin, 126,* 3–25.

Ryff, C. D. (1991). Possible selves in adulthood and old age. *Psychology and Aging, 6,* 286–295.

Teachman, B. A. (2006). Aging and negative affect: The rise and fall and rise of anxiety and depression symptoms. *Psychology and Aging, 21,* 201–207.

CHAPTER SEVENTEEN

Carson, R. (1962). *Silent spring.* New York: Houghton-Mifflin.

Sampson, E. E. (1993). Identity politics: Challenges to psychology's understanding. *American Psychologist, 48,* 1219–1230.

Sullivan, H. S. (1947). *Conceptions of modern psychiatry.* Washington, DC: William Alanson White Psychiatric Foundation.

CHAPTER EIGHTEEN

Angus, L. E., & McLeod, J. (Eds.) (2003). *The handbook of narrative and psychotherapy.* Newbury Park, CA: Sage Publications.

Frankl, V. (1946/1963). *Man's search for meaning.* New York: Washington Square Press. (Originally published 1946).

Hayes, S. C., Follette, V. M., & Linehan, M. M. (Eds.) (2004). *Mindfulness and acceptance.* New York: Guilford.

McAdams, D. (2006). The problem of narrative coherence. *Journal of Constructivist Psychology, 19,* 109–125.

Rogers, C. (1961). *On becoming a person.* Boston: Houghton-Mifflin.

Shainberg, L. (1996). *Ambivalent Zen.* New York: Pantheon.

CONCLUSION

Bosman, J. (2007, January 3). A Princeton maverick succumbs to a cultural shift. *New York Times,* pp. E1, E7.

COPYRIGHT INFORMATION

Excerpts from "Heroin," first appearing in the "Drug and Alcohol Use" chapter, written by Lou Reed; copyright 1966; believed to be owned by Lou Reed.

Excerpts from "The Needle and the Damage Done," first appearing in the "Drug and Alcohol Use" chapter, written by Neil Young; copyright 1971; believed to be owned by Neil Young.

Excerpts from "Casey Jones," first appearing in the "Drug and Alcohol Use" chapter, written by Jerome Garcia, Robert Hunter, Philip Lesch and Robert Weir; copyright 1971; believed to be owned by Ice Nine Publishing Company Inc.

Excerpts from "One Toke over the Line," first appearing in the "Drug and Alcohol Use" chapter, written by Charles Brewer and Thomas Shipley; copyright 1970; believed to be owned by Charles Brewer and Thomas Shipley.

Excerpts from "Sam Stone," first appearing in the "Drug and Alcohol Use" chapter, written by John Prine; copyright 1971; believed to be owned by John Prine.

Excerpts from "Lucy in the Sky with Diamonds," first appearing in the "Drug and Alcohol Use" chapter, written by John Lennon and Paul McCartney; copyright 1967; believed to be owned by Paul McCartney, Yoko Ono, Sean Ono Lennon, and Julian Lennon.

Excerpts from "I Wanna Be Sedated," first appearing in the "Drug and Alcohol Use" chapter, written by Douglas Colvin, Jeffrey Hyman, and John Cummings; copyright 1978; believed to be owned by Bleu Disque Music Company Inc. & Taco Tunes.

Excerpts from "Tequila Sunrise," first appearing in the "Drug and Alcohol Use" chapter, written by Don Henley and Glen Frey; copyright 1973; believed to be owned by Don Henley and Glen Frey.

Excerpts from "Dry Country," first appearing in the "Drug and Alcohol Use" chapter, written by J. Bon Jovi, R. Sambora, and D. Child; copyright 1992; believed to be owned by Polygram Records Inc.

Excerpts from "Addiction," first appearing in the "Drug and Alcohol Use" chapter, written by Kanye West; copyright 2005; believed to be owned by Chappell & Corporation, Please Gimmie My Publishing Inc., and Williamson Music Inc.

Excerpts from "She Talks to Angels," first appearing in the "Drug and Alcohol Use" chapter, written by Fred Ebb and John Kander; copyright 1989; believed to be owned by Def USA Music, Enough to Contend with Songs.

Excerpts from "Amelia," first appearing in the "Drug and Alcohol Use" chapter, written by Joni Mitchell; copyright 1976; believed to be owned by Joni Mitchell.

Excerpts from "Money," first appearing in the "Money" chapter, written by Pink Floyd; copyright 1973; believed to be owned by EMI Records Ltd.

Excerpts from "Conditions of the Heart," first appearing in the "Money" chapter, written by Prince; copyright information unavailable.

Excerpts from "Money Song," first appearing in the "Money" chapter, written by Fred Ebb and John Kander; copyright 1966; believed to be owned by John Kander.

Excerpts from "Money That's What I Want," first appearing in the "Money" chapter, written by Berry Gordy and Janie Bradford; copyright 1959; believed to be owned by Janie Bradford and Berry Gordy, Jr.

Excerpts from "Money Talks," first appearing in the "Money" chapter, written by The Alan Parsons Project; copyright 1982; copyright information unavailable.

Excerpts from "Working Man," first appearing in the "Money" chapter, written by Geddy Lee, Alex Lifeson, and Neil Peart; copyright 1968; believed to be owned by Core Music Publishing.

Excerpts from "Take It to the Limit," first appearing in the "Money" chapter, written by Don Henley and Glen Frey; copyright 1975; believed to be owned by Don Henley and Glen Frey.

Excerpts from "Can't Buy Me Love," first appearing in the "Money" chapter, written by John Lennon and Paul McCartney; copyright 1964; believed to be owned by Paul McCartney, Yoko Ono, Sean Ono Lennon, and Julian Lennon.

Excerpts from "The Message," first appearing in the "Money" chapter, written by Grandmaster Flash; copyright 1982; believed to be owned by Elektra/Asylum Records.

Excerpts from "This Charming Man," first appearing in the "Money" chapter, written by Steve Morrissey; copyright 1983; believed to be owned by Lotusdrive Ltd.

Excerpts from "Rocky Mountain High," first appearing in the "Religion and Spirituality" chapter, written by John Denver and Michael Taylor; copyright 1972; believed to be owned by Zachary Deutschendorf, Anna Kate Deutschendorf, Jesse Belle Denver.

Excerpts from "Come Here My Love," first appearing in the "Religion and Spirituality" chapter, written by Van Morrison; copyright 1986; believed to be owned by Van Morrison.

Excerpts from "God," first appearing in the "Religion and Spirituality" chapter, written by John Lennon; copyright 1971; believed to be owned by Yoko Ono, Sean Ono Lennon, and Julian Lennon.

Excerpts from "Box of Rain," first appearing in the "Religion and Spirituality" chapter, written by Robert Hunter; copyright 1990; believed to be owned by Ice Nine Publishing Company Inc.

Excerpts from "I Hope You Dance," first appearing in the "Religion and Spirituality" chapter, written by Lee Ann Womack; copyright 2000; believed to be owned by Ensign Music Corporation, Choice is Tragic Music, MCA Music Publishing, and Soda Creek Songs.

Excerpts from "The End of the Innocence," first appearing in the "Growing Up" chapter, written by Don Henley and B. R. Hornsby; copyright 1989; believed to be owned by Cass County Music and Zappo Music.

Excerpts from "Child of Innocence," first appearing in the "Growing Up" chapter, written by Kerry Livgren; copyright 1975; believed to be owned by Kerry Livgren.

Excerpts from "Try to Remember," first appearing in the "Growing Up" chapter, written by Tom Jones and Harvey Schmidt; copyright 1988; believed to be owned by Tom Jones and Harvey Schmidt.

Excerpts from "Puff the Magic Dragon," first appearing in the "Growing Up" chapter, written by Peter Yarrow and Leonard Lipson; copyright 1964; believed to be owned by William Nelson.

Excerpts from "Glory Days," first appearing in the "Growing Up" chapter, written by Bruce Springsteen; copyright 1984; believed to be owned by Bruce Springsteen.

Excerpts from "Jack and Diane," first appearing in the "Growing Up" chapter, written by John Cougar Mellencamp; copyright 1982; believed to be owned by Riva Music Ltd.

Excerpts from "For Today I Am a Boy," first appearing in the "Growing Up" chapter, written by Anthony and the Johnsons; copyright 2005; believed to be owned by Sanctuary Records.

Excerpts from "Coat of Many Colors," first appearing in the "Growing Up" chapter, written by Dolly Parton; copyright 1969; believed to be owned by Dolly Parton.

Excerpts from "Perfect," first appearing in the "Growing Up" chapter, written by Alanis Morissette; copyright 1995; believed to be owned by Music Corporation of America Inc., Vanhurst Place Music, MCA Music Publishing, and Aerostation Corporation.

Excerpts from "At Seventeen," first appearing in the "Growing Up" chapter, written by Janis Ian; copyright 1974; believed to be owned by Janis Ian.

Excerpts from "Rodeo Clowns," first appearing in the "Growing Up" chapter, written by Jack Johnson; copyright 2003; believed to be owned by Moonshine Conspiracy Records Inc.

Excerpts from "The Queen and the Soldier," first appearing in the "Growing Up" chapter, written by Suzanne Vega; copyright 1981; believed to be owned by Waifersongs Ltd. and AGF Music Ltd.

Excerpts from "Silent Legacy," first appearing in the "Growing Up" chapter, written by Melissa Etheridge; copyright 1992; believed to be owned by MLE Music.

Excerpts from "Stop This Train," first appearing in the "Growing Up" chapter; copyright information unavailable.

Excerpts from "Almost Grown," first appearing in the "Growing Up" chapter, written by Chuck Berry; copyright 1978; believed to be owned by Springboard International Records Inc.

Excerpts from "Kodachrome," first appearing in the "Growing Up" chapter, written by Paul Simon; copyright 1973; believed to be owned by Paul Simon.

Excerpts from "Another Brick in the Wall, Part 2," first appearing in the "Growing Up" chapter, written by Pink Floyd; copyright 1981; believed to be owned by CBS Inc.

Excerpts from "School's Out," first appearing in the "Growing Up" chapter, written by Alice Cooper; copyright 1972; believed to be owned by Alice Cooper and Michael Bruce.

Excerpts from "I'm Eighteen," first appearing in the "Growing Up" chapter, written by Alice Cooper; copyright 1971; believed to be owned by Alice Cooper, Michael Bruce, Neal Smith, Dennis Dunaway, Thomas Buxton, and Geraldine Buxton.

INDEX

About the Author

BARRY A. FARBER is Professor of Psychology and Education at Teachers College, Columbia University. He has twice served as Chair of the Counseling and Clinical Psychology Department at Teachers College. He has been the Program Coordinator and Director of Training in the Teachers College Clinical Psychology Program since 1990. He serves on the Editorial Boards for the journals *Psychotherapy, Journal of Clinical Psychology/In-Session* and *Psychotherapy Research*. He received his Ph.D. in clinical psychology at Yale University in 1978. Farber maintains a private practice in Westchester County, N.Y.

Chapter 11

THE DIFFICULTY OF CHANGE

And the course of a lifetime runs over and over again.
— Paul Simon, "Mother and Child Reunion"

Most everyone fantasizes about changing some aspect of him or herself, and most everyone comes to eventually realize that change is hard. Even when we are highly motivated to change an essential aspect of who we are—when we are given feedback by important others (friends, lovers) that there's a piece of us that really does need some altering—we struggle to find new ways. Or, more accurately, we either struggle to make changes that last for more than a few minutes or a few days, or we make cosmetic changes that have no signifi-cant effect on any really important parts of ourselves. The commitment may be there, even the sincerity, but remarkably we remain fundamentally who we are. The French have a wonderful proverb about this: "plus de la change, plus de la meme chose" ("The more things change, the more they remain the same"). Paul Simon expressed similar sentiments in his powerful and evocative song, "The Boxer": "After changes upon changes, we are more or less the same."

Psychologists know this. Indeed, it's not an overstatement to suggest that psychotherapists essentially exist because of this fact. If change were easy, few of us would need the help of professionals. Despite being the founder of psychoanalysis, Sigmund Freud was not an optimist about the possibility of significant change; indeed, he believed that life was inherently difficult and that people resisted change mightily. According to Freud, about the best we can do is to change "neurotic misery" (being victimized by our own repetitive missteps) into "common unhappiness" (being victimized by the inevitable hurts that life throws our way). And even this transformation might take many years of five times a week psychoanalysis!

So, why *does* the course of a lifetime run over and over again? Why for the most part, do we repeat the same screwups, make the same mistaken choices, reprise the same excuses, and fall into the same familiar traps? Why the same arguments with the same types of people, the same type of friends or lovers, the same reactions to the same temptations, the same relational messes, the same fears, and the same needs, wishes and fantasies? The simple answer is that who we are is dependent on both our genetic inheritance (virtually impossible to change) and the way we have internalized our early relationships with our parents (very resistant to change). I'll have more to say about both these factors later in the chapter, but for now, let's examine some remarkably smart lyrics that either confirm these basic facts or, even better, provide a new way of looking at why it's so remarkably hard to change our ways—evil or otherwise.

Back to Paul Simon, who seems to understand as well as any psychologist how remarkably consistent behavior tends to be, and seems to experience as intensely as any patient in therapy just how frustrating that phenomenon is. Moreover, he knows how to express these ideas in concise, expressive lyrics. In "Patterns," he notes that much of our behavior is not only inborn ("from the moment of my birth") but also enduring ("like a rat in a maze the path before me lies, and the pattern never alters until the rat dies"). Most psychologically astute, though, is his awareness that much of what we are and do cannot be changed very easily at all: "Like the color of my skin, or the day that I grow old, my life is made of patterns that can scarcely be controlled." In fact, Simon's words here imply that behavioral characteristics are as unalterable as biological imperatives. While this is not exactly the case—change is hard but not impossible—it's much closer to the truth than most of us would like to believe.

Among Freud's more provocative notions was the idea that there are no accidents—that even seemingly random events or bad breaks are the products of our unconscious wishes or patterns of behavior that are enacted out of awareness. Accordingly, one of the reasons it's so hard to change is because we're not even aware of how habitual most of our feelings, thoughts, and behaviors are. We're on automatic pilot a good deal of the time and tend to keep repeating familiar actions. Thus, Paul Simon's line under the chapter heading about how the "course of a lifetime runs over and over again." And thus, Billy Joel's very smart observation in "Don't Ask Me Why": "You are still a victim of the accidents you leave, as sure as I'm a victim of desire." Yes, *victim*—a perfect word here, reflecting cynically but so accurately the extent to which we are often blind to the fact that we create situations we profess to abhor. Note, too, the wonderful equivalence here between biological expressions of desire and apparent accidents: we are equally culpable and helpless in both cases. We often cannot help but act in a certain way, regardless of conscious intent. The Eagles, in "Hotel California," also found a quite clever way of articulating this same point: "We are all just prisoners here, of our own device." The metaphor of "prisoners of our own device" is a perfect reflection of Freud's ideas.

The Eagles have also noted (in "Lyin' Eyes") the tendency we have to believe that relatively easy external changes will somehow result in profound psychological differences in our behavior, feelings, or attitudes. Similar to Paul Simon's earlier-noted observation that we remain the same following "changes after changes," the Eagles sang the following: "ain't it funny how your new life didn't change things, you're still the same old girl you used to be." How often we observe that, even when people move to another town or job, they still manage to find the same type of inappropriate friends or dead-end relationships as before. And, in the same vein, back in "Hotel California" (arguably the cleverest, most lyrically brilliant song of the past 30 years), the Eagles observed that "you can check out any time you want, but you can never leave"—a line that fans seem to really resonate with at concerts, and a line that, while a bit too pessimistic, still suggests a fundamental psychological problem. There are many pieces of us, especially our sense of ourselves and our patterns of relating to others, that stay with us regardless of where we are, and, because they often operate out of conscious awareness, much sustained work is necessary to change them.

Rock stars of a more contemporary vintage than Paul Simon, Billy Joel, and the Eagles have also understood how change, even in adulthood, is often limited by our parents' values, needs, and sensitivities. They've grasped the fact that despite our best efforts, we often become replicas of who our parents are or have been. They've even understood that we may model our parents in ways that we don't particularly like but seem unable to change. And not surprisingly, the words of these artists suggest strongly that they have been there, have themselves struggled with these dynamics. Ani DiFranco, a hard-edged performer familiar to most every woman who graduated from college in the late 1990s, sings in "Out of Range" of being "locked into being my mother's daughter." Similarly, Mike and the Mechanics in "The Living Years" sing of being "a prisoner to all my father held so dear," of being "a hostage to all his hopes and fears." There's that prisoner motif again, a reminder of just how powerful early influences are and how they get in the way of our choosing independent identities or even adopting autonomous beliefs.

More than a few rock stars, then, have apparently gotten it. Their lyrics conform to scientists' belief that the combination of nature (genetic/biological inheritance) and nurture (the way we were brought up) determine who we are, that our characteristic ways of being in the world get laid down very early, and that these patterns are heartily resistant to modification. None of this should be surprising. Our genetic endowment, affecting everything from our basic temperament to intelligence to body type, limits change in many areas. Consider this line from the Allman Brothers (written by Dickie Betts): "when it's time for leavin' I hope you'll understand, that I was born a ramblin' man." Of course, it's an exaggerated truth and self-serving in the context of the song (used as justification for dubious behavior), but it's also a reflection of a fundamental reality. Temperament is essentially hardwired.

Furthermore, the way our parents nurtured us in those first three years also affects us profoundly throughout life—these relationships result in enduring psychological templates ("mental models" for psychologists; "patterns" for Paul Simon) that affect our sense of security in the world, our view of ourselves, and our basic way of relating to others. John Bowlby (1988), the great British psychiatrist of the twentieth century, studied the ways in which mothers respond to their infants and found three essential types: those who were consistently responsive to their babies' needs, those who were unpredictably responsive to these needs, and those who were predictably unresponsive. Each of these types of mothering yields a different mental model in children (what he termed *attachment style*) that turns out to be fairly predictive of later behavior, especially the ability to effectively deal with anxiety and to negotiate mutually satisfying friendships and intimate relationships. For example, individuals whose mothers tend to be predictably responsive to their needs in childhood tend to be especially capable of sustaining a satisfying long-term relationship; they trust their partners and value intimacy. On the other hand, individuals whose mothers tended to be predictably unresponsive to their needs in childhood often struggle with long-term relationships; they tend not to regard romantic relationships as central to their lives and prefer to limit intimacy, affection, and commitment.

And thus, as some of our better rock lyricists have noted, we tend to repeat basic patterns of behavior learned early in life. Although not quite indelible, these patterns are nonetheless highly resilient. One group of psychotherapists (behaviorists) suggests that because the people in our usual environment tend to reward, or at least subtly encourage, the maintenance of old patterns, we should change environments if we're serious about changing behavior. On the other hand, more psychodynamically and existentially oriented psychologists tend to concur with the sentiments of Paul Simon and the Eagles, believing that this strategy doesn't work that well at all. They contend that by the time we're adults we've already internalized a set of behaviors, feelings, attitudes, and thoughts that we take with us wherever we are. Jon Kabat-Zinn, a psychologist and student of Buddhism, wrote a book (1994) whose title reflects this idea quite well: *Wherever You Go, There You Are.*

Freud—who's hard to get away from when discussing psychological phenomena—invoked the concept of repetition compulsion to denote the